Commentary on the Book of Causes

THOMAS AQUINAS IN TRANSLATION

EDITORIAL BOARD

Jude P. Dougherty, The Catholic University of America

Thérèse-Anne Druart, The Catholic University of America

David M. Gallagher, The Catholic University of America

Jorge J. E. Gracia, The State University of New York at Buffalo

David J. McGonagle, The Catholic University of America

Timothy Noone, The Catholic University of America

Kevin White, The Catholic University of America

John F. Wippel, The Catholic University of America

ST. THOMAS AQUINAS

Commentary on the Book of Causes

[*Super Librum De Causis Expositio*]

❖o❖

Translated and annotated by

Vincent A. Guagliardo, O.P.

Charles R. Hess, O.P.

Richard C. Taylor

Introduction by

Vincent A. Guagliardo, O.P.

The Catholic University of America Press
Washington, D.C.

Copyright © 1996
The Catholic University of America Press
All rights reserved
Printed in the United States of America

The paper used in this publication meets the minimum
requirements of American National Standards for
Information Science—Permanence of Paper for
Printed Library materials, ANSI Z39.48–1984.

∞

Library of Congress Cataloging-in-Publication Data

Thomas, Aquinas, Saint, 1225?–1274.
 [Super librum de causis expositio. English]
 Commentary on the Book of causes / St. Thomas Aquinas ;
translated and annotated by Vincent A. Guagliardo, Charles R.
Hess, Richard C. Taylor ; introduction by Vincent A. Guagliardo.
  p. cm. — (Thomas Aquinas in translation)
 Includes bibliographical references and index.
 1. Liber de causis. 2. Causation—Early works to 1800.
I. Guagliardo, Vincent A., 1944–1995. II. Hess, Charles R.,
1922– . III. Taylor, Richard C., 1950– . IV. Title. V. Series.
BD530.L533T47 1996
122—dc20
 95-22559
ISBN 0-8132-0843-2 (cl). — ISBN 0-8132-0844-0 (pa)

CONTENTS

Introduction	ix
A Note on the Translation	xxxiii
Outline of the *Book of Causes*	xxxvi

COMMENTARY ON THE BOOK OF CAUSES

Preface	3
Proposition 1 [*The Principle of the Entire Work*]	5
Proposition 2 [*The Three Grades of Universal Causes*]	12
Proposition 3 [*The Unity of Universal Causes through the Ultimate Cause*]	19
Proposition 4 [*Intelligences*]	28
Proposition 5 [*Souls*]	37
Proposition 6 [*The First Cause*]	45
Proposition 7 [*The Substance of an Intelligence*]	53
Proposition 8 [*An Intelligence's Knowledge of Higher and Lower Things*]	60
Proposition 9 [*An Intelligence's Knowledge of What Is above It*]	64
Proposition 10 [*How an Intelligence Knows*]	74
Proposition 11 [*An Intelligence Knows Eternal Things*]	81
Proposition 12 [*Intelligences Know One Another*]	87
Proposition 13 [*How an Intelligence Knows Itself*]	91

Proposition 14   94
[*The Soul in Relation to Other Things*]

Proposition 15   98
[*The Soul in Itself*]

Proposition 16   103
[*The Dependency of Unlimited Powers on the First Infinite Power*]

Proposition 17   109
[*The Assimilation of Unlimited Powers to the First Infinite Power*]

Proposition 18   111
[*Universal Dependence on the First Cause*]

Proposition 19   116
[*Degrees of Participation in the First Cause*]

Proposition 20   120
[*Divine Rule*]

Proposition 21   125
[*Divine Abundance*]

Proposition 22   128
[*Divine Excellence*]

Proposition 23   131
[*Rule of an Intelligence*]

Proposition 24   134
[*Perfections Diversely Received*]

Proposition 25   139
[*Ingenerable Substances*]

Proposition 26   143
[*Incorruptible Substances*]

Proposition 27   146
[*Corruptible Substances*]

Proposition 28   148
[*The Simplicity of Steadfastly Abiding Substances*]

Proposition 29   151
[*The Steadfast Abidingness of Simple Substances*]

Proposition 30   153
[*Temporal Things*]

Proposition 31   158
[*Eternal Things*]

Proposition 32   161
[*The Condition of the Soul*]

Appendices

1. Another Proposition 29	167
2. St. Thomas's Citations of the *Book of Causes*	169
Bibliography	179

INTRODUCTION

The *Commentary on the Book of Causes*, composed during the first half of 1272,[1] is among the last works of St. Thomas (1220–74). Why he undertook to write such a commentary while he was in the midst of composing his chief theological work, the *Summa Theologiae*, as well as a series of philosophical commentaries on Aristotle's major works could be explained by his new and important realization upon reading William of Moerbeke's recent translation of Proclus's *Elements of Theology*:[2] that the *Book of Causes*, which had become rather problematically attributed to Aristotle, was in great part derived from the former work.

The *Book of Causes* entered medieval Europe presumably via Spain through a translation by Gerard of Cremona (d. 1187),[3] under the title: *Liber de Expositione Bonitatis Purae*, the "Book on the Exposition of Pure Goodness."[4] The work also circulated under a second title, *Liber de Causis*, presumably due to the frequent citing of it by the opening proposition, which speaks about primary and secondary causes.[5] But under whichever title, the work was commonly understood to be the completion of Aristotle's metaphysics. Although its association with Aristotle made it sus-

---

1. See James Weisheipl, O.P., in *Friar Thomas D'Aquino: His Life, Thought and Works* (Washington, D.C.: The Catholic University of America Press, 1983), p. 284. Also, see H.-D. Saffrey, *Sancti Thomae de Aquino Super Librum de Causis Expositio* (Fribourg: Société Philosophique, 1954), Introduction, pp. xxxiii–xxxvi. According to Weisheipl, the commentaries on Aristotle's major works stem from 1269–73.

2. The translation was completed May 18, 1268. See Weisheipl, *Friar Thomas d'Aquino*, p. 235. For a more extensive introduction to the *Book of Causes* and St. Thomas's commentary, beginning with the thought of Proclus, see Cristina D'Ancona Costa, *Tommaso D'Aquino: Commento al "Libro delle cause"* (Milan: Rusconi, 1986), pp. 7–120. For those interested in correlating the Latin to the Arabic terms, see her index of terms, pp. 437–63.

3. See Dennis Brand, trans., *The Book of Causes* (Milwaukee: Marquette University Press, 1984), p. 4. According to Pattin, there is some evidence that Dominicus Gundissalinus was also involved in this translation. See Adriaan Pattin, "Over de schrijver en de vertaler van het Liber de causis," *Tijdschrift voor filosofie* 23 (1961), pp. 503–26.

4. See Brand, trans., *Book of Causes*, p. 4.

5. See Saffrey's introduction, p. xviii.

pect from the viewpoint of its compatibility with Christian faith, it nevertheless was widely read and studied during the "ban" on the works of Aristotle.[6] Because this work, which deals monotheistically with a First Creating Cause, was amenable to a biblical view of the universe, its contents spoke tellingly to the Christian mind.

Almost immediately after the introduction of the *Book of Causes* into the University of Paris, the question of its authenticity as a work of Aristotle was raised. Albert the Great, for example, suspected the author to be a certain Ibn Daoud, a Jewish author living in Spain and a contemporary of Gerard of Cremona.[7] St. Thomas referred to the author as the "philosopher" in his earlier works, such as the *Commentary on Boethius' On the Trinity* (1258–59),[8] but with perhaps a bit of uncertainty, if not intentional vagueness. Aquinas's suspicion that this was not a work of Aristotle might have preceded his awareness of Proclus's *Elements of Theology* as the primary source for this work, for in the *De Veritate* (1256–59), Q. 21, A. 5, he first vaguely refers to the "author" of the *Book of Causes*, then a few lines later uses the term "philosopher" to refer to the same author. Noting this, Vansteenkiste questions the commonly made assumption by asking whether ". . . in the writings of St. Thomas the term 'philosopher' indicates exclusively Aristotle. No one has proven that as a fact, and I believe it could be a pure fantasy."[9]

Soon after its entry into the medieval university, the *Book of Causes* became standard fare in the curriculum as the Masters expounded upon it. A number of commentaries began to spring up, notably those of Roger

---

6. The ban of Paris in 1210 states: "Neither Aristotle's books, nor the commentaries thereon, are to be read." Although renewed by Innocent IV in 1263, the situation became completely reversed when in 1366 Urban V required the study of all the works of Aristotle as part of the university curriculum. See M-D. Chenu, O.P., *Toward Understanding Saint Thomas* (Chicago: Henry Regnery Co., 1964), pp. 37–39.

7. See Brand, trans., *Book of Causes*, p. 6. Also see Léon Elders, "S. Thomas et la métaphysique du 'Liber de causis,'" *Revue thomiste* 89 (1989), p. 428.

8. See *In Boeth. de Trin.*, Q. 6, A. 1, 3.2a.

9. See, Vansteenkiste, "Il Liber de Causis negli scritti di San Tommaso," *Angelicum* (1958), p. 365. Weisheipl, however, understands St. Thomas's applying the term "philosopher" to the author of the *Book of Causes* to mean Aristotle. (See Weisheipl, *Friar Thomas d'Aquino*, p. 383.) On Vansteenkiste's side, it must be said that none of St. Thomas's references to the *Book of Causes* explicitly mentions "Aristotle" as the author.

Bacon (c. 1212–92), Giles of Rome (1247–1316), Henry of Ghent (?–1293) and the Latin Averroist, Siger of Brabant (1235–92).[10]

St. Albert the Great (1206–80), St. Thomas's teacher, also composed a commentary. While the precise dating of his commentary remains conjectural (between 1265 and 1272), it seems clear that St. Albert wrote his commentary without knowledge of either Moerbeke's translation of Proclus or Aquinas's commentary, since he evidences no awareness of the connection of the *Book of Causes* with Proclus.[11] Albert's viewpoint assumes the continuity of Aristotelian thought with the development of Arabic philosophy. He remarks that this work

> ... was assembled by a certain David the Jew from sayings of Aristotle, Avicenna, Algazel and Alfarabi. He put them in order according to the style of theorems, to which he himself attached comments in the manner in which Euclid proceeded in geometry. In the same way, in effect, that Euclid in his comments demonstrates theorems one after the other, David has added comments which are nothing other than the demonstrations of the proposed theorems.[12]

As a result, Albert views the text through a hermeneutic quite opposite that of Aquinas, in which the approach of the author to the text is decidedly one more of harmonizing than critiquing.[13] Although Albert's attitude to this work differs considerably from that of Aquinas, the end result coincides with the intent of Aquinas as well: a more thoroughly Aristotelianized understanding of the philosophical issues involved than the *Book of Causes* suggests by itself.[14]

10. See bibliography, primary sources, section 5.
11. See Leo J. Sweeney, S.J., "Esse Primum Creatum in Albert the Great's Librum de Causis et Processu Universitatis," *The Thomist* (1980), p. 603 and note 13.
12. *Liber de Causis et de Processu Universitatis*, ed. Borgnet (Paris: Vivès, 1890–99), v. 10, Lib. II, Tract. 1, Cap. 1.
13. Alain de Libera remarks, "Thomas lit le Liber de causis à la lumière de Proclus, pour rejoindre la terre ferme de la théologie dionysienne; Albert l'interprète dans le cadre d'un péripatétisme total qui, ici ou là, intègre certaines thèses de Denys. Thomas voit dans le Liber de causis une adaptation critique de la théologie platonicienne; Albert y voit une somme du 'péripatétisime antique.' On ne peut faire coincider deux herméneutiques aussi radicalement distinctes" ("Albert le Grand et Thomas d'Aquin interprètes du Liber de Causis," *Revue des sciences philosophiques et théologiques* 3 [1990], pp. 375–76).
14. "Si l'on regarde bien, l'interprétation albertinienne n'est pas dans son résultat opposée à celle de Thomas . . ." De Libera, "Albert le Grand," p. 375.

While Albert the Great attributes the work to a Jewish author, St. Thomas, as we have seen, in the preface to his commentary surmises it to be the work of an unknown Arabic author who had excerpted it from the *Stoicheiosis theologike*, the "Elements of Theology," written by Proclus (410–85), a Neoplatonist. But regardless who the author might be, St. Thomas had discovered the primary source, by means of which he could shed a needed light upon this mysterious work. Accordingly, he employs Proclus's *Elements of Theology* as a constant companion volume in his dissection and elucidation the *Book of Causes*.[15]

Since neither Proclus nor the author of the *Book of Causes* is a Christian author, Aquinas also employs the writings of Pseudo-Dionysius (also influenced by Proclus) to evaluate both.[16] Further elements for comparison throughout the commentary are provided by the views of Aristotle, to which St. Thomas in the main adheres, in contrast to the rather straightforward Neoplatonism espoused by the author of the *Book of Causes*. Fi-

---

15. Unbeknown to St. Thomas, the author of the *Book of Causes* also draws upon the *Enneads* of Plotinus for Props. 4–5(4), 9(8), and 22(21). See the introductory notes to these propositions on S{26}, S{57}, and S{114}.

16. Pseudo-Dionysius himself employs an overall Neoplatonic framework in his use of the triadic scheme: the one, which remains within itself as the principle; the emanation of beings from the one; the return of beings to the one as their source. St. Thomas adapts this in the *exitus/reditus* schema of his systematic works: God in Himself, the procession of creatures from God, the return of creatures to God as their end. See the *Commentary on the Sentences of Peter Lombard* (I Sent., D. II, Divisio Textus & III Sent., Prologue), the *Summa contra Gentiles* (Book I, Ch. 9, n. 4 & Book IV, Ch. 1, nn. 1–2) and the *Summa Theologiae* (I, Q. 2).

St. Thomas's commentary on the *Divine Names* of Pseudo-Dionysius is presumed to have been written before he had read Moerbeke's translation of Proclus's *Elements* (see Weisheipl, *Friar Thomas d'Aquino*, p. 174). Because Aquinas understood the works of Pseudo-Dionysius to be of almost apostolic antiquity (Weisheipl, p. 175), they served as an important gauge for evaluating the thought of Proclus. But, as Chenu notes, the works of Pseudo-Dionysius were also not without controversy: ". . . on the very eve of Saint Thomas's entrance into academic affairs at Paris, there occurred the great incident of 1241. At that time, the Parisian masters condemned several propositions inspired by a neo-Platonism of Dionysian vintage, and undoubtedly many Dominican professors at Saint Jacques were implicated." (Chenu, *Toward Understanding Saint Thomas*, p. 51.)

For a study of the relationship between the thought of Pseudo-Dionysius and that of St. Thomas, see Fran O'Rourke, *Pseudo-Dionysius and the Metaphysics of Aquinas* (Leiden: E. J. Brill, 1992).

nally, there are issues from the side of Catholic faith that need to be addressed.

St. Thomas's commentary, as we can see, is an involved study of several juxtaposed currents of thought being counterbalanced, evaluated and reappraised, making it somewhat more than the usual exposition.[17] As a result, the commentary emerges as a distinct philosophical work in its own right. But before proceeding further into Aquinas's commentary, we need first to look briefly at the *Book of Causes* itself, especially with a view to its doctrinal contents.

The *Book of Causes*

The identity of the author of the *Book of Causes*, or *Book on Pure Goodness*, remains an issue still debated by scholars. Pattin, for example, has argued for Jewish authorship in twelfth-century Spain. Others, like Saffrey and Anawati, have argued for Arabic authorship at an earlier date.[18] If we follow the Arabist view, the work belongs together with a number of other writings circulating in the Arabic world that were of pseudonymous origin, in which greater authority, if not survivability, could be assured for a work by attaching some well-known and accepted name to it.[19] The writings of the so-called "Dionysius the Areopagite" fall into this cate-

17. Saffrey remarks: "Saint Thomas, lorsqu'il commentait le Liber de causis, avait trois livres ouverts devant lui: la texte du Liber, un manuscript de l'Elementatio et un corpus dionysien. Les textes de ces trois livres sont cité ad litteram, les autres auteurs utilisés, et principalement Aristote, sont cités ad mentem. . . . Mais la véritable intentio de Saint Thomas dans ce commentaire est de comparer les trois textes. C'est là tout l'argument de l'ouvrage et c'est peut-être un cas unique dans l'oeuvre du saint" (*Sancti Thomae*, pp. xxxvi & xxxvii).
18. See Brand, *Book of Causes*, pp. 5–6. Citing the work of A. Badawi, Richard C. Taylor, and F. W. Zimmermann, de Libera considers the hypothesis of twelfth-century Spain to have been refuted (see de Libera, "Albert le Grand," p. 350). In a recent article, however, Pattin, examining the issue again, continues to argue his position: "Notre conviction est que cet auteur se nomme Ibn Daud" (Pattin, "Auteur du *Liber de causis*: Quelques réflexions sur le récente littérature," *Freiburger Zeitschrift für Philosophie und Theologie* 41, 3 [1994], p. 388).
19. Saffrey remarks, ". . . l'attribution à Aristote elle-même serait alors une pieuse supercherie, s'il est vrai que, à partir du VIe siècle, toute oeuvre platonicienne pour survivre dût se couvrir d'un pseudonyme quelconque: nous avons l'exemple de ces fragments d'Ennéades, et aussi celui de la fiction dionysienne" (*Sancti Thomae*, p. xxiv).

gory; the Christian writer of these works presents himself as the Athenian convert of St. Paul mentioned in Acts 17:34. While the writings of Pseudo-Dionysius are thought to have come from late fifth-century Syria, the *Book of Causes*, following the Arabist view, is suspected of having come from the vicinity of Baghdad around 850.[20]

Evidence for the Procline inspiration of the *Book of Causes* is undeniable. As St. Thomas progresses through his commentary, he documents no fewer than 37 of the 211 propositions found in Proclus's *Elements* that are relatable to this work. In this light, the *Book of Causes* appears at first sight to be no more than a compendium of Proclus's work, with the essentials abstracted and highlighted. But that, as St. Thomas clearly recognizes, is only half the story of this rather puzzling work. The author of the *Book of Causes* has formulated much of the Procline, and thus Neoplatonic, view of reality in conformity with a creationist, and thus more biblical, view.[21] Any interpretation of this work, then, requires careful attunement to a reworked and sometimes inconsistent hermeneutical grid upon which the author has superimposed the thought of Proclus.[22]

20. The works of Pseudo-Dionysius are first quoted at the Council of Constantinople in 533. For the place and dating of the *Book of Causes*, following the Arabist view, see Elders, "Saint Thomas d'Aquin," p. 428, and de Libera, "Albert le grand," p. 350.

21. In his "Doctrine of Creation in Liber De Causis," in *An Etienne Gilson Tribute* (Milwaukee: Marquette University Press, 1959), p. 289, Sweeney concludes: "If this interpretation is accurate, then, the impact of the divine revelation upon our author has been strong enough to break through an otherwise rather rigid neoplatonism and his Supreme Cause becomes the 'First Creative Being.' Whereas Proclus' One causes all things to be unified, the *Esse Creans* of the *Liber de Causis* makes every thing simply to be by an act of genuine creation." In footnote 77 Sweeney further remarks, "This interpretation is confirmed by Father Anawati's brief survey of creation in the Arabic text . . ." He then quotes Anawati: "L'intention de l'auteur est nettement d'affirmer une 'création' au sens monothéiste de mot. L'expression employée est abda'a (64,2) que les Latins ont traduit par creans, avec ses dérivés . . ." (In G. C. Anawati, "Prolégomès à une nouvelle édition du De Causis arabe," *Mélanges L. Massignon* [Paris: A. Maissoneuve, 1957], p. 93).

22. This is not to say that the recognition and explanation of this hermeneutical grid is without difficulties. As Sweeney notes in "Research Difficulties in the Liber de Causis," *The Modern Schoolman* 36 (1959): "Almost every proposition in the *Liber* exemplifies that disconcerting use the author makes of the pagan Greek philosopher . . . so near and yet so far from Proclus" (p. 111), so that we find ". . . puzzling statements concerning items on every level of his Neoplatonic universe . . . enough to make one's journey through the *Liber* slow and painstaking" (p. 115).

Outwardly the author proceeds in the highly formulaic style of Proclus's *Elements*, introducing a proposition and then following it with appropriate comments and corollaries. The procedure is "mathematized" in the style of Euclid's geometry, a priori in fashion, proceeding deductively, downward from the higher to the lower, from cause to effect, from the general to the particular. The order of these propositions—thirty-one in all[23]—gives the impression of a "logically" flowing cosmos descending necessarily from an ideal pattern. The airtightness of such a procedure might seem questionable to a contemporary mind, and indeed, for reasons not always clear, the method itself seems to break down in the hands of the author as the work unfolds. But the author, while externally conforming to this "Euclidean style," seems in truth not wholly concerned about adhering strictly to this method, violating it at times, as St. Thomas observes,[24] without apology for any inconsistency. One might be inclined to take this as an "internal weakness" of the work, but that would be to judge it by criteria to which it seems interested in conforming only loosely. It would be, furthermore, to miss the real novelty, if not intent, of the work: to be something more than an abstract of Proclus.

The author states the first principle of the entire work: "Every primary cause infuses its effect more powerfully than does a universal second cause." Causality operates hierarchically in the universe: the first and ultimate cause, who is God, gives being to all. Some of these beings are temporal, i.e., generable and corruptible. Others, i.e., higher souls, are on the horizon between the temporal and the eternal, eternal in their being but temporal in their activities. Still others are intelligences, i.e., minds alone, immobile and "abiding steadfastly" as eternal. While the first cause is the cause of the being (*esse*) of all beings (*entia*), other transcendent beings, such as intelligences and higher souls, are also universal causes, not with respect to being (which the first creating cause alone infuses), but with respect to the forms and activities of other things. In this regard, souls know due to higher intelligences, which are knowers, infusing them with knowledge, while things in the temporal world move due to higher souls animating them. The threefold Procline scheme of

---

23. The Latin translation used by St. Thomas incorrectly divides Prop. 4 in two (a fact that St. Thomas notes), giving the work thirty-two propositions. See the introductory notes at Props. 4 and 5.

24. E.g., S{27}.

being, living, and knowing (*esse, vivere, intelligere*) is accordingly expressed by these three descending orders of universal causes.

In view of this chain of causality, the fourth order, the temporal world of bodies, is passive, informed entirely by what transcends it, having the relation of image to exemplar. Thus nothing in this passing world is explainable simply in terms of itself, but everything must be explained in terms of its higher causes, which temporal things participate with respect to their being, nature, and activities. All goodnesses, or perfections, that the things of this world possess are infusions from the realm of higher causes, which, because they are eternal, are more truly in being than the temporal things, which receive and share these perfections from them. All the various orders of being, by reason of cause-effect relations, touch, one upon the other, leaving no gaps between them.

The first cause itself is understood in the style of apophatic theology: above description and knowledge by any lower being, including higher intelligences and souls. It is signified and named only by its first effect, an intelligence. It is "infinite power," upon which all other powers depend, and it rules all things without being "mixed" with them. The author is rather silent on the question whether the first cause, although seemingly the creating God of Scripture, is personal and free.[25]

While the first cause alone gives being to all, the author's conception of being is not expressed altogether unproblematically.[26] It is not put forward in terms of the Aristotelian notion of act in contrast to potency, more familiar and acceptable to St. Thomas. It definitely includes matter as what minimally belongs to the existing things of this temporal world, but it cannot be just matter, since being is given to intelligences and souls as well. The notion of being, which the first cause alone creates and gives to all, does, however, seem relatable to the Platonic notion that what is more common than and therefore ontologically prior to everything else is being. This can be said of anything existing, whether as inanimate thing, as soul or as intelligence. More problematic is his stating that being and life in

---

25. See Sweeney, "Doctrine of Creation," p. 288.

26. Saffrey remarks: "Car il y a bien une création au sens fort de la cause première à la prima rerum creatura, qui est l'esse, mais cet esse est l'esse superius, c'est-à-dire une espèce de primum esse, qui sera cause de cette perfection dans les autres êtres. Cependant, il est difficile d'apprécier exactement la position de l'auteur du Liber . . ." (*Sancti Thomae*, p. xxxi). Also, see Sweeney, "Doctrine of Creation in Liber De Causis," pp. 285–89.

an intelligence are "two intelligences," being and intelligence in life "two lives," and intelligence and life in being "two beings."[27]

Another point of difficulty has to do with "higher being" (*esse superius*) and intelligences as eternal, in contrast to which the first cause, who is God, is before and above eternity, just as he is above time. While such expressions as "before and above eternity" serve to distinguish the first cause from other eternal beings, the author leaves insufficiently addressed the question of whether or not these latter beings always were. The extent to which the author remains wedded to the ancient view of the "philosophers" on the eternity of higher beings on this point remains, then, unclear.[28]

Intelligences are "full of forms," i.e., they know a priori. They are described as pure knowers, who, in knowing, "turn to themselves." By this the author means the total immanence of such knowing. This kind of knowing is possible only for immaterial beings, which are simple in their being, without division and thus parts.

If the being of an intelligence is self-knowing, reverting only to itself to know in circular fashion, then the "motion" of the soul is self-motion, not having to be moved by what is outside it, but itself moving other things. Heavenly bodies, then, have souls, and "noble souls" move earthly bodies. They turn to what is higher, intelligences, in order to know, but turn to what is lower in their activities. In this, however, the author modifies the view of Proclus: human souls are also higher souls, on the ho-

27. See S{77} and St. Thomas's comments on S{79}.
28. See S{12ff} and S{74ff}. While St. Thomas acknowledges that the term "eternity" is sometimes used to mean "unfailingness and immobility of being," this still does not remove the difficulty. See S{12}. St. Thomas clearly distinguishes elsewhere in his writings the question of creation as ontological dependence in being from the question of the duration of the world. Accordingly, ". . . although Plato and Aristotle did posit that immaterial substances or even heavenly bodies always existed, we must not suppose on that account that they denied to them a cause of their being. For they did not depart from the position of the Catholic faith by holding such substances to be uncreated, but because they held them to have always existed—of which the Catholic faith holds the contrary" (*De Subst. sep.*, IX, 52; Lescoe trans., p. 63.) (See *ST* I, Q. 44–45 & 46.) Also, see Mark F. Johnson, "Did St. Thomas Attribute a Doctrine of Creation to Aristotle?" *The New Scholasticism* 63 (Spring 1989), pp. 129–55.

Sweeney, as we have seen, argues for the compatibility of the Book of Causes with the Christian view, "Although our author would have to be much more generous with relevant data to enable us to answer affirmatively with complete certainty, nevertheless our reply is yes" ("Doctrine of Creation," p. 289).

rizon of eternity and time. Animals and plants have lower souls, and are not the mere "icons" of some higher soul, as Proclus has it.[29]

There are other points on which it is quite clear that the author thinks differently than Proclus and than Neoplatonism as a whole. The first, and perhaps most crucial, is, as we have already mentioned, the question of the first cause as the one God who creates. The author removes the polytheistic overtones of Proclus, whose depersonalized gods, the henads, serve as the ideas with which intelligences themselves become informed by what are higher than they. Proclus, in Platonic fashion, preserves the world of subsisting ideas through such henads or gods, impersonally conceived but nonetheless needed as exemplars for all beings, knowing and otherwise. Consequently, between the one and the multiplicity of beings Proclus inserts a world of forms, or ideas, in the scheme of (1) the unparticipated as such (the one and good); (2) the participated (ideas, henads or gods); and (3) what participates (knowingly—intelligences and higher souls—or unknowingly—animate and inanimate things of the temporal world). The author of the *Book of Causes* simply eliminates this intermediary category (as St. Thomas notes), and does so without comment,[30] presumably because it is unnecessary from a creationist viewpoint, where the first cause itself, and not self-subsisting ideas, is the direct and sufficient explanation of both knowing and being. In removing such ideal subsisting forms between the One and the many, the author also removes Proclus's ideal intellect, by the participation of which all intelligences are supposed to know.[31]

This point of divergence profoundly restructures the entire key notion of participation. For Proclus everything is participable except one, "the one and good," which is above all. This means, as we have seen, that it can be participated by other beings only indirectly through the interven-

---

29. See S{35}. Also, see S{36}, note 148. For a discussion of the meaning of the corrupted term "*yliatim*" applied to intelligences and the common misunderstanding of it as "matter" in Prop. 9, along with St. Thomas's insightful treatment of this textual difficulty, see Richard C. Taylor, "St. Thomas and the *Liber de Causis* on the Hylomorphic Composition of Separate Substances," *Medieval Studies* 41 (1979), pp. 506–13. Also, see Cristina D'Ancona Costa, "Causa prima non est yliatim. *Liber de Causis*, Prop. 8 (9): le fonte e la dottrina." *Documenti e studi sulle tradizione filosofice medievale* (Spoleto) 11 (1990), pp. 327–51.

30. See Prop. 3 and S{20}; Prop. 4 and S{29}.

31. See Prop. 13 and S{83}.

ing abstract and universal forms or ideas below it. In the world of the *Book of Causes* this triadic view is replaced by a dyadic one which distinguishes between the first creating cause and created being, but in which the first creating cause is not "mixed" with created being. So, too, Proclus's triad of being, life, and intelligence, while not supplanted, is somewhat curtailed and interrupted by the same dyadic view. If the one is now the God who as pure goodness creates all, without which there is neither being, life, nor intelligence, then "all is in all" in a descending order of goodnesses, or perfections, where each kind of being receives finitely from the "richnesses" of the infinite one according to its capacity to receive, and multiplicity is explained by the diverse recipients. The only actual infinite is the pure one, or pure goodness itself, which participates nothing. All other beings are, to use St. Thomas's categories, a mixture of *esse* as what is received and limited by form (and matter) and form as what receives and limits *esse*. In the case of such beings, the "infinitude" of form is not a hyper-real, self-subsisting abstraction vis-à-vis concretely existing being (*ens*), but only a potency which receives being (*esse*) from the unlimitedness which is God.

St. Thomas's *Commentary*

In his opening remarks in the preface to his commentary St. Thomas notes how what is first in the order of being is last in the order of human knowing. With this casual remark, St. Thomas is signaling an approach different from that of the *Book of Causes*. From an Aristotelian perspective St. Thomas does not consider what the *Book of Causes* talks about to be something immediately and self-evidently knowable. On the contrary, the topics discussed in this work are reserved for the end of philosophical inquiry rather than the beginning. They presuppose a knowledge of logic and method, then a knowledge of the natural things of our experience, which Aristotle deals with in his physical treatises, and finally a knowledge of the human, both in terms of what is proper to human cognition (the nature of material things) and in terms of the end of human nature in that which transcends it. For this reason, the subject matter of this treatise is reserved for the "mature" part of a person's life.

Furthermore, even this "final" knowledge remains imperfect in this life, limited in its content to what is naturally knowable by the unaided use of human reason, rather than based upon anything like revelation.

While this treatise does deal with "divine" things, it is for St. Thomas metaphysics rather than theology proper. Thus St. Thomas interprets the first proposition of this work in terms of Aristotle's four causes, in which the meaning of the proposition reduces to a statement about efficient causes that are universal and per se (eliminating the need for separated forms as causes, as Platonism would have it). St. Thomas, following the author, remarks how this principle is verifiable by experience, for when the "use of reason" is lost in a human person, "life" may still remain, as does "breathing" in a comatose person. And when "life" is withdrawn, so, too, "being" in some sense remains, as in the case of a lifeless body. While being is granted to all that is, in any way, life is found only in some being(s). So, too, with respect to intelligence.

While St. Thomas does not raise the issue here of what is precisely meant by "being," it is clear as the commentary proceeds that he would have us understand "being" (*esse*) in terms of a more technical notion derived from Aristotle, namely "act" (*actus*), specifically the act that all beings (*entia*) participate from the self-subsisting "to be" (*ipsum esse subsistens*) which is God.[32] So, too, what God creates is not just being (*esse*), but the total being (*ens*) of the creature as the subject of creation, where "to be" is the object, or end, of creation.[33] Consequently, the view that the *Book of Causes* espouses—that higher intelligences and noble souls give other things their form and activity—is qualified by Aquinas to involve only some of the predisposing conditions for their nature and activity, and that only in a *per accidens* way.[34]

Proposition by proposition, St. Thomas's commentary brings to surface and explains the various propositions from Proclus's *Elements* that relate to the *Book of Causes*. Several times St. Thomas remarks that Proclus

---

32. See especially the commentary to Props. 4, 6 and 18. From the other side, it could also be said that St. Thomas somewhat "Platonizes" this notion: "Hence Plato said that unity must come before multitude," so that the act of "to be" is ". . . multiplied by its recipients," and ". . . because from the fact that a thing has being by participation, it follows that it is caused . . ." (*ST* I, Q. 44, A. 1; Benzinger trans.). See *De Subst. sep.*, 3, where Aquinas asserts that both Plato and Aristotle agree in the basic idea of participation. Fran O'Rourke remarks that once he has "[f]reed [it] from its separatist nature, Aquinas fully embraces the Platonist principle of causality and participation; in particular he makes his own much of the vision of the *Liber de Causis*, which he continuously relates to the *Corpus Areopagiticum*" (*Pseudo-Dionysius*, p. 127.)

33. See *ST* I, Q. 45, A. 4.

34. See S{9–10}. Also, see S{23–24, 37–39, 62}.

more clearly and coherently states the view that the author of the *Book of Causes* is advancing. Sometimes this is due to the faulty or unclear translation which St. Thomas has before him.[35] At other times Proclus simply evidences himself as the more proficient philosopher.[36] Still, at other times St. Thomas notes how the view of the author of the *Book of Causes* is actually closer to the view of Christian faith, as a text from Pseudo-Dionysius or another Church Father shows,[37] or how the author departs from Proclus.[38] At other times, Aquinas uses such "Christian texts" to correct the author or Proclus in the direction of a view more consonant with Christian faith.[39] Finally, St. Thomas also uses Aristotle in places as a philosophical "correction" of some Platonic view.[40]

From all of this one might get the impression that St. Thomas is using questionable measuring sticks to interpret and evaluate this work, but his thinking here needs to be understood in its historical context. First of all, concerning any issue touching upon faith, Aquinas as a Christian theologian will uphold only that view which is compatible with faith. If a certain philosophical view is opposed to faith, then according to Aquinas's hermeneutic, the choice must be made in favor of faith. The conflict is seen as due ultimately to some error of human reason.[41] On this score, Pseudo-Dionysius functions in the commentary as the primary theological authority (and so theological correction) for certain philosophical positions, especially "Platonic positions."[42]

35. E.g., S{51, 52, 73, 93}.
36. E.g., S{7, 47, 79}.
37. E.g., S{16, 20, 28, 33, 41}. Vansteenkiste notes 23 citations in St. Thomas's other works where he couples Pseudo-Dionysius and the author of the *Book of Causes* as authorities holding a particular view in common. See "Il *Libro de causis* negli scritti di San Tommaso," p. 369.
38. S{13–14, 29, 33, 41, 44, 58}. In S{21} and S{80} St. Thomas acknowledges the monotheism of the author, in clear contrast to the thought of Proclus.
39. E.g., S{16, 24}.
40. E.g., S{24, 38}.
41. See *In Boeth. de Trin.*, Q. 3, A. 1, ad 3.
42. The commentary ". . . is not merely a reading of the text; there is, in addition, a determination of truth and here Dionysius is the principal *auctoritas* for correction as well as confirmation. It is most significant that Dionysius is invoked precisely in the central points of Platonic doctrine . . . in which . . . the *De Divinis Nominibus* becomes an anti-Platonic work. This commentary, therefore, continues the work of that on the *De Divinis Nominibus* and with it constitutes an interrelated body of criticism

But when it is a matter of philosophy, then reason itself must decide the issue; thus Aquinas repeatedly refers to "Platonic positions" (*positiones Platonicae*). One might, again, think that this phrase serves as a "red flag," isolating Platonism from Aquinas's Aristotelianism only to reject it.[43] But, if one examines the texts more closely, one discovers operative here a subtle and at times involved method developed by St. Thomas for approaching "Plato" and "the Platonists."[44] That Aquinas needed to work out such a method seems inescapable, given the fact that Christian theology in the West, as it had been received by Aquinas, had long been developed along Augustinian, and therefore basically Platonic, lines. That framework was thought to be more acceptable to express certain Christian themes than the more recent and suspect Aristotelian approach employed by the Averroists.[45] On this score, it would oversimplify our understanding

---

directed precisely at the main theses dependent upon the via Platonica" R. J. Henle, S.J., *Saint Thomas and Platonism. A Study of "Plato" and "Platonici" Texts in the Writings of St. Thomas* (The Hague: Martinus Nijhoff, 1956), p. 384.

Also, de Libera: "La critique du platonisme au nom d'Aristote et de Denys est un leitmotiv de l'interprétation thomiste du Liber de causis. . . . Thomas réaffirme qu'il faut suivre la thèse d'Aristote et non celle de Proclus, car la position aristotélicienne est davantage conformé aux exigences de la foi—magis consona fidei christianae . . .'" ("Albert le Grand," p. 370). And, "Le sens de la stratégie interprétative de Thomas apparait ici clairement: si la thèse du Liber de causis a un sens, et elle en a un, c'est à condition d'effacer en elle toute trace des positiones platonicas, qu'elles soient inauthentiques ou authentiques . . .'" (p. 372).

43. As A. E. Taylor, in *Philosophical Studies* (London: Macmillan, 1934), pp. 231–32, points out, the issues were no clearer with respect to Aristotle: "Here again there was a definite tradition confronting him [Aquinas] . . . decidedly in favour of a pantheistic and naturalistic interpretation of Aristotle . . .'"

44. St. Thomas knew little Plato firsthand (see Henle, *Saint Thomas and Platonism*, p. xxi). Due to sparse historical information, he frequently placed under the collective term "the Platonists" a lengthy and varied development beyond Plato (see the criticisms of C. J. De Vogel in "Some Reflections on the Liber de causis," *Vivarium* 4 [1966], pp. 69–70). Acknowledgement of this difficulty is certainly not the same as the removal of it. Nevertheless, what we have to deal with in the commentary is St. Thomas's understanding of Platonism—itself an historical matter. But see Henle, p. 447, note 4, for a list of texts in which St. Thomas acknowledges differing views among the Platonists.

45. See Chenu, *Toward Understanding Saint Thomas*, pp. 50–58, on this Augustinian tradition. As Chenu remarks: "St. Thomas himself, in those very passages where he admits that Augustine was influenced by the opinions of the Platonists, was most careful not to take exception to his texts, and he respectfully applied to them the

of Aquinas to see him as a wholesale rejector of Platonism in favor of Aristotelianism.[46] The task facing Aquinas was more complex, and the tools demanded to accomplish it, more subtle.

The formulaic statement "Platonic positions," with all its variants expressed in the verb forms of *ponere* (usually *ponebant*),[47] involves the structure of a *ratio* (or *radix, fundamentum,* or *principium*) in which the *positio* (or *opinio* or *suppositio*) is a conclusion flowing from such a reason, principle, or foundation.[48] In this light several possible approaches open up. St. Thomas might critique and reject: (1) the *ratio,* or (2) the *positio,* or (3) both in the *via* that the *ratio-positio* itself expresses. A *ratio,* then, might be maintained, such as the principle of reducing a many to a one, but with a position drawn from it that differs from the usual "Platonic position." Or the position might be maintained, freed from its Platonic basis,

---

procedure of reverential exposition" (p. 52). We find a triadic scheme operative in Augustine's thought similar to the one in the *Book of Causes*: ". . . a God who was at once, for his creatures, the *causa essendi* [cause of their being], the *ratio intelligendi* [principle of their understanding], and the *ordo vivendi* [norm of their living]" (p. 56). So, too, ". . . Augustine was led to see created beings less in their own proper consistency than in their representative value. The dichotomy of *res et signa* [things and signs], in which all objects of knowledge were ranged, lay at the base of his whole methodology" (pp. 55–56).

46. A. E. Taylor remarks: "It is not true that he [Thomas] changed the existing philosophical tradition by dethroning one uncritically accepted and enthroning another. It would be much truer to say that he retained and built upon the thought which had been accessible to his own age by the recovery of Aristotle. . . . For the first time in the life of the modern world he attempted something like a critical and thoroughly historical appreciation of past philosophy in its entirety" (*Philosophical Studies,* pp. 230–31). Henle (*Saint Thomas and Platonism,* pp. 309–12) speaks of the more historical approach to philosophy developed by St. Thomas, especially in the late work, *De Substantiis separatis* (1271–73), in which he refers to Proclus by name. This work also serves as another companion piece to the commentary on the *Book of Causes,* where both Plato and Aristotle can be cited together by St. Thomas against the positions of other philosophers.

47. In the present translation *ponebant* usually appears as "maintained" or "asserted" to avoid the awkward and otherwise frequent use of "posited." Any appearance of the phrase "positio Platonica" ought not be understood to insinuate automatically St. Thomas's use of this *ratio-positio* method.

48. See R. J. Henle, S.J., "St. Thomas's Methodology in the Treatment of 'Positiones' with Particular Reference to 'Positiones Platonicae,'" *Gregorianum* 36 (1955), pp. 391–409, and the expanded treatment of this in his *Saint Thomas and Platonism,* already cited.

where it is rooted in some other principle. In approaching these texts, then, it is important to realize how St. Thomas deals with the "root" as well as the "position," accepting, rejecting, or modifying the one, the other, or both. Since a *via* exhibits a *ratio* and a *positio*, in which the *ratio* is the premise and the *positio* the conclusion of a self-contained reasoning process, a *via* in Aquinas indicates a purely philosophical method, distinguishable from and ancillary to the quite different method of *auctoritas*, which he employs in theological matters.[49]

The need for some such strategical method on Aquinas's part appears more clearly when we realize that

[m]edieval discussion was carried on under the double rubric of a profound reverence for tradition and a profound respect for reason. The medieval philosopher or theologian was, therefore, forced to substantiate his teaching by placing it under great names—the *Sancti et philosophi*—of the past, while, at the same time, supporting it on a solid rational structure. His weapons of debate were twofold: *auctoritates* and *rationes*. Saint Thomas employed both. . . . By using every variation of the *auctoritas*-technique he was able to maintain his solidarity with Saint Augustine and so enjoy protection of the same great name his adversaries invoked. At the same time, by using the *via-positio* technique in his handling of Platonism he was able to attack directly the fundamental principles which were Plato's source of error and were still at work within Augustinianism. Thus it was that he could borrow the *auctoritates* of his Augustinian adversaries while, without offending the Christian veneration for Saint Augustine, he could, through Plato, destroy their *rationes*.

In addition, however, the application of the *auctoritas*-technique to the free *positio* [i.e., a position freed from its Platonic *ratio*] enabled him, on due occasion, to invoke the great name of Plato in witness of his own positions. His varying handling of the subsistence of Ideas furnishes pertinent examples.[50]

That St. Thomas sees himself as a corrector of a number of "Platonic positions" in his doing of theology, especially with reference to the chief

---

49. See Henle, "St. Thomas' Methodology," p. 401; *Saint Thomas and Platonism*, pp. 301 and 307–8, 400 and 405. The idea of a *via* is also operative in St. Thomas's "five ways" of arguing for the existence of God in *ST* I, Q. 2, A. 3. Henle isolates 24 such uses of this *ratio-positio* method in St. Thomas's *Commentary on the Book of Causes*: Props. 1, 2 (2 uses), 3 (4 uses), 4 (3 uses), 5 (2 uses), 6, 9, 10, 12, 13, 14, 15, 16 (2 uses), 18, 19, 32 (see Henle, *Saint Thomas and Platonism*, pp. 183–95).

For a discussion of the *auctoritas* approach and St. Thomas's use of it as a method, see Chenu, *Toward Understanding Saint Thomas*, pp. 126–55.

50. Henle, *Saint Thomas and Platonism*, p. 304.

theological authority, St. Augustine, can be seen from a rather "unguarded" text in the *Summa Theologiae*: "For this manner of speaking [that is to say, that charity, love, and the like, are not something really in the creature but only a participation in God] is common among the Platonists, with whose doctrines Augustine was imbued; and the lack of adverting to this has been to some an occasion of error."[51]

The Platonic view found in Augustine is that of some kind of extrinsicism. St. Thomas would have us see the above as involving not just an extrinsic formal relation to God Who essentially is charity (love), but also an *intrinsically formal* relation, so that charity, grace, and the like, when present, are *really* in the creature as the term of divine activity: "God is effectively the life both of the soul by charity, and of the body by the soul: but formally charity is the life of the soul, even as the soul is the life of the body."[52]

St. Thomas's treatment of the same basic Platonic approach in the *De Veritate* is somewhat instructive on this score. He asks, in Question 21, Article 4, "Is everything good by the first goodness?" He responds:

There have been various positions concerning this question. . . . The Platonists . . . said that all things are formally good by the first goodness, not as by a conjoint form, but as by a separated form. For an understanding of this point it should be noted that Plato held that all things that can be separated in thought are separated in reality. . . . Hence he asserted that good is separate from all particular goods, and he called it "good-in-itself" or "the idea of the good." By participation in it, all things are called good. . . .

This Platonic position was in a sense followed by the Porretans. . . . A creature is called good simply, they said, not by any inherent goodness but by the first goodness—as if good taken absolutely and in general were the divine goodness . . .[53]

51. *ST* II–II, Q. 23, A. 2, ad 1.
52. Ibid., ad 2 (Benzinger trans.). Also see *De Veritate*, Q. 21, A. 4, 3a & ad 3. Cornelio Fabro puts the matter this way: While the truth of Neoplatonism lies in maintaining that ". . . the real that we experience exists by means of that higher formality that maintains and penetrates everything with its power . . . the difficult point for all of this speculation lies in the divergence that remains between the formal unification of the real in itself and the concrete unity of the real of our experience. While Platonism opted for formal unity and lost real unity, Aristotelianism, on the other hand, opted for real unity but lost formal unity . . ." ("The Overcoming of the Neoplatonic Triad of Being, Life, and Intellect," in *Neoplatonism and Christian Thought* [Albany: University of New York Press, 1982], p. 105).
53. *De Veritate*, Q. 21, A. 4 c. (Schmidt trans.)

St. Thomas's position, in contrast, incorporates Aristotle on the one hand with respect to intrinsic form, and a "corrected" Plato on the other hand with respect to God as the first efficient and exemplary cause:

> If, therefore, the first goodness is the effective cause of all goods, it must imprint its likeness upon the things produced; and so each thing will be good by reason of an inherent form because of the likeness of the highest good implanted in it, and also because of the first goodness taken as the exemplar and effective cause of all created goodness. In this respect the opinion of Plato can be held.[54]

Some of the "Platonic positions" found in Proclus—and the author of the *Book of Causes* insofar as he follows them as well—that St. Thomas "corrects" in the commentary are the following:

1. The "similitude" principle of knowledge, which presupposes that being must be isomorphic with human knowing, so that what is abstract and universal in our knowledge is also abstract and universal in reality, constituting a separate world of ideas, or forms. In contrast, St. Thomas's position is that how a thing is in reality (particularly and concretely) and in the one knowing (abstractly and universally) are not the same. Following Aristotle, abstracting and universalizing for Aquinas pertain to our way of knowing due to the activity of the agent intellect in us. Knowing and being (except in God) are not the same. On this score, St. Thomas is able to use the author of the *Book of Causes* as a correction of the Platonic "root" for this position by asserting another principle: that "whatever is received is received according to the mode of the recipient."[55]

2. Another Platonic position is that abstract universals as prior self-subsisting forms are the cause not only of our knowledge of things but also of the very things that participate them. St. Thomas accepts the Platonic principle that, wherever there exists a many having some form in

---

54. Ibid. But see the following article, where St. Thomas asks, "Is a created good good by its essence?" to which he answers in the negative. The author of the *Book of Causes* is cited twice in the solution, where the question is no longer one of a received and limited form inhering in a created thing but one of what is something essentially (God) rather than participatively (the creature).

55. See S{77} & S{108}. Although Boethius is frequently cited as the source for this principle, the author of the *Book of Causes* more clearly and decisively articulates it. See Vansteenkiste, "Il *Libro de causis* negli scritti di San Tommaso," pp. 369–70. Also, see Henle, *Saint Thomas and Platonism*, p. 331. See *In Met.* I, Lect. 10, n. 158, for a succinct critique of this "similitude" principle in Plato.

common, there must be a one that is their source and explanation.[56] But he consistently rejects the "position" that the Platonists drew from it: that there is a first, self-subsisting idea or form for every class of being in which others exhibiting that form participate. Instead, St. Thomas places all such ideas in God as the first efficient, exemplary, and final cause of things. The author of the *Book of Causes* also has already made this correction (for the most part), placing all such forms in the unlimitedness of the first cause and, to a lesser extent, in the limitedness of intelligences and higher souls.[57] Common being for St. Thomas, then, is no longer "rooted" in a Platonic idea but in God: what God is essentially (and thus does not participate), creatures have participatively. But this must be understood analogously. Common being, which is shared and so finite, is not God. Creatures constitute common being, composed of act (existence, which is received) and potency (essence, which receives). Common being, then, is always an effect, viz., the creature that actually exists, really related to God as its cause, while God, in turn, is related to the creature only by a relation of reason. Things are in one another "only in the way that they can be in one another."[58] In this context, the role of intermediary Platonic ideas hierarchically arranged according to greater universality or commonality between the One and the many as what the many variously participate, is "corrected" by being eliminated.[59]

3. The doctrine of the triad of being, life, and intelligence, explicitly a doctrine of Proclus, is "corrected" by St. Thomas through his use of Pseudo-Dionysius and Aristotle. He places this triad formally in God alone as the very "nature" of God as the one who alone is being, life, and in-

---

56. See *ST* I, Q. 45, A 4. Also see Henle, *Saint Thomas and Platonism*, pp. 404–407.
57. See S{44} and S{20}.
58. See S{66 and 77}. For the ideas in God, see *ST* I, Q. 15, A. 1–3; for God as exemplary cause, see *ST* I, Q. 44, A. 3.
59. See S{64–65, 67–68}. St. Thomas accepts three basic kinds of participation: (1) participation in predication, which is only logical and therefore univocal, involving the ideas of species, genus, etc.; (2) participation of form in matter or of accidents in a subject, which is real and univocal, where such forms, whether substantial or accidental, exist only in the individuals with such forms, rather than as self-subsisting, as the Platonist view has it; (3) participation of effects in a universal cause, which is real but analogous, involving the relation of creature to Creator with respect to perfections that pertain to the creature participatively, but to God essentially. See *In Boeth. de Heb.*, Lect. 2. Also, see *In Met.* I, Lect. 10, n. 154; *ScG*, II, Cap. 52 & 54.

telligence "essentially."⁶⁰ So, too, the "Platonic position" of "the one and good" as transcending being (*esse*) is also corrected through the use of Pseudo-Dionysius: God's essence is simple, self-subsisting "to be," which is goodness itself.⁶¹

4. As a result of (3), the positing of an ideal intellect, which all intellects are supposed to participate in order to know, is no longer necessary, as the author of the *Book of Causes* also recognizes.⁶² So, too, the first infinite power is God, not an abstract Platonic idea after the one and good,⁶³ and God alone is absolutely self-sufficient.⁶⁴

5. The doctrine that intelligences (angels) create the nature of intellectual souls and inform them with knowledge, which the author of the *Book of Causes* espouses, is "corrected" by St. Thomas: creation of the intellectual or human soul is due to the direct activity of God alone. Any informing of the human soul with knowledge through the mediation of intelligences is only accidental, not essential.⁶⁵ So, too, any causal influence of intelligences and the heavenly bodies on the formation of the human being is restricted to the human body, insofar as matter is susceptible of being affected by such higher beings.⁶⁶

6. The position of the author of the *Book of Causes* that higher souls

---

60. See S{20, 23, 80, 103}.
61. See S{47}. This view, however, is more strictly speaking that of St. Thomas. For Pseudo-Dionysius, "to be" is the primary perfection of finite reality, caused by God and from which God is named as from his first proper effect. But God as the Good for Pseudo-Dionysius is above "to be" (see Fran O'Rourke, *Pseudo Dionysius*, pp. 123 and 275). In this regard, Aquinas could be said to be offering a "correction" of Pseudo-Dionysius, insofar as for Aquinas "to be" is not simply the primary effect caused by God as Creator but God's essence, and so God's most proper name.
62. See S{83}.
63. See S{92 and 94–95}.
64. See S{112}.
65. See S{23–24, 38, 62}. It is this doctrine which St. Thomas seems to have found the most objectionable of all held by the author of the *Book of Causes*: ". . . we find that certain people strayed from the truth by taking away from spiritual substances an origin in a first and highest Author." Applied specifically to the author of the *Book of Causes*: "Still others admit that all these substances have the origin of their being immediately from the First Principle; but in the case of their other attributes, for example, in that they are living, intelligible and the like, the higher substances are as causes for the lower ones" (*De Subst. sep.*, IX, 46; Lescoe trans., p. 56.) Also, see III Sent., D. 18, Q. 2, A. 2, ad 1 & ad 5.
66. See S{37–39}.

know in the way that intelligences do is "corrected" by a modification based on Aristotle: while intelligences are "full of forms," receiving intelligible species directly from God, the human intellect, Aquinas says, following Aristotle, is a "blank tablet," which in its dependence upon the senses needs to turn to phantasms in order to form concepts and thereby know its proper object, the quiddity of material things.[67]

Other positions, ones common to the "philosophers," also surface in the commentary, such as that the world is eternal, a view about which the author of the *Book of Causes* remains unclear. Aquinas examines the position of Averroes, who argues for the eternity of the world on the basis of the impossibility of a new effect coming about from an unchangeable and eternal will. Aquinas counters that in God, whose being is outside time and whose understanding is sempiternal, sempiternal understanding and producing a new effect are not opposed, just as similarly in us someone ". . . can, with his will remaining unchanged, defer his work to the future, so that he does it at a predetermined time."[68]

Another view common to the "philosophers," such as Plato and Aristotle, one which the author of the *Book of Causes* shares, is that the heavenly bodies are animated. Faith does not speak about it, and St. Thomas leaves the matter undecided. Elsewhere he argues that the motion of such bodies can be sufficiently explained by their heavenly bodies being guided by God as the first unmoved Mover, a Mover which, as a single superior immaterial substance, understanding many things at once, can also produce many simultaneous effects among material things.[69] But since the view that the heavenly bodies are animated is an opinion and has the status of probability, the sense in which that view can be maintained is, not that these bodies are themselves ensouled, but that intelligences direct their motion.[70]

67. See S{69 and 92}.
68. See S{74–77}.
69. See S{25 41}. See *In Met.* XII, Lect. 9, n. 2560.
70. See *Quaest. Disp. de spir. Creat.*, A. 6. Aquinas, recognizing the differing views on the subject of the heavenly bodies, the number of celestial motions, and the way in which all this motion is to be explained, remarks, ". . . if some view should appear later on in addition to those which are now stated . . . we must follow the opinion of those who have attained the truth with greater certitude" (*In Met.* XII, n. 2566). Also, see *ST* I, Q. 32, A. 1, ad 2.

Although St. Thomas rejects, qualifies, or recasts a number of views expressed, implied, or left undetermined by the author of the *Book of Causes*, he also acknowledges a number of other views which do not need rejection or "correction." In these instances St. Thomas offers an approving rather than critical interpretation of the text.

This brings us to our final point of consideration: the views expressed in the *Book of Causes* that St. Thomas takes over as themes expressive of his thought as well, citing them frequently in his other writings. One finds echoes of the author of the *Book of Causes* in some of the most common themes we have come to associate with the metaphysics of Aquinas:[71] (1) that the first being, God, is the "cause of causes," giving being (*esse*) to all others by way of creation; (2) that being (*esse*) as the "first of created things" is the most proper effect of God, and, in St. Thomas's metaphysics, is the perfection by which all other perfections are in the creature's real participation in what God essentially is; (3) that God as the first cause is "innermostly" present in all things by His abiding power as cause, preserving each thing in being; (4) that the higher a cause is, the more extensive and intensive its effects, so that the highest cause, God, is truly the first cause of all; (5) that the more united a power is, the more powerful and unlimited in its power it is, God alone having infinite power; (6) that second causes, while real causes, do not act without the first cause, and whatever power they have is due to the power of the first cause; (7) that God as being (*esse*) alone is infinite in that being, individuated by His own being as "pure goodness;" (8) that God is above every name and description; (9) that God rules all things without being mixed with them; (10) that intelligences or angels, which are "form and being" (essence and existence), are simple substances, undivided in being, diversified by their forms; (11) that such intelligences are "full of forms," i.e., they know a priori; (12) that higher angels possess a greater number of universal forms of knowledge, by which they know more things than do lower angels; (13) that every intellectual knower reverts to its essence in order to know (although Aquinas qualifies this when it comes to the human, who knows not by essence but by an intellect that turns to phantasms in order to form concepts of material things; (14) that the human

71. For a similar listing, see Elders, "Saint Thomas d'Aquin," pp. 438–39. For a listing of St. Thomas's citations of the *Book of Causes* in his other writings (including those passages cited unfavorably), see Appendix 2.

soul is free from the conditions of matter both in its being able to subsist as incorporeal and in its material activity of knowing; (15) that the human soul is on the "horizon" of the eternal and above the temporal, sharing in both worlds; (16) that what is received is received according to the mode of the recipient, and not as it exists in itself—a principle that applies to the various modes of both being and knowing; (17) that "all is in all" in the sense in which one thing may be in another, a cause in its effect in the mode proper to it and an effect in its cause in the mode proper to the latter.

Since many of these ideas found in the *Book of Causes* emerged out of a "communally" worked out and so continually developing philosophical heritage, the "originality" of the author of the *Book of Causes* cannot be claimed for each and every one of them. Still, their formulation and development in the *Book of Causes* bears the author's unique and undeniable stamp. When they are taken up by Aquinas into his thought, though often expressed in the very words of the author of the *Book of Causes*, they, too, bear Aquinas's unique and undeniable stamp as well.[72]

The influence of the *Book of Causes* has extended beyond St. Thomas to other medieval thinkers and, beyond and through them, to modern philosophy. There, this "Platonic heritage" finds applications quite different from and often contrary to those made by St. Thomas. One finds echoes of it in Descartes's *Meditations*, in particular in his "ontological proof" for the existence of God, according to which the idea of the perfect that exists innately in my understanding contains more objective reality than does my thought of it. Other echoes are present in the notion of the true idea found in Spinoza's *Ethics* and "On the Improvement of Human Understanding," as well as in Leibniz's conception of the monad, which corresponds in so many ways to the intelligences in the *Book of Causes* and to St. Thomas's angelology. So, too, in Kant, the notions of the architectonic function of pure reason, of the idea of the Ideal as the indeterminate source

---

72. As Fran O'Rourke remarks, "It is a hazardous endeavor to chart the history of intellectual influence; and in attempting to clarify the role of a chosen author, there is an unconscious temptation to extol his importance beyond due measure" (*Pseudo-Dionysius*, p. 276.) Determining the extent to which the author of the *Book of Causes* directly influenced St. Thomas is, of course, a matter beyond the scope of an introduction. The intent here is merely to point to a commonality of themes open to further historical study.

of all determinate predications, and of the faculty of understanding a priori constructing knowledge—all bear traces of such an influence. Finally, Hegel's triadic system as the life of Spirit unfolding itself in creation and returning back to itself in reconciliation seems undeniably indebted to the continued undercurrents of such a tradition, stretching back at least to Plotinus and Proclus.[73]

In an interesting "repetition" of history, Hegel sought to encircle religion, and especially the Christian religion, within the compass of his philosophy as the Idea of the Absolute, just as Plotinus and Proclus centuries before had sought in their philosophy to encircle Greek religion within the compass of the One as they understood it. Perhaps the absence of any such "grand" philosophy today shows itself in the difficulty of finding in the "many" any "One" by which they are and are united, as Plato and the Neoplatonists did in their own way, St. Thomas and the medievals in theirs, the moderns yet again in theirs. Even if we are post-moderns at the "end of philosophy," to use Heidegger's phrase, we at the same time still find ourselves asking the question of being, of life, and of intelligence—on none of which, from the viewpoint of science today, can we pronounce any too securely. So, too, the question of religion in relation to these three questions arises.

In an age preoccupied so often with the hermeneutics of suspicion, the critique of ideology, and deconstruction, the *Book of Causes* and St. Thomas's commentary on it turn our attention to the indication of something else as a motivating force in the history of human endeavors: the quest for Pure Goodness in the unity of Being, Knowing, and Life Itself.

---

73. As A. E. Taylor remarks: "It was from these sources [the Neoplatonic writings of Pseudo-Dionysius and the *Book of Causes*] that the schoolmen of the golden thirteenth century derived the peculiar theory of causality upon which their conception of the Universe rests, and it is most instructive, as an illustration of the impossibility of drawing any real dividing line between ancient and modern thought, to find Descartes, in the very act of professing to construct a new way in philosophy, assuming as his fundamental principle and treating as evident 'by the natural light' of the understanding just this same theory" ("The Philosophy of Proclus," in Taylor, *Philosophical Studies*, p. 152). And: "The manner and method of Proclus are, in fact, much those of the great rationalists of the seventeenth century from Descartes to Leibniz and Locke. In method, in particular, he recalls at once at least two famous names in modern philosophy, Spinoza and Hegel. Of Spinoza, he reminds us by the care with which his method is based on Euclid and the geometers, of Hegel by his insistence upon the grouping of notions in triads" (ibid., pp. 157–58).

A NOTE ON THE TRANSLATION

A translation of St. Thomas's *Super Librum de Causis Expositio* (*Commentary on the Book of Causes*) presents an unusual set of difficulties: St. Thomas commenting through the lens of a sometimes opaque Latin translation of an Arabic work, itself drawn in great part, but departing in significant ways, from an earlier Greek work, that of Proclus. The text chosen for our translation is the one provided by Fr. H.-D. Saffrey, O.P., who attempted a critical edition of the text by comparing the then-known available manuscripts. Since Saffrey's edition (1954), further work on both the Arabic and Latin manuscripts of the *Book of Causes*, as well as on St. Thomas's commentary, has been done. Therefore, in translating, we have followed Saffrey's text *except* in those places, always noted, where another reading of the text is now indicated. Numbers appearing in the text bold and in brackets { } refer to the pagination of Saffrey's edition and are designated S{ } in the footnotes.

In translating, we have sought to remain close to the literal meaning of the text, occasionally at the expense of some awkwardness in the English. This involves retaining the inaccuracies and occasional omissions in the Latin translation that St. Thomas presumably had before him, in order to show the difficulties he himself experienced in trying to comment on this work, as his remarks in the exposition from time to time indicate. In these cases we have provided the necessary footnotes to help the reader understand the correct text or the omissions.

As is the case with any translation, certain key terms have a nuance in one language that is lost in another, or a technical meaning in one language that they do not have in another. The latter is especially the case with the term *esse* (the verb "to be" in Latin), which translates a nontechnical term from the *Book of Causes*, but which in the thought of St. Thomas often has a more technical meaning. For the sake of simplicity, however, we have translated this term as "being," both in the *Book of Causes* and in St. Thomas's exposition, and footnoted passages that are possibly ambiguous; we have changed the translation to the inelegant "to be" only in a few instances in the exposition, when St. Thomas clearly intends it in his more technical meaning (e.g., see Proposition 6). The word *ens*, indicating being in the substantive rather than the verbal sense, we also translate as "being." Used less frequently than *esse*, it is usually accompanied by an article or other qualifying adjective. The word "being" with the possessive "its" or without any qualifier, except where noted, indicates *esse* in the Latin text.

The Latin expression *influere*, in its various forms, is translated as "to infuse," etc.; *influentia* usually as "infusion," but occasionally as "influence." *Causatum* is rendered "effect." *Superior* is usually rendered "higher," but occasionally as "transcending." We follow the conventional way of translating the expression *converti ad seipsum*, in its various forms, which in the Latin has the sense of a middle voice, with the active voice and the reflexive pronoun as "to turn to itself," etc. We render *reditio* and its various forms as "reversion," etc. The reader who wants to compare the translation of further terms with the Latin, as well as Arabic and Greek terms, should consult the footnotes throughout.

In St. Thomas's exposition, quotations taken from the *Book of Causes* are given in italics to distinguish them from other quotations, e.g., those from Proclus and Dionysius, which are placed in quotation marks. Each proposition from the *Book of Causes* is given a brief explanatory footnote, which relates it to comparable propositions in Proclus, and in some cases to Plotinus's works, and then lists St. Thomas's citations of this proposition elsewhere in his writings. Since footnotes as a rule refer to primary sources, the reader is advised to consult the bibliography for secondary sources.

For the convenience of the reader we provide the outline of the *Book of Causes* that St. Thomas indicates as he interprets this work in the progress of his exposition. This outline also provides a rationale for our assigning a "title" in brackets to each proposition in the table of contents. The reader, however, should be cautioned that the *Book of Causes* itself contains no such titles to designate the subject matter of each proposition and that St. Thomas's division of the text is not the only one possible. Consequently, such titles indicate St. Thomas's understanding of this work rather than the expressed thought of the author of the *Book of Causes*.

Two appendices are provided at the end of the work: (1) another version of Proposition 29 (30) of the *Book of Causes*, unknown to St. Thomas;

and (2) a listing of texts from St. Thomas's other works that cite the *Book of Causes* and various propositions from it.

Special thanks must be given to The Dominican School of Philosophy and Theology at the Graduate Theological Union, Berkeley, and to Marquette University for their support in this project. Special thanks also to Fr. Hilary Martin, O.P., and Fr. Owen Carroll for their involvement in the earlier stages of this work, to Fr. Lawrence Dewan, O.P., for some suggestions about the translation, and to Fr. Saffrey, O.P., for his encouragement of the undertaking of this collaborative translation. Finally, special thanks to the Director of The Catholic University of America Press, Dr. David McGonagle, for his patience in understanding the delays that invariably seem to accompany translations.

As a final point of clarification, I note that Appendix 2 and the documentation in the footnotes with respect to both the Arabic and Latin manuscripts of the *Book of Causes* and the influence of Plotinus's *Enneads* are the work of Professor Richard Taylor, who has devoted much of his academic career and talents to sorting out the many difficulties contained in this sometimes baffling, but nevertheless fascinating and influential work.

OUTLINE OF THE *BOOK OF CAUSES*
according to St. Thomas's Division of the Text

The principle of the entire work respects the order found in causes, expressed in a threefold way:
1. The first cause infuses the effect more powerfully than does a second cause.
2. The impression of the first cause recedes from the effect last.
3. The impression of the first cause reaches the effect first. (Prop. 1)

    I. How universal causes are distinguished (Props. 2–15)
1. He distinguishes universal causes (Props. 2–5)
   a. into three grades:
      1) the first cause, which is God
      2) intelligences
      3) souls (Prop. 2)
   b. How they are united through a certain participation in the ultimate cause (Prop. 3)
   c. He distinguishes intelligences (Prop. 4)
   d. He distinguishes souls (Prop. 5)
2. He investigates these one at a time (Props. 6–15)
   a. the first cause, God, is inexpressible whether
      1) through a cause
      2) through itself or
      3) through an effect (Prop. 6)
   b. an intelligence (Props. 7–13)
      1) as regards its substance (Prop. 7)
      2) as regards its knowledge (Props. 8–13)
         a) how it knows things other than itself (Props. 8–12)
            [1] it knows both higher and lower things (Prop. 8)
            [2] it knows what is above it (Prop. 9)
            [3] in general, how it knows things other than itself (Prop. 10)
            [4] in particular, what it knows
               [a] it knows eternal things (Prop. 11)
               [b] intelligences mutually understand one another (Prop. 12)
         b) how it knows itself (Prop. 13)

c. the soul (Props. 14 & 15)
   1) its relation to other things (Prop. 14)
   2) in itself (Prop. 15)

   II. How lower things depend upon higher causes and how higher causes relate to one another (Props. 16–32)
1. How lower things depend upon higher things (Props. 16–19)
   a. according to power (Props. 16 & 17)
      1) all unlimited powers depend upon the first infinite power (Prop. 16)
      2) how they are assimilated to it in greater or lesser degrees (Prop. 17)
   b. according to substance and nature (Props. 18 & 19)
      1) the universal dependence of things upon the first cause (Prop. 18)
      2) the different degrees of closeness to the first cause according to the participation of some natural perfection (Prop. 19)
2. How higher things infuse lower things with perfections (Props. 20–23)
   a. on the universal rule of the first cause (Props. 20–22)
      1) the manner of divine rule (Prop. 20)
      2) the sufficiency of divine abundance (Prop. 21)
      3) the excellence of divine goodness (Prop. 22)
   b. on the rule of an intelligence, whose power is due to the power of the first cause (Prop. 23)
3. How lower things diversely receive perfections from the first cause infusing them (Props. 24–32)
   a. in general (Prop. 24)
   b. in particular (Props. 25–32)
      1) on the difference between corruptible and incorruptible things (Props. 25–27)
         a) ingenerable substances (Prop. 25)
         b) incorruptible substances (Prop. 26)
         c) corruptible substances (Prop. 27)
      2) on the difference between simple and composed things (Props. 28 & 29)
         a) a steadfastly abiding substance is simple (Prop. 28)
         b) conversely, a simple substance is steadfastly abiding (Prop. 29)
      3) on the difference between eternity and time (Props. 30–32)
         a) the order of temporal things to one another (Prop. 30)
         b) the order of eternal things to one another (Prop. 31)
         c) the condition of the soul as one between eternity and time (Prop. 32)

ST. THOMAS AQUINAS

Commentary on the Book of Causes

PREFACE

As the Philosopher says in Book 10 of the *Ethics*,[1] ultimate human happiness lies in the noblest human activity, that of our highest faculty, the intellect, in relation to the noblest intelligible reality. Since an effect is known through its cause, it is clear that a cause is by its nature more intelligible than an effect, although effects are sometimes better known than causes from our perspective,[2] because we acquire knowledge of universal and intelligible causes from sensible particulars. Speaking unqualifiedly, then, the first causes of things must be those intelligible realities which are in themselves[3] the greatest and noblest in that they are beings and true to the greatest degree, {2} since they are the cause of the essence and truth of other things, as the Philosopher makes clear in Book 2 of the *Metaphysics*,[4] even though first causes of this sort are known less well and later from our perspective. Our intellect relates to them as an owl's eye does to sunlight, which it cannot perceive well because of the sun's intense brightness.[5] Therefore, the ultimate human happiness possible in this life must lie in the consideration of first causes, because what little we can know about them is worthier of devotion and nobler than all that we can know about lower things, as the Philosopher makes clear in Book 1 of *On the Parts of Animals*.[6] However, as this knowledge [of first causes] becomes complete after this life, we shall then be made perfectly blessed, according to the words of the Gospel, "This is eternal life, that they know You, the one true God."[7]

Thus, the aim of the philosophers was principally that, through everything that they considered in [their study of] things, they might arrive at a knowledge of first causes. Accordingly, they placed the science of first causes last, reserving it for the mature part of their life. First they began

---

1. Aristotle, *Nicomachean Ethics*, X 7, 1177a12–14.
2. *quoad nos*.
3. *secundum se*. On the distinction of things more knowable to us from those more knowable in themselves, see Aristotle, *Posterior Analytics*, I 2, 71b33–72a5; and *Metaphysics*, VII 3, 1029a34–b11.
4. Aristotle, *Metaphysics*, II 1, 993b26–31.
5. Aristotle, *Metaphysics*, II 1, 993b9–11.
6. Aristotle, *On the Parts of Animals*, I 5, 644b32–34.
7. John 17:3.

with logic, which deals with the method of the sciences. Next they proceeded to mathematics, which even children can have the capacity for. Third to natural philosophy, which requires time for experience. Fourth to moral philosophy, which young people are not ready for.[8] And last they turned to the study of divine science,[9] which treats the first causes of beings.

{3} Thus we find a collection of writings on first principles that are divided into different propositions, in a way similar to the procedure of those examining certain truths one at a time.[10] And in Greek we find handed down a book of this type by the Platonist Proclus, which contains 211 propositions and is entitled *The Elements of Theology*. And in Arabic we find the present book which is called *On Causes* among Latin readers, [a work] known to have been translated from Arabic and not [known] to be extant at all in Greek. Thus, it seems that one of the Arab philosophers excerpted it from this book by Proclus, especially since everything in it is contained much more fully and more diffusely in that of Proclus.

The aim, then, of this book called *On Causes* is to delineate the first causes of things. And since the word "cause" implies an order of some kind, and in causes we find an ordering of one to another, [the author] introduces as the principle of the entire work that follows a certain proposition concerning the order found in causes. The proposition is:

---

8. Cf. Aristotle, *Nicomachean Ethics*, I 3, 1095a2. This reference is supplied by Fr. Saffrey in a corrected copy of his edition.

9. I.e., metaphysics, first philosophy or philosophical theology. See Aristotle, *Metaphysics*, I 2, 983a6–10; VI 1, 1026a10–33. See St. Thomas, *In Eth.*, VI, Lect. 7. St. Thomas makes a distinction between two kinds of divine science, or theology: metaphysics, which considers divine being as the principle and cause of all things, in which divine being is not the subject of metaphysics but a cause that transcends the subject, known only through its effects; and Christian theology (*sacra doctrina*), which is based on Scripture as revealed knowledge of God as He is in Himself. See *In Boeth. de Trin.*, Q. 5, A. 4, c.

10. That is, the geometrical method of Euclid, which is imitated by Proclus in the *Elements of Theology*. See Dodds, p. xi.

{4} PROPOSITION 1[1]

Every primary cause infuses its effect more powerfully[2] than does a universal second cause.

Now when a universal second cause removes its power from a thing, the universal first cause does not withdraw its power from it. This is because the universal first cause acts on the effect of the second cause before the universal second cause, which follows the effect,[3] acts on it. So when the second cause which follows the effect acts, its act is not independent of the first cause, which is above it. And when the second cause is separated from the effect that follows it, the first cause, which is above it, is not separated from the effect, because it is its cause.[4]

    1. This proposition is derived from Props. 56 and 70 of Proclus's *Elements*. Cf. Dodds, p. 54.4–5; p. 66.14–16, 66.18–30. St. Thomas relates it specifically to Props. 56 and 57. He refers to this proposition in a number of his writings, e.g. *ST* I–II, Q. 2, A. 6, 2a; III, Q. 6, A. 4, 3a; *De Veritate*, Q. 5, A. 8, s.c. 9; Q. 5, A. 9, 10a; Q. 6, A. 6c; Q. 24, A. 1, 4a; Q. 24, A. 14c; *De Potentia*, Q. 3, A. 4c & 7c; Q. 5, A. 8c. In Aristotelian fashion, St. Thomas analyzes the application of this proposition in terms of the four causes, where the efficient cause expresses the primary sense of this principle. Elsewhere St. Thomas relates infusion (*influentia*) to creation (". . . the infusion of the first agent, which is creation . . ." [. . . *influentia primi agentis, quae est creatio* . . .] [*II Sent.*, D. 1, Q. 1, A. 3, ad 4]) and to God's both causing and conserving the existence of things (*esse rei*) (*II Sent.*, D. 15, Q. 3, A. 1, ad 5).
    2. *plus est influens super causatum suum*. Literally, "pours forth more abundantly on its effect." This key notion is here translated by forms of "infuse," a word derived from the past participle of *infundere*, "to pour in." The modern English "to influence" or "to exercise influence" fails to capture the notion that the power of the first cause— as source for the second cause—both constitutes and thoroughly permeates the second cause and all that proceeds from the second cause.
    3. *quae sequitur ipsum*; literally, which follows it (*causatum*: the effect). As A. Pattin has noted (Pattin, "De hierarchie," pp. 130–31), this reading of the Latin entails the more than awkward consequence that the second cause is said to follow the effect that it causes. It is for this reason that Pattin adopted the reading, *quae sequitur ipsam*: which follows it (*causa prima*: the first cause). Nevertheless, the correct reading is *quae sequitur ipsum*, in which the Latin verb *sequi* is used incorrectly to render the Arabic verb *waliya*, here found in the form of *talihi*. *Waliya* here means "to be [immediately] adjacent to" or "to be near," not "to follow." For detailed discussion of this, see Richard C. Taylor, "A Note on Chapter 1 of the *Liber de Causis*," *Manuscripta* 22 (1978), pp. 169–72. Note also that St. Thomas omits this clause when he quotes this passage in his commentary.
    4. The Latin and two of the Arabic manuscripts here omit a version that is pre-

We find an example of this in being,[5] living, and man, for it is necessary that something be first of all a being, next a living thing, and afterward a man. Therefore, living is man's proximate cause and being is his remote cause. Being then is more powerfully the cause of man than is living, because it is the cause of living, which is the cause of man. Likewise, when you assert rationality to be the cause of man, being is more powerfully the cause of man than is rationality, because it is the cause of his cause. The indication of this[6] is that, when you remove the rational power from a man, a man does not remain, but living, breathing, and sensible remain. And when you remove living from him, living does not remain, but being remains, because being is not removed from him, but living is removed, since the cause is not removed through the removal of its effect. As a consequence, the man remains a being. So when the individual is not a man, it is an animal, and, if it is not an animal, it is only a being.

It is, therefore, now clear and plain that the first remote cause is more comprehensively and more powerfully the cause of a thing than the proximate cause. For this reason, its activity comes to adhere more powerfully to the thing than the activity of the proximate cause. It happens in this way only because a thing first of all is affected by the remote power alone and then is secondly affected by the power that is below the first.

The first cause aids the second cause in its activity, because the first cause also effects every activity that the second cause effects, although it effects it in another way [which is] higher and more sublime. When the second cause is removed from its effect, the first cause is not removed from it, because the first cause adheres more greatly and more powerfully to the thing than does the proximate cause. The effect of the second cause is only through the power of the first cause. This is because, when the second cause makes a thing, the first cause, which is above it, infuses that thing with its power, so that it adheres powerfully to that thing[7] and conserves it.

---

served in the oldest of the three Arabic manuscripts: "because it [the first cause] is cause of its cause. The first cause, then, is more the cause of the thing than its proximate cause, which is [immediately] adjacent to it." See Taylor (1981), pp. 437–38.

5. *Esse* is the translation of the Arabic *anniya*, which for the author of the *De Causis* does not have the technical meaning of the act of "to be" that it does for St. Thomas. Rather, for him it is the formal substrate upon which life and intelligence are received. See Taylor (1979), p. 506.

6. Saffrey, reprinting Bardenhewer's edition of the Latin text, has *Et illius quod dicimus significatio*. Instead, read *Et illius quidem significatio* with six important manuscripts (Aosta and Pattin's LOSTV) and the Arabic text.

7. *quare adhaeret illud rei adhaerentia vehementi*. The corresponding Arabic has: "so

It is, therefore, now clear and plain that the remote cause is more powerfully the cause of a thing than the proximate cause that follows it,[8] *and that the remote cause infuses the thing with its power, conserves it, and is not separated from it by the separation of its proximate cause. Rather, it remains in it and adheres to it powerfully, as we have shown and explained.*

COMMENTARY

{5} Every primary cause infuses its effect more powerfully than does a universal second cause.

To make this clear [the author] introduces a corollary through which he clarifies the first point as through a certain sign. So he adds: *Now when a universal second cause removes its power from a thing, the universal first cause does not withdraw its power from it.* To prove this he introduces a third point, saying: *This is because the universal first cause acts on the effect of the second cause before the universal second cause acts on it.* From this he infers what he asserted in the corollary, and rightly so, because what arrives first must depart last, for we see that those things that are prior in composition are last in resolution. The meaning of this proposition, therefore, consists in these three points: (1) that the first cause infuses the effect more powerfully than does the second cause; (2) that the impression of the first cause recedes later from the effect; (3) that it reaches the effect first. Proclus makes these three points in two propositions. The first is in Proposition 56 of his book, which is as follows: "Everything that is produced by what is secondary is produced more eminently by what is prior and more causally efficacious, by which what is secondary is also produced."[9] He makes the other two points in the next proposition, which is as follows: "Every cause both acts prior to its effect and is the basis of more things after it."[10]

---

that it [the first cause] strongly adheres to that thing." This grammatically problematic passage of the Latin is based on a literal rendering of a corruption in the Arabic manuscript used for the twelfth-century Latin translation. The reading of the Latin suggested by Pattin (I 17.61–62) must be rejected in favor of this *lectio difficilior.*

8. *quae sequitur eam.* While in Latin the referent of the pronoun *eam* may be either cause (*causa*) or thing (*res*), in Arabic the text is unambiguous: "which is [immediately] adjacent to the thing."

9. Proclus, Prop. 56, Dodds, p. 54.4–6; Vansteenkiste, p. 286.

10. Proclus, Prop. 57, Dodds, p. 54.23–24; Vansteenkiste, p. 286. *Substitutiva,*

After making these three points, the author proceeds to clarify them, first through an example, second through an argument, at: *The first cause aids.*

Now the example seems to pertain to formal causes in which the more universal a form is the greater priority it seems to have. {6} So, if we take a *man,* [for example,] his specific form is observed in the fact that he is rational. But the generic form is observed in the fact that he is *living* or animal. Finally there is that which is common to all, *being.* Now it is clear that in the generation of one particular man, the first thing found in the material subject is being, then living, and after that man, for he is animal before he is man, as is said in Book 2 of *On the Generation of Animals.*[11] Again, in the process of corruption he first loses the use of reason, while living and breathing remain. Second he loses life, while being itself remains, because he does not corrupt into nothing. And in this way the example can be understood with reference to the generation and corruption of some individual. That this is his intent is clear from what he says: *So when the individual is not a man,* that is, according to the act proper to man, *it is an animal,* because animal activity, which consists in movement and sense, still remains in it, and when *it is not an animal, it is only a being,* because a completely inanimate body remains. This example is verified in the very order of things, for existing things are prior to living things and living things are prior to men, because when man is removed what animal entails is not removed. Instead, the opposite[12] is the case, because, if there is no animal, there is no man. The same argument applies to animal and being.[13]

Then, when he says, *The first cause* etc., he proves the three points mentioned above by an argument. Now he proves the first point, that the first cause infuses more powerfully than does the second, in this way. Any characteristic belongs more eminently to the cause {7} than to the effect. But the activity by which the second cause causes an effect is caused by the first cause, *for the first cause aids the second cause,* making it act. Therefore, *the first cause* is more a cause than the second cause of that *activity* in

---

which Moerbeke uses to render the Greek *hypostatikon,* seems to mean "standing as a basis for" or "constitutive of" as a difficult literal rendering of the Greek into Latin.

11. Aristotle, *On the Generation of Animals,* II 3, 736a24.
12. We read *e contrario* with Saffrey's corrected copy instead of the printed *e converso.*
13. For use of this analysis by St Thomas, see, e.g. *ST,* I–II, Q. 67, A. 5, ad 1.

virtue of which an *effect* is produced by *the second cause*. Proclus, however, proves this more explicitly as follows.[14] The second cause, since it is the effect of the first cause, has its "substance" from the first cause. But from that from which something has substance, it also has the "potency," or power, to act. Therefore, the second cause has its potency, or power, to act from the first cause. But the second cause is the cause of the effect through its potency, or power. Therefore, that the second cause is the cause of its effect is due to the first cause. To be the cause of the effect, therefore, lies primarily in the first cause and only secondarily in the second cause. Now what is prior in all things is greater, since more perfect things are prior by nature. The first cause, therefore, is more the cause of the effect than the second cause.

He proves the second point, that the impression of the first cause recedes later from the effect, at: *When the second cause is removed* etc. He puts forward this argument: What is more powerfully in a thing inheres more [profoundly]. But the first cause impresses more powerfully upon the effect than does the second cause, as was proved. Therefore, its impression inheres more [profoundly]. Consequently, it recedes later.

He proves the third point, that the first cause arrives first, at: *The effect of the second cause is only* etc., with this argument. The second cause acts {8} on its effect only by the power of the first cause. The effect, then, proceeds from the second cause only through the power of the first cause. The power of the first cause thus enables the effect to be affected by the power of the second cause. Therefore, it is affected first by the power of the first cause. But Proclus proves this[15] with one middle term in the following way. The first cause is more a cause than the second. Therefore, it has more perfect power. But the more perfect the power of any cause is, the more things to which it extends itself. Therefore, the power of the first cause extends itself to more things than does the power of the second cause. But what is in more things is first in arriving and last in receding. Therefore, the impression of the first cause arrives first and recedes last.

We should now consider the [kinds of] causes for which this proposition is true. If the question refers to the kinds of causes, it is clear that it is true in its own way in every kind of cause. An example has already been presented in the case of formal causes. But a similar argument is

14. Proclus, Prop. 56, Dodds, p. 54.7ff; Vansteenkiste, p. 286.
15. Proclus, Prop. 57, Dodds, p. 54.25ff; Vansteenkiste, p. 286.

found in the case of material causes, for what first underlies as matter is the cause of more proximate matter by materially underlying it, as prime matter underlies the elements, which are in a certain way the matter of mixed bodies. Both of these, in addition, show that the same is the case with efficient causes. For it is clear that the extent to which some efficient cause is prior, to that extent does its power extend itself to more things. Hence its proper effect must be more common. But the proper effect of the second cause is found in fewer things. So it is more particular. For the first cause itself produces or moves the cause acting secondarily and so becomes the cause of its acting.

Therefore, the three previously mentioned points we have touched upon are found originally in efficient causes. From this it is clear that this principle applies to formal causes by derivation. For this reason [the author] uses the word "infusing"[16] here, while Proclus employs the word "production,"[17] {9} which expresses the causality of an efficient cause. But that this principle applies by derivation from efficient causes to material causes is not so clear, because the efficient causes of our experience produce not matter but form. Yet, if we consider the universal causes from which the material principles of things proceed, this order must also apply to material causes by derivation from efficient causes. For, because the efficacy, or causality, of the first and supreme cause extends itself to more things, it is necessary that what first underlies all things[18] be from the first cause of all things. Then second causes add the dispositions in virtue of which matters are made suitable to singular things.[19] This appears in one way or another in the things of our experience, for nature provides prime matter for all artificial things. Then certain prior arts dispose natural matter to make it suited to the more particular arts. The first cause of all things, however, is compared to the whole of nature as nature is to art. Hence that which first underlies the whole of nature is from the first cause of all things, and the function of second causes is to make it suitable for singular things.

16. *influendi*.
17. *productionis*. Proclus, Prop. 56, Dodds, p. 54; Vansteenkiste, p. 286. In Moerbeke's translation of this proposition, forms of *producere* are used to render forms of the Greek *paragein*.
18. *subsistit in omnibus*.
19. That is, unformed matters created by the first cause have their being specified by secondary causes, and from this process singular things are originated.

It is clear that everything we have said above is also verified in final causes, for because of the ultimate end, which is universal, other ends are sought. The desire for these other ends comes after the desire for the ultimate end and ceases before it. But the explanation of this order leads back to the genus of efficient cause, for the end is a cause inasmuch as the end moves the efficient cause to act; thus, insofar as [the end] has the character of a mover, it belongs in a certain sense to the genus of efficient cause.

If, however, someone asks whether for every genus of causes the above prove true in all causes regardless of how they happen to be ordered, it is clear that this is not the case. For we find causes to be ordered in two ways: in one way *per se* and in another *per accidens*. The order is *per se* when the intention of the first cause respects the ultimate effect {**10**} through all the mediating causes, as when a craftsman's art moves the hand, and the hand a hammer that pounds out the iron, to which the intention of the art reaches. The order is *per accidens*, however, when the intention of the cause proceeds only to the proximate effect. But that something else is in turn brought about by that effect lies outside the intention of the first agent, as, when someone lights a candle, it is outside his intention that the lighted candle in turn light another, and that one another. What lies outside an intention, however, we say to be *"per accidens."* Therefore, this proposition is true for causes that are ordered *per se* in which the first cause moves all the mediating causes to the effect. But in causes ordered *per accidens* it is the opposite, for the effect produced *per se* by the proximate cause is produced *per accidens* by the first cause, being outside its intention. Now what is *per se* is more powerful than what is *per accidens*. For this reason he expressly says "universal cause," which is a *per se* cause.

PROPOSITION 2[1]

Every higher being is higher than eternity and before it[2] or is with eternity or is after eternity and above time.

The being that is before eternity is the first cause, since it is the cause of eternity. The being that is with eternity is an intelligence,[3] since it is second being. Existing in a single state,[4] it neither undergoes change nor is subject to destruction. The being that is after eternity and above time is the soul, since it is lower on the horizon of eternity and above time.

The indication that the first cause is before eternity itself is that being in eternity is acquired. And I say that all eternity is being but not all being is eternity.[5] So being is more common than eternity. The first cause is above eternity because eternity is its effect. An intelligence is placed at or made equal to eternity because it is

---

1. This proposition is derived from Props. 88 and 87 respectively in the *Elements*. Cf. Dodds, p. 80.25–27, 80.22–23, 80.15, 80.22. St. Thomas relates it to these, as well as to Props. 169 and 191. He cites it regarding God in *ST*, I, Q. 10, A. 2, 2a; regarding intelligences in *De Veritate*, Q. 8, A. 14, 12a; *ST*, I, Q. 57, A. 3, 2a; Q. 61, A. 2, 2a; and regarding the intellectual soul in *SCG*, II, 68; III, 61; *De Potentia*, Q. 3, A. 9, 27a and A. 10, 8a.

2. *Omne esse superius aut est superius aeternitate et ante ipsam*. Less literally, "Every transcendent being transcends eternity and is before it. . . ." *Esse superius*, "higher being" or "superior being," might be translated as "transcendent being," since this more readily conveys in English the notion expressed by the Latin: those beings that are not restricted to the temporal realm but transcend time in one or more of the ways mentioned. Here and in most of this work, however, we retain the more literal translation.

3. For St. Thomas these intelligences or separate substances are understood as angels: ". . . in some works translated from the Arabic, the separate substances that we call angels are called intelligences, and perhaps for this reason, that such substances are always actually understanding. But in works translated from the Greek, they are called intellects or minds" (*ST*, I, Q. 79, A. 10c; Benzinger trans.).

4. *esse secundum; secundum habitudinem unam, non patitur neque destruitur.* This Latin text is based on a minor but significant corruption (missing or misplaced diacritical marks) in the Arabic manuscript tradition. The Latin translator read *al-anniyah al-thaniyah* ("second being," *esse secundum*) while the correct reading is *al-anniyah al-thabitah* ("being standing stable"). Thus the Arabic has a commonplace, formulaic description of the nature of an intelligence: "It is being standing stable in a single state, neither being acted upon nor undergoing transformation." See Taylor (1981), pp. 145; 355–56; 442–43.

5. *omnis aeternitas est esse sed non omne esse est aeternitas.*

coextensive with eternity and neither changes nor is subject to destruction. The soul is joined to eternity in a lower way, since it is more susceptible to impression than is an intelligence, and it is above time, since it is the cause of time.

COMMENTARY

{11} After setting down the first proposition, which serves as a certain principle for the entire treatise that follows, [the author] begins here to treat of the first causes of things. He divides [the treatment] into two parts. In the first part he treats of the distinction of first causes. In the second part he treats of their coordination or dependence upon one another, in Proposition 16, at: *All the powers* that *have no limit* etc. He further divides the first part into two parts. In the first part he distinguishes first causes. In the second part he delineates them individually, in Proposition 6, at: *The first cause transcends*[6] etc.

Now the universal causes of things are of three kinds: (1) the first cause, which is God, (2) intelligences, and (3) souls. Regarding the first division he does three things: (1) he distinguishes these three kinds, in which the first is undivided because there is only one first cause; (2) he distinguishes intelligences, in Proposition 4, at: *The first of created things* etc.; (3) he distinguishes souls, in Proposition 5, at: *The higher intelligences* etc.

Regarding the very first division he makes, he does two things. First, he distinguishes the three kinds just mentioned. Second, he shows how they are united through a certain participation in the ultimate, in Proposition 3, at: *Every noble soul* etc.

With regard to the first division he asserts the following proposition: *Every higher being is higher than eternity and is before it, or is with eternity, or is after eternity and above time.* To understand this proposition it is necessary first to see what eternity is, then in what way the above proposition is true.

Now the word "eternity" implies a certain unfailingness or unendingness,[7] for to be eternal means to exist, as it were, without {12} limits.

---

6. *superior est.*

7. *interminabilitatem,* which contrasts in Latin with *extra terminos,* "without limits," in the same sentence.

But because, as the Philosopher says in Book 8 of the *Physics*,[8] in every motion there is some corruption and generation, inasmuch as something begins to be and something ceases to be, there must be some deficiency[9] in any motion whatsoever. Thus all motion is repugnant to eternity. True eternity, along with unfailingness of being, then, implies immobility as well. Now because the before and after in the duration of time result from motion, as is clear in Book 4 of the *Physics*,[10] it is therefore necessary, third, that eternity be existing all at the same time, without a before and after, as Boethius defines it at the end of *On the Consolation of Philosophy*, saying: "Eternity is the simultaneously total and perfect possession of unending life."[11]

Therefore, any thing with unfailingness of being that has immobility and is without temporal succession can be called eternal. The Platonists and the Peripatetics called immaterial separate substances eternal in this sense, adding to the notion of eternity that it always had being.[12] But this is not in accord with Christian faith,[13] for eternity in this sense belongs to God alone.[14] We call them eternal, however, as things that begin to obtain from God perpetual and unfailing being without motion and temporal succession. So Dionysius also says, in Chapter 10 of *On the Divine Names*,[15] that the things that are called eternal in Scripture are not ab-

8. Aristotle, *Physics*, VIII 3, 254a11–12.
9. *deficientia*, which contrasts with *indeficientia*, "unfailingness" below.
10. Aristotle, *Physics*, IV 11, 219a17–19.
11. Boethius, *On the Consolation of Philosophy*, V, Prosa 6; CSEL LXVII, p. 122.12–13; PL 63, 858 A. Testor (1973), p. 423: "Eternity, then, is the whole, simultaneous and perfect possession of boundless life . . ." Also, see *I Sent.*, D. 8, Q. 2, A. 1 for St. Thomas's discussion of Boethius's definition.
12. Cf. St. Augustine, *City of God*, X, Chap. 31; PL 41, 311. See *II Sent.*, D. 1, Q. 1, A. 5 and *SCG*, II, 32–37 for St. Thomas's discussion of such arguments.
13. Cf. *Concilium Lateranense IV*, cap. 1: Firmiter; Denzinger, *Enchir. Symb.*, n. 428; and S. Th., *In Decret. Iam Exp.*, p. 333 (Mandonnet).
14. Regarding the eternity of God, see *ST*, I, Q. 10, A. 1–3 and *I Sent.*, D. 19, Q. 2, A. 1–2.
15. Pseudo-Dionysius, *On the Divine Names*, Chap. 10, 3; *Dionysiaca* I, 492; PG 3, 940 A. "It is therefore necessary that we do not conceive those which are called eternal to be co-eternal with the God which is before eternity. But, following the most august writings, we should understand 'eternal' and 'temporal' according to the characteristics that agree with them. Further, we should interpret those beings that in some way [partake in] eternity and in some way [partake in] time to be intermediate between those which are and those which come to be." Pseudo-Dionysius Areopagite, *The Divine Names and Mystical Theology*, tr. John D. Jones (Milwaukee: Marquette University Press, 1980), p. 194.

solutely coeternal with God. For this reason some call eternity taken in this sense {13} *aevum*, which they distinguish from eternity taken in the first sense. But, if one considers the matter correctly, *aevum* and "eternity" differ no more than do *anthropos* and "man." For in Greek eternity is called *evon*,[16] just as man is called *anthropos*.

So, in light of these distinctions, we should realize that this proposition is found in Proclus's book as Proposition 88 in these words: "Every beingly," or existential, "being is before eternity or in eternity, or participating eternity."[17] Now "beingly being" is said [here] in contrast to mobile being, just as to be abiding steadfastly[18] is said in contrast to to be changing.[19] Accordingly, we can understand by this what *every higher being* means in this book, namely, that it is above motion and time. For, according to the authors of both books, being of this kind is divided into three grades, although it is not for altogether the same reason for each [author].

For Proclus presents this proposition according to the theories of the Platonists, who, in maintaining the abstraction of universals, held that the more abstract and universal something is, the greater priority it has. For it is clear that this mode of expression, "eternity," is more abstract than "eternal," since the word "eternity" designates the very essence of eternity, but the word "eternal" designates what participates eternity. Furthermore, being itself is more common than eternity, for "every eternal thing is being, but not every being is eternal."[20] So, in accord with what was previously said, separate being itself is {14} before eternity, while sempiternal being is with eternity, and everything that participates eternal being participates eternity and is, as it were, after eternity.

Now, first of all, the author of this book agrees to some extent with

---

16. Thus in the manuscript for the Greek word *aion*. See Saffrey, p. 13, note. For a fuller discussion of the distinction between eternity and *aevum*, see *ST* I, Q. 10, A. 5; *I Sent.*, D. 8, Q. 2, A. 1 and 2; *II Sent*, D. 2, Q. 1. A. 1–3; *Quodlibet*. V, Q. 4, A. 7; *In de div. Nom.* V, Lect. 1 and X, Lect. 3.

17. Proclus, Prop. 88, Dodds, p. 80.25–26; Vansteenkiste, p. 298: *Omne enter ens aut ante aeternitatem est, aut in aeternitate, aut participans aeternitate*. *Enter ens* renders the Greek *to ontos on*. *Enter* and *existenter* are translated by "beingly" and "existential" respectively to reflect equally in English the awkwardness of these words in thirteenth-century Latin.

18. *esse stans*.

19. *moveri*.

20. Proclus, Prop. 87, Dodds, p. 80.15; Vansteenkiste, p. 298.

the positions just mentioned. So he explains that *The being that is before eternity is the first cause because it is the cause* of eternity. To prove this he introduces the idea that *in it*, i.e., in eternity, *being is acquired*, i.e., participated. He proves this by arguing that things that are less common participate things that are more common. But eternity is less common than being. So he continues: *And I say that every eternity is being but not every being is eternity. Therefore, being is more common than eternity.* In this way he proves that eternity participates being. But abstract being itself is the first cause whose substance is its own being. So it remains that the first cause is the cause from which anything always existing acquires sempiternal being.

But in [explaining] the other two members[21] of the division the author of this book departs from the intention of Proclus and approaches more the common opinions of the Platonists and Peripatetics. For he explains the second grade [of higher being] by saying that *the being with eternity is an intelligence*. For, because eternity, as was said,[22] implies unfailingness with immobility, whatever is unfailing and immobile in every way wholly attains eternity. But the above-mentioned philosophers hold that an intelligence, or separate intellect, has unfailingness and immobility in being, in power, and in activity. So Proposition 169 of Proclus is: "Every intellect {15} has substance, potency and activity in eternity."[23] And in accord with this the author proves here that *an intelligence is with eternity* because it is altogether *in a single state* so that *it neither undergoes* any change of power or activity *nor is it* as well *subject to destruction* in substance. For this reason he later also says that *it is made equal* to eternity *because it is co-extensive with it and does not change* because eternity extends itself to everything that has the character of an intelligence.

Finally he explains the third grade as soul, which has higher being, i.e., as [being that is] above motion and time. For such a soul more closely approaches motion than does an intelligence, because an intelligence is clearly not touched by motion in either [its] substance or [its] activity. But the soul in [its] substance surpasses time and motion and touches eternity, while in its activity it touches motion because, as the philoso-

21. I.e., intelligences and the soul.
22. Cf. above, S{12}.
23. Proclus, Prop. 169, Dodds, p. 146.24–25; Vansteenkiste, p. 515. Also, see St. Thomas, *De Subst. sep.*, Cap. 20 (vol. 40 D Leon.), p. 79b, 307–10.

PROPOSITION 2

phers prove,[24] whatever is moved by another must be reduced to something first, which moves itself. Now for Plato it is the soul that moves itself,[25] but for Aristotle it is the animated body, whose principle of motion is the soul.[26] Thus on either account the first principle of motion must be the soul. So motion is an activity of the soul itself.

Because motion is in time, time touches the activity of the soul itself. Hence Proclus also says in Proposition 191: "Every participable[27] soul has an eternal substance, but its activity is in time."[28] So the author says here that *it is conjoined*[29] *with eternity in a lower way, conjoined* to eternity in substance, but *in a lower way* because it participates eternity in a lower way {16} than an intelligence does. He proves this by saying that *it is more susceptible to impression than is an intelligence*. For the soul not only receives the impression of the first cause, as does an intelligence, but it also bears the impression of an intelligence. But the more removed something is from the first, which is the cause of eternity, the more weakly it participates eternity. And, although the soul attains the lowest level of eternity, still *it is above time*, as a cause is above [its] effect, for *it is the cause of time* inasmuch as it is the cause of the motion upon which time follows.

[The author] also speaks here of the soul that philosophers attribute to heavenly bodies. For this reason he says that *it is on the horizon of eternity in a lower way and above time*. For a horizon is a circle marking off the boundaries of what is seen. It is the lowest boundary of the upper hemisphere, the starting point, however, of the lower. Similarly, the soul is the last boundary of eternity and the starting point of time. Dionysius also agrees with this opinion in Chapter 10 of *On the Divine Names*,[30] but with this exception: he does not assert that the heavens have soul, because Catholic faith does not assert this. So he says that "God is before the

---

24. Aristotle, *Physics*, VIII 4ff.; Proclus, Props. 14–20.
25. As Saffrey (p. 15, note) indicates, this Platonic teaching is found in the *Phaedrus*, 245 C–E. But Aristotle, *De Anima*, II 4, 404a21 and 406a1 ff, was probably the source for St. Thomas here.
26. Aristotle, *De Anima*, II 4, 415b8–28.
27. Or "able to be participated." *Participabilis* here renders the Greek *to methekte*.
28. Proclus, Prop. 191, Dodds, p. 166.26–27; Vansteenkiste, p. 524.
29. *connexa*. Here in his commentary St. Thomas has *connexa* while the Latin text of the *De Causis* has *annexa*.
30. Pseudo-Dionysius, *On the Divine Names*, X 3; *Dionysiaca* I 492–493; PG 3, 937C–940A.

eternal" and that, according to the Scriptures, some things are called "eternal and temporal." But this must be understood "according to the ways" that Sacred Scripture assumes. "Between things that exist and things that are made," i.e., generable things, are "whatever things participate in one way in the eternal but in another way in time."

{17} PROPOSITION 3[1]

Every noble soul has three activities, for its activities consist of animate activity, intellectual activity, and divine activity.

The activity is divine because soul provides for[2] nature with the power present in it from the first cause. Its activity is intellectual because [soul] knows things through the power of the intelligence present in it. And, the activity is animate because soul moves the first body[3] and all natural bodies, since it is the cause of the motion of bodies and the cause of nature's activity.

Soul carries out these activities only because it is an image[4] of a higher power. This is because the first cause created the being of soul with the mediation of an intelligence. As a result, soul came to carry out a divine activity. Thus, after the first cause created the being of soul, it placed it as something subject[5] to an intelligence on which it carries out its activities. Because of this, then, an intellectual soul carries out an intellectual activity.

Since the soul receives the impression of an intelligence, it came to have an activity inferior to [that of] an intelligence in its impression upon what is under it.

---

1. This proposition is derived from Prop. 201 in Proclus, as St. Thomas indicates in the opening paragraph of his commentary. Cf. Dodds, p. 176.1–5, 176.10–13, 176.11, 176.13–16. St. Thomas refers favorably to this proposition in *ST*, I, Q. 45, A. 5c; *SCG*, III, 66; *De Veritate*, Q. 5, A. 9, 7a and ad 7; *De Potentia*, Q. 3, A. 1c. But, since some had interpreted this proposition to mean that intelligences created souls, he identifies the proposition with this position in *De Potentia*, Q. 3, A. 4c and ad 10 and in *De Subst. sep.*, X. What the proposition says in this regard Aquinas accepts only in a very restricted way.

2. *praeparat* is the reading that St. Thomas had in his text, though other manuscripts have *parat*. The sense is that soul, that is, *every noble soul*, provides nature with order of direction.

3. For the meaning of "first body," see Aristotle, *On the Heavens*, I 2–3, 268b12–270b31. Aristotle remarks: "And so, implying that the primary body is something else beyond earth, fire, air, and water, they gave the highest place the name of *aether*, derived from the fact that it 'runs always' [*aei thein*] for an eternity of time" (270b21–24; McKeon trans).

4. *exemplum*.

5. *stramentum*. This Latin word is used to denote straw or something suitable for spreading under foot, a sense quite in accord with the Arabic *bisat*. See Taylor (1981), pp. 48; 366. Many of the manuscripts of the Latin tradition contain the corruption, *instrumentum*. See Pattin (1966) p. 140, III 33.17.

This is because [soul] impresses things only through motion, since what is under it receives its activity only if soul moves it. For this reason, then, it happens that soul moves bodies. For it is characteristic of soul to vivify bodies, since it infuses them with its power and brings them directly to right activity.[6]

It is therefore clear now that soul has three activities because it has three powers: a divine power, an intellectual power, and the power of its essence,[7] *as we have described and shown.*

COMMENTARY

What belong to higher things are present in lower things according to some kind of participation. For this reason, after [the author] divided the three grades of higher beings, one above eternity, God, another with eternity, intelligence, and the third after eternity, soul, he intends now to show how the third participates both what belongs to the first and what belongs to the second, saying: *Every noble soul has three activities, for its activities consist of animate activity,* {18} *intellectual activity and divine activity.* We can understand what he means by a *noble soul* from what Proclus says in Proposition 201: "All divine souls have activities that are threefold: some as souls, others as receptive of divine intellect, and still others as joined extrinsically to gods."[8] From this it is evident that what [the author] calls *noble soul* is what Proclus calls "divine soul."

To make this clear we ought to realize that Plato maintained that the universal forms of things were separate and *per se* subsistent. Because, according to him, such universal forms have a certain universal causality over particular beings that participate them, he consequently calls all such forms subsisting in this way "gods." For the word "god" implies a certain universal providence and causality. Furthermore, among these forms he articulates this order: the more universal any form is, the more simple and prior a cause it is, for it is participated by later forms, as when we

---

6. The corresponding Arabic reads somewhat differently: "For it is characteristic of soul that it give life to bodies, since it infuses them with its power, and also [that] it guide them to the right activity." See Taylor (1981), p. 149.

7. A minor corruption in the Latin translator's Arabic manuscript no doubt led to this understanding. The Arabic manuscripts have "and an essential power," as might be expected. See Taylor (1981), p. 150.

8. Proclus, Prop. 201, Dodds, p. 176.1–3. *Extraiunctae* is Moerbeke's Latin rendition of Proclus's term, *exertemenai* ("derived from").

assert that animal is participated by man and life by animal and so on. But the last, which is participated by all and itself participates nothing else, is the separate one and good itself, which he calls "the highest god" and "the first cause of all things."[9] So Proclus also introduces Proposition 116 of his book as follows: "Every god is able to be participated," that is, participates,[10] "except one."[11] Forms of this kind, which they call "gods," are intelligible[12] in themselves, but an intellect becomes intelligent in act through an intelligible species. Thus they placed below the order of gods, i.e., of the forms mentioned above, an order of intellects that participate {19} these forms in order to be intelligent, and the ideal intellect is among these forms.[13] But the intellects mentioned above participate these forms in an immobile way insofar as they understand them. Thus they placed under the order of intellects a third order, that of souls, which, with the mediation of intellects, participate these forms through motion insofar as they are the principles of corporeal motions through which corporeal matter participates the higher forms. And so the fourth order of things is that of bodies.

The higher intellects they call divine intellects. But they call the lower ones intellects, though not divine, because the ideal intellect, which according to them is a god *per se*, is participated by the higher intellects in both ways: insofar as it is intellect and insofar as it is god. The lower intellects participate it only insofar as it is intellect, and so they are not divine intellects. For the higher intellects gain not only their intellectual

---

9. But see *ST,* I, Q. 65, A. 4, where St. Thomas argues with regard to Plato and those of a like opinion, "Yet these opinions seem to have a common root. They are seeking the cause of forms as if forms as such came into being. As Aristotle proves, however, what properly comes into being is not the form but the composite. . . . since like produces like, an immaterial form should not be sought as the cause of corporeal forms; rather a composite of matter and form should be sought, as in the case where one fire is started by another" (Blackfriars trans., vol. 10, p. 21).

10. *participat*: The sense seems to require *participat* to be understood as "allows participation of itself."

11. Proclus, Prop. 116, Dodds, p. 102.13. Vansteenkiste, p. 496.

12. *intelligibiles*. This term requires flexibility for proper translation in context, since it can mean "intellectual" or "intelligible." Here it is rendered "intelligible," since these higher intellects are intellectual as *per se* intelligible and intellectually self-sufficient, while lower intellects are intellectual or intelligent in act only through participation in the higher intellects through intelligible species.

13. Cf. St. Thomas, *In de Caelo II*, Lect. 4 and *De Subst. sep.*, I.

character but also their divine character. Similarly, when souls are joined[14] to gods by mediating intellects, [which are] as it were, nearer the divine, the higher souls themselves are also divine, because of the divine intellects to which they are joined or which they participate. Lower souls, however, as joined to nondivine intellects are not divine. Because bodies receive motion through the soul, it also follows, according to them, that higher bodies are divine, while lower bodies are not divine. So Proclus says in Proposition 129: "Every divine body is divine through a deified soul; but every soul is divine owing to a divine intellect, while every intellect is divine through a participation of divine unity."[15] Because they call the first separate forms "gods" insofar as they are in themselves universal, {20} they consequently also call intellects, souls, and bodies "divine" insofar as they have a certain universal influence[16] and causality over the things of their own genus and of lower genera that follow after them.

Dionysius, however, corrects this position when they assert that the different separate forms, which they call "gods," exist in succession, so that one would be *per se* goodness, another *per se* being, another *per se* life, and so on with regard to the others. For it must be said that all these are essentially the first cause of all things itself, from which things participate all such perfections. In this way we will not assert that there are many gods, but one. And this is what he says in Chapter 5 of *On the Divine Names*: "Now it," namely, Sacred Scripture, "does not say that good is one thing, existent[17] another, and life or wisdom another, nor that there are many causes and that there are other transcending[18] and yet subject deities that produce other things, but that all good processions are of the one [God]."[19] How this can be he shows subsequently from the fact that, since God is being itself and the very essence of goodness, whatever belongs to the perfection of goodness and being belongs essentially to him as a whole, so that he is the essence of life, wisdom, power, and the rest. So further on he adds: "For God is not somehow existent, but he pre-

---

14. *applicentur.*
15. Proclus, Prop. 129, Dodds, p. 114.12–14. Vansteenkiste, p. 501.
16. *influentia.* 17. *existens.*
18. *excedentes.*
19. Pseudo-Dionysius, *On the Divine Names*, V, 2; *Dionysiaca* I, 326–327; PG 3, 816 C–D.

possesses[20] the whole of being in himself in an absolute and uncircumscribed way."[21] The author of this book adheres to this as well. For we do not find him introducing any multitude of deity.[22] Rather, he establishes unity in God and distinction in the order of intellects, souls, and bodies. Accordingly, then, he speaks of the noble soul, i.e., the divine soul {21} of a heavenly body, in accord with the opinion of those Philosophers who held that the heavens are animated. For, according to them, this soul has a certain universal influence over things through motion. Due to this they called it *divine* in the same way that others call "divine" those in society who have charge of the universal care of the common welfare.[23]

Consequently, he says that this most nobly divine soul has a divine activity. Explaining this further, he says that its *activity is divine* because *it provides for nature*, inasmuch as it is the principle of the first motion to which all nature is subject. It has this through the *power* that it participates *from the first cause*, which is the universal cause of all things, from which it gains a certain universal causality over natural things. And so, assigning the reason for this activity that belongs to the divine soul, he says that *it is an image*,[24] i.e., a likeness[25] of *higher*, i.e., divine, *power*. For the universality of the divine power is exemplified in that soul because, just as God is the universal cause of all beings, so that soul is the universal cause of natural things that are in motion.

He asserts that the second *activity* of a noble or divine soul is *intellectual*, which, as he explains, consists in the fact that *it knows things* insofar as it participates *the power of an intelligence*. And why it participates *the power of an intelligence* he shows through the fact that the *soul is created* by *the first cause, with the mediation of an intelligence*. Hence the soul is from God as the first cause, but from an intelligence as the second cause. Now, every effect participates something of the power of its cause. So it remains that the soul, just as it performs {22} a divine activity insofar as it is from the first

---

20. *praeaccipit*.
21. Pseudo-Dionysius, *On the Divine Names*, V, 4; *Dionysiaca* I, 333–34; PG 3, 817 C.
22. That is, deity plural in number.
23. Cf. Plato, *Meno*, 99 D 8 and Aristotle, *Nicomachean Ethics*, VII 1, 1145a29. Also, see St. Thomas, *In Polit. I*, Lect. 4, p. 380 b (ed. Parm.): ". . . the error of the gentiles who called rulers 'gods.'"
24. *exemplum*.
25. *imago*.

cause, so too it performs the activity of an intelligence insofar as it is from [an intelligence] and participating its power.

Some, however, wrongly understanding what he says here, that *the first cause created the being of the soul, with the mediation of an intelligence*, thought that the author of this book had held the opinion[26] that intelligences are creative of the substance of souls.[27] But this is contrary to the positions of the Platonists. For they maintain that such causalities belonging to simple beings are according to participation. But what is participated is not the participating thing but what is first such through its essence. For example, if whiteness were separate, simple whiteness itself, and not something participating whiteness, would be the cause of all white things insofar as they are white. Accordingly, then, the Platonists maintained that being itself is the cause of existing for all things, while life itself is the cause of living for everything [that lives], and intelligence itself is the cause of understanding for everything [that understands]. So Proclus says in Proposition 18 of his book: "Everything that dispenses being to others is itself originally that which it gives to the recipients of the dispensation."[28] Aristotle agrees with this opinion when he says in Book 2 of the *Metaphysics*[29] that what is first and a being to the greatest degree is the cause of subsequent beings. So, according to what was previously said, we should understand that the soul's very essence was created by the first cause, which is its very own being.[30] But [the soul] has subsequent participations {23} from some later principles, such that it has living from the first life and understanding from the first intelligence. Hence in Proposition 18 of this book [the author] also says: *All things have essence through the first being, living things are through the first life, and intellectual things have*

---

26. In his corrections to the printed text, Saffrey deletes *secundum* and adds <*sensuisse*>. It is this corrected version that is translated here.

27. Cf. below, S{62} and S{104}. Also, see St. Thomas, *ST,* I, Q. 47, A.1 and Q. 90, A. 3; *De Potentia*, Q. 3, A. 7; *De Subst. sep.*, X. St. Thomas identifies Avicenna as the chief proponent of this view. But for others as well, see Saffrey's note, p. 22.

28. Proclus, Prop. 18, Dodds, 20.3–4. *Derivans,* which is translated as "dispensing," is Moerbeke's Latin rendition of Proclus's term, *choregoun.* Note also that the Latin reflects the reading *to einai* which is found in all but one of the Greek manuscripts. The reading adopted by Dodds, *to tō einai,* is not found in any of the Greek manuscripts.

29. Aristotle, *Metaphysics*, II 1, 993b24–25.

30. *Esse* here and throughout the paragraph.

knowledge because of the first intelligence.[31] This is how he understands that *the first cause created the being of the soul with the mediation of an intelligence,* since the first cause alone created the essence of the soul. But that the soul is intellectual is due to the activity of an intelligence. That this is what he means he shows clearly by the words that follow: *Therefore,* he says, *after the first cause created the being of the soul, it placed it as something subject to an intelligence,* i.e., it made it subject to the activity of an intelligence, for the intelligence to perform its activity in it, giving it its intellectual character. Hence he concludes that *because of* this *an intellectual soul carries out intellectual activity.* This also agrees with what he said in Proposition 1: the effect of the first cause pre-exists the effect of the second cause and is more universally diffused.[32] For being, which is most common, is diffused into all things by the first cause. But understanding is not communicated by an intelligence to all things but only to some, presupposing the being that they have from the first.

But even this position, if it is not soundly understood, is repugnant to the truth as well as to the opinion of Aristotle, who argues in Book 3 of the *Metaphysics*[33] against the Platonists, who hold for such an order of separate causes in terms of what we predicate of individuals. For [otherwise] it follows that Socrates will be many animals: Socrates himself, separate man and also separate animal. For separate man participates animal and so is an animal. And Socrates participates both, so he is a man and he is an animal. Therefore, Socrates would not be truly one, if from one thing he were an animal and from another {24} he were a man. Hence, since intellectual being belongs to the very nature of the soul as its essential difference, if [the soul] had being from one thing and an intellectual nature from something else, it would follow that it would not be absolutely one. Therefore, one has to say that the soul not only has essence but also [has] intellectuality from the first cause. This accords with the opinion of Dionysius, which we quoted above:[34] that good itself, being itself, life itself, and wisdom itself are not different but one and the same thing, which is God, from whom things derive that they are, that they live, and that they understand, as he shows in the same place. So, too, in Book 12

---

31. Cf. below, S{100}.
32. *diffunditur.* Cf. above, S{7}.
33. Aristotle, *Metaphysics*, III 6, 1003a11ff. Also, cf. below, S{79}.
34. Cf. above, S{20}.

of the *Metaphysics*[35] Aristotle expressly attributes to God both understanding and living, saying that he is life and intelligence, so that he excludes the previously mentioned Platonic positions. Nevertheless [what is said here] can be true in a sense, if it refers, not to an intellectual nature, but to the intelligible forms that intellectual souls receive through the activity of intelligences. So Dionysius says in Chapter 4 of *On the Divine Names* that "through angels" souls "become participants of illuminations emanating" from God.[36]

Continuing, he states that the third activity of the noble or divine soul is an animate one. He explains that *the activity is animate* in that it *moves the first body and,* as a consequence, *all natural bodies.* For *it is the cause of the motion* in things. He afterwards gives the reason for this. For because the soul, as what *receives the impression of an intelligence,* is inferior to an intelligence, it consequently acts *upon* those things that are *under it* in a way that is *inferior* to the way in which an intelligence impresses things subject to itself, since the primary cause infuses more powerfully than the second cause, as is clear from Proposition 1.[37] Furthermore, an intelligence impresses souls without motion, inasmuch as it makes the soul know, which is without motion. But the soul *impresses* bodies {25} *through motion.* What is under it, a body, *receives* the impression of the soul *only* insofar as it is moved by it. Consequently, he indicates the *reason* why we must say that *the motion of* natural *bodies* is due to the *soul.* For we see that all natural bodies *directly* arrive at their fitting ends through their activities and motions, which could not happen unless they were directed by something intelligent. From this it seems that the motion of bodies is due to the soul, which *infuses* bodies *with its power* by moving them.

This position, i.e., that the motion of the heavens is due to a soul, has also not been confirmed in faith, and Augustine leaves this in doubt in Book 2 of *On the Literal Interpretation of Genesis.*[38] But Augustine in Book 3

---

35. Aristotle, *Metaphysics,* XII 7, 1072b24ff. Also, cf. below, S{79} and S{103}.

36. Pseudo-Dionysius, *On the Divine Names,* IV 2; *Dionysiaca* I, 154–55; PG 3, 696 C.

37. Cf. above, S{6}.

38. We take this title from the translation by Roland J. Teske, S.J., Fathers of the Church series, vol. 84 (Washington, D.C.: The Catholic University of America Press, 1991). St. Augustine, *Super Genesim ad Litteram,* II 18; CSEL, XXVIII, p. 62.4; PL 34, 279f.

of *On the Trinity*[39] and Gregory in Book 4 of the *Dialogues*[40] assert that [this motion] is from God directing the whole of nature and that God moves corporeal creation, with the mediation of intelligences, or angels.

Finally the author concludes with what he had proposed, i.e., that the noble *soul has* the *three* previously mentioned *activities*. Now the opinion of Dionysius agrees with what [the author] said about the divine intellect and the divine soul when in Chapter 4 of *On the Divine Names* he calls the higher angels divine "minds," i.e., intellects, through which "souls" also "participate the godlike gift in accordance with" their "power."[41] But he understands[42] divinity only in virtue of the connection to God, not in virtue of the universal influence upon created things.[43] For the former is more properly divine, because in God himself what he himself is is greater than what he causes in other things.

39. St. Augustine, *On the Trinity,* III 4; PL 42, 873.
40. St. Gregory, *Dialogues,* IV 6; PL 77, 328 C.
41. Pseudo-Dionysius, *On the Divine Names,* IV 2; Dionysiaca I, 153–55; PG 3, 696 C.
42. *accipit*.
43. That is, he accepts the use of the notion of divinity regarding those higher angels or minds only because of their relationship to God, not because they have universal influence on things below.

{26} PROPOSITION 4[1]

The first of created things is being, and there is nothing else created before it.

This is because being is above sense, above soul, and above intelligence, and after the first cause there is no effect more extensive or prior[2] to it. As a result, then, it came to be higher[3] than all [other] created things and to be more powerfully united. It came to be so only because of its nearness to the pure being and the true one, in which there is no multiplicity of any sort.[4]

Although created being is one, nevertheless it comes to be multiple because it receives multiplicity. And, it became many only because, although it is simple and

---

1. This proposition and the one that follows are a single proposition in the Arabic manuscript tradition. In the Latin manuscript tradition, as St. Thomas notes (cf. S{31}), some manuscripts have 31 propositions while others have 32, where Prop. 4 has been divided into two. These "two" propositions are related to Prop. 138 and perhaps Prop. 177 in Proclus, both of which St. Thomas refers to in his commentary. Cf. Dodds, p. 122.7–12, 122.16–17, 122.12–14; p. 156.7–9, 156.1–4. Like Propositions 9(8) and 22(21), these "two" propositions are also inspired by the thought of Plotinus, though his *Enneades* is not quoted. Cf. (a) *Enneades* IV 8, 3.6–4.10 = PA *Dicta* MS Marsh 539, ff. 22v1–25v13; Lewis, pp. 235–37, nos. 47–68. (Lewis omits most of folio 25v10–11 from his translation.) (b) *Enn.* IV 9, 4.2–3 and 4.19–20; 9, 1.16–18; 9, 2.3–8; and 9, 3.1–4 = PA *Dicta* MS Marsh 539, ff. 38v2–39v8; Lewis, p. 255, nos. 50–56. (c) *Enn.* VI 7, 14 = PA *Theologia* pp. 97.7–99.8, Lewis pp. 471–473, nos. 38–51. The author of the *De Causis* departs from Proclus in two fundamental ways: the first cause, which is God, is explicitly said to *create* being; and the intelligible forms are in intelligences and not prior to them as gods. (In contrast, cf. Proclus, Props. 125, 129, 137, and 161–163.) St. Thomas frequently cites this proposition. See, e.g. , *ST*, I, Q. 5, A. 2 s.c.; Q. 45, A. 1, 1a; *De Veritate*, Q. 1, A. 4 s.c. and Q. 21, A. 2, 5a; *De Potentia*, Q. 3, Q. 5, 2a and A. 8, 19a; Q. 6, A. 1, 5a; Q. 7, A. 2c; *Quaest. Disp. de Anima*, Q. 9c. Certain portions of the explanation are cited in *De Potentia* Q. 7, A. 2, ad 5; Q. 3, A. 4, 10a.

2. As his commentary on this proposition indicates, the Latin text of St. Thomas had *prius*, *"prior."* The original Latin translation almost certainly had *plus*, reflecting the Arabic manuscript tradition's *akthar*. The singular *causatum*, *"effect,"* was probably in the original Latin translation, though it differs in number from the Arabic *ma'lulat*. The corresponding Arabic can be rendered, "there is nothing more extensive and having more effects than it." See Taylor (1981), pp. 151; 368; 447.

3. *superius*.

4. For *aliquorum modorum* read *aliquo modorum* with the Arabic and several key Latin manuscripts.

there is nothing among created things more simple than it, it is nevertheless composed of the finite and the infinite. All the part of it that follows the first cause is achili,[5] *that is, an intelligence, complete and ultimate in power*[6] *and all the other goodnesses. And the intelligible forms in it are more extensive and more powerfully universal. The part of it that is lower is also an intelligence, though it is below the former intelligence in completeness, power, and goodnesses. The intelligible forms in it are not as extended in their breadth as they are in the former intelligence. First created being is wholly intelligence, yet intelligence in it is diverse in the way we have said. And because intelligence is diversified, the intelligible form there becomes diverse. And, just as from one form, because it is diversified in the lower world, there proceed individuals infinite in multitude, so too from the first created being, because it is diversified, there appear infinite intelligible forms. Yet, although they are diversified, they are not distinct from one another as are individuals. This is because they are united without corruption and are separated without distinction, for they are a one possessing multiplicity and a multiplicity in unity. And the first intelligences infuse the second intelligences with the goodnesses they receive from the first cause, and they spread*[7] *goodness in them until they reach the last of them.*[8]

COMMENTARY

After the author of this book has distinguished the threefold grade of higher being and has shown how the whole is found in the lowest of them by participation, he intends now to show the distinction of the second

5. *achili* or *alachili*, as it appears in some of the Latin manuscripts of the *De Causis*, is a transliteration of the Arabic *'aql* or *al-'aql*, "intelligence," "the intelligence." It is not clear precisely why the translator chose to transliterate this term, though the simplest explanation, the term's importance, may be the answer. The only other term transliterated is the problematic Arabic term *hilyah*, apparently transliterated as *helyatun* in Proposition 8(9). The important Aosta manuscript containing the *De Causis* has forms of *alachl* or *alachli* preceding or following *intelligentia* throughout the entire text.
6. *potentia.*
7. *intendunt.*
8. As indicated in the Introduction, the Arabic text has 31 propositions, but in some manuscripts of the Latin tradition the text of the *De Causis* is found to have 31 propositions, while in others it is found to have 32. It is here that the difference between the two versions begins. St. Thomas follows the tradition of 31 propositions in his commentary. As he notes, it is clear that this is not a distinct proposition, since the conclusion of Prop. 5 deals with what is treated in both Props. 4 and 5. Cf. below, S{35}.

grade, namely, that being that is with eternity. For the first grade, that of the first cause existing before eternity, he passes over {27} as undivided, as was said.[9] Now in this proposition he proceeds in a different way than in the other propositions. For in all the other propositions he presents the proposition and then proves the proposition offered with the explanation he gives. But here, in the fashion of those making divisions, he (1) presents what is common; (2) divides it, at: *Although created being is one* etc.; and (3) indicates the difference between the parts of the division, at: *All the part of it that follows* etc.

Now what is common to all the distinct[10] intelligences is first created being. Regarding this he presents the following proposition: *The first of created things is being, and there is nothing else created before it.* Proclus also asserts this in Proposition 138 of his book, in these words: "Being is the first and supreme of all that participate what is properly divine[11] and of the deified."[12] According to the positions of the Platonists the reason for this is that, as was said above,[13] [the Platonists] maintained that the more common something is the more it is separate and, as it were, in a prior way participated by what is posterior, and, thus, that it is cause of posterior things. Furthermore, in the order of predication, they maintain that the most common is the one and good, and even more common than being. According to them, good or one are found predicated of something of which being is not predicated, namely, prime matter, which Plato associates with nonbeing, not distinguishing {28} between matter and privation, as is noted in Book 1 of the *Physics*.[14] Still, he attributes unity and goodness to matter inasmuch as matter is ordered to form. For we call "good" not only the end but also what is ordered to the end. In this way, then, the Platonists place the separate one itself and good itself as the highest and first principle of things. But after the one and the good nothing is found as common as being. For this reason they maintain that sep-

---

9. Cf. above, S{11}.
10. *distinctis*, i.e., individual and separate.
11. *divina proprietate*.
12. Proclus, Prop. 138, Dodds, p. 122.7–8; Vansteenkiste, p. 505. *Ens* is used here by Moerbeke (rather than *esse* as in the *De Causis*) to translate Proclus's *on*.
13. Cf. above, S{13}.
14. Aristotle, *Physics*, I 9, 191b35–192a16.

arate being itself is created, since it participates goodness and unity, but they maintain that it is first among all created things.

Dionysius did away with the order of separate things, as was said above,[15] maintaining the same order as the Platonists in the perfections that other things participate from one principle, which is God. Hence in Chapter 4 of *On the Divine Names* he ranks the name of good in God as the first of all the divine names and shows that its participation extends even to nonbeing,[16] understanding by nonbeing prime matter. For he says: "And, if it is permitted to say it, even the nonexisting itself[17] desires the good that is above all existing things."[18] But among the other perfections from God that things participate, he puts being first. For he says this in Chapter 5 of *On the Divine Names*: "Being is placed before the other participations" of God "and being in itself is more ancient than the being of *per se* life, than the being of *per se* wisdom, and than the being of *per se* divine similitude."[19]

The author of this book also seems to understand this in the same way. For he says that this *is so because being is above sense, above soul and above intelligence.* How it is above these he shows, adding: *There is nothing after the first cause* {29} *more extensive*, i.e., anything more common, and in consequence *no effect prior to it.* But the first cause is more extensive, because it even extends itself to nonbeings, according to what was previously said. From this he concludes that, *as a result* of what was said, being itself *came to be higher than all [other] created things*, because it is more common than the other effects of God, *and* is also *more powerfully united*, i.e., more simple. For those things that are less common seem to be related to the more common by way of some addition.[20] Nevertheless, it seems that it is not

---

15. Cf. above, S{20}.   16. *non ens.*
17. *ipsum non existens.*
18. Pseudo-Dionysius, *On the Divine Names*, IV 3; *Dionysiaca* I, 158–59; PG 3, 697 A.9.
19. Pseudo-Dionysius, *On the Divine Names*, V 5; *Dionysiaca* I, 337; PG 3, 820 A. For further discussion on this, see *ST*, I, Q. 5, A. 2, where St. Thomas remarks, ". . . in idea being is prior to goodness" but ". . . goodness, as a cause, is prior to being, as is the end to the form. Therefore, among the names signifying the divine causality, goodness precedes being" (Benzinger trans., vol. I, p. 24).
20. On the notion of addition, such as that of form, which specifies being (*esse*), see *De Ente et Essentia*, 4. The resulting being (*ens*) which participates being (*esse*) is

his intention to speak about some separate being, as the Platonists did, nor about the being that all existing things participate commonly, as Dionysius did, but [rather] about being participated in the first grade of created being, which is higher being. And, although higher being is both in intelligence and in soul, nevertheless in intelligence itself being itself is considered to be prior to the specific nature[21] of intelligence, and likewise for the soul. For this reason he asserted that it is above soul and above intelligence. So he gives the reason why the being that intelligences participate is the most united.[22] He says that this happens *because of its nearness* to the first cause, which is *pure* subsistent *being* and is *truly one*, unparticipated, *in which* there can*not* be found any *multiplicity* of things differing in essence. But what is nearer to what is *per se* one is more united, as participating unity to a greater degree. Hence the intelligence that is nearest to the first cause has the most united being.

Then, when he says: *It became many only* etc., he shows the reason for the distinction that there can be in intelligences according to essence. Here we ought to note that, if there is some form or nature altogether separate and simple, no multiplicity can occur in it, as, if there were some separate whiteness, there would be only one. Now many diverse whitenesses are found that participate whiteness. In this way, therefore, if first created being were {30} abstract being, as the Platonists maintained, such being could not be multiplied, but would be one only. But, because first

---

"contracted," i.e., both composed of the two principles, essence (*essentia*) and being or existence (*esse*), and yet finite, by reason of its essence specifying it to be this or that kind of a being, this or that individual in the case of intelligences, or angels (while signed, or quantified, matter individuates those beings whose essence is composed of matter and form). On the notion of contraction, see *I Sent.*, D. 43, Q. 1, A. 1. Participated being (*esse participatum*) for St. Thomas, then, does not involve an addition of some form over, and thus contraction of, God's existence, but is, as in the *De Causis*, created. A creature, or a being which participates existence, can approach God as absolutely one, or simple, only to the degree it is itself more in act than in potency and thus more united in its being and in that way more like God. In contrast to the author of the *De Causis*, St. Thomas does not conceive being (*esse*) as a substrate upon which a form can be added but as a co-principle, along with essence (simple or composed), in which being stands to essence as act to potency, in which it is the individual which is the subject of creation, while being is the object of creation. See *ST*, I, Q. 45, A. 4c and ad 1.

21. *ratio.*
22. *maxime unitum.*

created being is being participated in the nature of an intelligence, it can be multiplied according to the diversity of those that participate it. And this is what he says: *It*, namely, first created being, *became many*, i.e., divided into many intelligences, *only because*, although *it is simple and there is nothing among created things more simple than it, it is itself, nevertheless, composed of the finite and the infinite*. Proclus also asserts such a composition in Proposition 89, saying: "All beingly being is of the finite and the infinite."[23] He explains this in the following fashion: all immobile being is infinite in its power of being. For, if what can endure longer in being is of greater power, then what can endure into infinity is, to this extent, of infinite power. Hence he stated in Proposition 86: "All beingly being is infinite, not according to multitude[24] or magnitude, but according to power alone," namely, [the power] of existing, as he himself explains.[25] But, if something were to have infinite power of being such that it does not participate in being from another, then it alone would be infinite. Such is God, as is said below in Proposition 16.[26] But, if there be something that has infinite power for being according to being that is participated[27] from another, insofar as it participates being it is finite, because what is participated is not received in the one participating according to its entire infinity but in the manner of a particular. Therefore, an intelligence is composed of the finite and the infinite in its being to the extent that the nature of an intelligence is said to be infinite in its power of being, but the very being that it receives is finite. From this it follows that the being of an intelligence can be multiplied insofar as it is participated being, for the composition of the finite and the infinite signifies this.

{31} Next, when he says: *All the part of it that follows* etc., he shows the difference between the members of the division, i.e., between the multiplied intelligences. He does this in a threefold way: (1) as regards their diverse perfection; (2) as regards the infusion of some upon others, at: *The first intelligences* etc.; (3) as regards the effect of the intelligences in

---

23. Proclus, Prop. 89, Dodds, p. 82.1. Vansteenkiste p. 298. Regarding *enter ens* ("beingly being") as the translation of *to ontos on*, see note 46. For an explanation of the meaning of the finite (*peras*) and the infinite (*apeiron*) and their union (*mikton*) in Proclus, see Dodds, pp. 246–48.
24. That is, according to number.
25. Proclus, Prop. 86, Dodds, p. 78.19–20. Vansteenkiste, p. 297.
26. Cf. below, S{95}.
27. *ad essendum secundum esse participaturm.*

souls, and this in the following proposition, which is found in some books conjoined with his commentary here, and begins: *Higher intelligences* etc. With regard to the first point he does two things: (1) he shows the difference; (2) he removes a certain doubt, at: *Because it is diversified* etc.

Regarding the first point, then, we ought to note that he indicates a twofold difference of intelligences: one regarding their nature and the other regarding the intelligible species through which they understand. Regarding their natures, it is necessary for their natures to be diversified according to a certain order. For the difference in them is not material but formal, for they are composed, not of matter and form, but of a nature, which is form, and participated being, as was said.[28] In those things, however, that differ materially, nothing prevents many being found equal to one other, for in substances the individuals of one species equally participate the nature of the species. Likewise in accidents it is possible for diverse subjects to participate whiteness equally. But in those things that formally differ, a certain order is always found. For, if one considers it carefully, in all the species of one genus one will always find one more perfect than another, such as whiteness among colors and man among animals. This is so because the things that differ formally differ according to some contrariety, for {32} contrariety is a difference according to form, as the Philosopher says in Book 10 of the *Metaphysics*.[29] Now in contraries one is always more noble and another more base, as he says in Book 1 of the *Physics*.[30] This is so because the first contrariety is "privation and habit," as Book 10 of the *Metaphysics* says.[31] Because of this the Philosopher says in Book 8 of the *Metaphysics*[32] that the species of things are like numbers, which are diversified by species according to the addition of one over the other. It is clear that to the extent that something is more perfect, to that extent is it nearer to the one that is the most perfect. Hence [the author] asserts this difference as regards the nature of intelligences, that the intellectual being that immediately *follows* upon *the first cause is a complete intelligence ultimate* in completion as regards created being *in the power of being and* in *all the other* subsequent *goodnesses,* while that intellectual

28. Cf. S{30}.
29. Aristotle, *Metaphysics*, X 9, 1058b1ff.
30. Aristotle, *Physics*, I 5, 189a3–4.
31. Aristotle, *Metaphysics*, X 4, 1955a33ff.
32. Aristotle, *Metaphysics*, VIII 3, 1043b36–1044a2.

being that *is lower* in the order of intelligences retains the nature and specific character[33] of *intelligence, but yet it is below* the higher *intelligence in the completeness* of nature *and* in *the power* of being and acting *and* in all *goodnesses,* or perfections.

However, regarding the second difference, which is from the intelligible species, he supposes that intelligences understand through certain intelligible species and that intelligible species of this kind [i.e., in the higher intelligences] have a greater breadth and universality than they do in the lower intelligences. But he dismisses this now undiscussed, for he will clarify this below in Proposition 10, which deals exclusively with this.[34]

Next, when he says: *Because intelligence is diversified* etc., he removes a certain doubt. For because he had said that the intelligible species in higher and lower intelligences are different, {33} this could seem false to someone, due to the fact that the thing understood is one. So he shows how intelligible species of this kind are diversified. First he presents a certain example of this. Second he shows the difference, at: *Yet, although they are diversified* etc. Concerning the first point we ought to note that, as was said above,[35] the Platonists held that there were separate forms of things through whose participation intellects become intelligent in act, just as, through participation of them, corporeal matter is constituted in this or that species. But the result is the same if we do not hold for many separate forms, but in place of them all assert one first form from which all else is derived, as was said above[36] in regard to the opinion of Dionysius, which the author of this book seems to follow when he does not place any distinction in divine being. So, since the intelligences are diverse in essence, as was said above,[37] intelligible participated forms must be diverse and different in the diverse intelligences, just as the diverse participated forms in this sensible world are also found according to the diversity of individuals that participate them.

Next, when he says: *Yet, although they are diversified* etc., he shows the diversity found in the previously mentioned example. For the sensible forms that diverse individuals participate are individuated forms and are distinct from each other by that distinction by which one individual is

33. *rationem*.
34. Cf. below, S{67}.
35. Cf. above, S{18}.
36. Cf. above, S{20} and S{28}.
37. Cf. S{29}.

distinguished from another, so that both forms belong to the existence, not of one thing, but of diverse things. But intelligible forms are not similarly multiplied by the fact that they are present in diverse intelligences or intellects, since they are not made individual forms through this. Rather, they retain the force of their universality inasmuch as each of them causes universal knowledge of the same understood thing in the intellect in which it is. The reason for this is apparent from what was said above. For, since the forms of things, whether they be separately[38] abiding steadfastly *per se* or united in {34} the one first, have being that is the most universal and divine, it is clear that the more the forms approach this most universal being of forms the more universal they are. In accord with this, he said[39] that the forms participated in higher intellects are more universal. But what is lowest in things is corporeal matter. Hence it receives such forms as particular without any universality. And this is what he says: *although* the intelligible forms *are diversified* in diverse intelligences, nevertheless they are *not* in this way divided *from one another like* diverse *individuals* are divided in sensible things. For they have *one* together with *multiplicity,* one on the part of universality, *multiplicity* according to the diverse mode of participation in diverse intellects. Through this he removes totally the argument of Averroes, who wanted to prove the unity of the intellect through the unity of the intelligible form. For [Averroes] thought that, if intelligible forms are diverse in diverse intellects, then they are individuated and intelligible in potency, not in act. But this is evidently frivolous, from what has been said.[40]

Next, when he says: *The first intelligences* etc., he states the second difference, which follows from the first. For we find in any order of things whatsoever that what is in act acts on what is in potency. But what is more perfect is always compared to the less perfect as act to potency. Therefore, it is of the nature of the more perfect things in any genus whatsoever to act upon the more imperfect. So, since higher intelligences are more complete in power and all the other goodnesses than are lower intelligences, it follows that, just as the first cause infuses higher intelligences, so higher intelligences infuse the lower, and so down to the last.

38. *divisim.*   39. Cf. above, S{32}.
40. See Averroes, *In III de Anima*, Comm. 5, pp. 411–13. Also, see St. Thomas, *De Unitate Intellectus*, Cap. 5.

{35} PROPOSITION 5[1]

The first higher intelligences, which follow the first cause, impress second,[2] steadfastly abiding forms which are not destroyed, so that they might need to be repeated again. The second intelligences impress declining, separable forms, such as the soul.

For the soul results from the impression of a second intelligence, which follows created being more lowly. Souls are multiplied only in the way in which intelligences are multiplied, because the being of the soul likewise has limit, but the part that is lower is infinite.

Souls, therefore, that follow an intelligence are complete, perfect, of slight declination and separation. But souls that follow being more lowly are below the higher souls in completeness and declination. Higher souls infuse lower souls with the goodnesses they receive from an intelligence. Every soul that receives more power from an intelligence is stronger in its impression. What is impressed by it is fixed, abiding steadfastly, and its motion is regular, continuous motion. But that [soul] in which the power of an intelligence is less is below the first souls in impression,[3] and what is impressed by it is weak, evanescent and destructible. Nevertheless, although it is so, its impression still persists through generation.

It has now, therefore, been shown why the intelligible forms came to be many,

---

1. While this proposition is related to concerns discussed in Props. 182 and 183 in Proclus, both of which St. Thomas quotes in his commentary, it seems not to be explicitly dependent on particular texts in Proclus. The ultimate source is the thought of Plotinus. For references see the note at the beginning of Prop. 4. As St Thomas indicates, this should be read as the continuation of Prop. 4. The transcendent souls spoken of here are the souls attributed to heavenly bodies, i.e., the supposed souls of planets and stars. (For a discussion of such souls in Neoplatonic thinking, see Dodds, pp. 294–96.) St. Thomas does not accept the existence of such souls and for this reason, it seems, does not cite this proposition in his other works. St. Thomas also diminishes the role given the intelligences by the author of the *De Causis* in the generation of the human, allowing for the influence of heavenly bodies and angels only in the disposition of the human body as receptive of the soul, not in the creation of the soul itself. But St. Thomas follows the author in his dismissal of the Neoplatonic notion of an astral body for souls.

2. The Latin *secundas* is a translation of the Arabic, *al-thaniyah*. This Arabic, however, is a corruption of *al-thabitah*, "stable." See Taylor (1981), p. 156.

3. More literally, "And that part of it in which the power . . ."

while there is only one simple being [belonging to them all], and why souls came to be many, some of which are stronger than others, while there belongs to them one simple being in which there is no diversity.

COMMENTARY

After showing the distinction between intelligences in the preceding proposition, the author here treats of the distinction between souls, which he allots according to the difference between intelligences as in some sense causing these souls, according to his view. So what he treats here in terms of the distinction of souls can be traced back to the distinction between intelligences inasmuch as a distinction in effects manifests a distinction of causes. For this reason in some texts this proposition is not placed on its own but is joined to the commentary of the preceding proposition. This is also apparent from the epilogue, which the author places here as common to both propositions.

{36} The proposition is as follows: *The first higher intelligences [which follow the first cause][4] impress second forms steadfastly abiding, which are not destroyed so that they might need to be repeated again. The second intelligences impress declining, separable forms, such as the soul.* Proclus gives two propositions that correspond to this proposition: 182, which reads as follows: "Every divine intellect is participated by divine souls,"[5] and 183, which reads as follows: "Every participated intellect that is solely intellectual is participated by souls that are neither divine nor made to alternate between intelligence and unintelligence."[6] To make this proposition evident we should consider three things: (1) the impression of the soul; (2) the distinction between souls; (3) the difference between distinct souls. With

---

4. St. Thomas omits the bracketted words.
5. Proclus, Prop. 82, Dodds, p. 160.5–6; Vansteenkiste, p. 521.
6. Proclus, Prop. 83, Dodds, p. 160.13–15; Vansteenkiske, p. 521. Moerbeke's translation for the Greek *metabole* is *transmutatio*, which we have rendered "to alternate"; *ignorantia* is his translation for the Greek *anoias*, which we have rendered "unintelligence." The souls spoken of here are the higher souls of heavenly bodies midway between higher intelligences, which always know, and the "lower" or human soul, which knows only intermittently. For Proclus, unlike Aristotle, plants and animals have no soul but are only "images" or "reflections of souls" (*eidola ton psychon*) (see Prop. 64, Dodds, p. 62.11–12; also, see p. 296). Neither the author of the *De Causis* nor St. Thomas, however, follows Proclus in this. For them lower souls are the souls of plants and animals impressed and perpetuated through generation.

regard to impression of the soul we should consider: (1) how it belongs to the soul to be impressed; (2) what impresses it.

That it belongs to the soul to be impressed appears clear if one considers the nature of impression, for which two things are required: (1) that what is impressed exist in something; (2) that it not be in it superficially according to extrinsic contact alone, but that it be intimate to it, penetrating, as it were, into its depths. And these two things do belong to the soul according to its proper nature. For it was said above in Proposition 3[7] that the proper activity of the soul is to move the body, in that the activity of the soul itself is below the activity proper to an intelligence, to which it belongs to know things without motion. But a principle of motion must be applied to a mobile thing because, as {37} Book 7 of the *Physics* proves, mover and moved are [present to one another] simultaneously.[8] Hence, according to its proper nature, it belongs to the soul to be in a mobile body. But the motion by which the soul moves the body is a living body's motion, which is not from an extrinsic mover, as in the case of violent motion or the motion of light and heavy things from what generates them, but from an intrinsic mover. Hence living things are said to move themselves. Therefore, the soul that moves the body must be in the body, intrinsically united to it. For this reason is it said to be impressed.

But if we ask what impresses it, according to the opinion of the author of this book, it is an intelligence that impresses it. For he says, *For the soul,* namely, a lower soul, *results from the impression of a second intelligence,* i.e., of the second order of intelligences, *which,* namely, a second intelligence, *follows created being more lowly,* i.e., in the lower part of the first created being itself, which is the being of intelligences. Or when he says: *which follows [created] being* etc., this can be taken to refer to the soul, which is below the eternity of an intelligence, as was said in Proposition 2.[9] But this opinion is not valid on all counts. For we can speak of the impression of the soul in two ways: in one way, from the viewpoint of the impressed soul itself; in another way, from the viewpoint of the matter upon which it is impressed. This distinction applies to any soul abiding steadfastly in it-

---

7. Cf. above, S{24}.

8. Aristotle, *Physics,* VII 2, 243a4. Cf. St. Thomas, *In Phys. VII,* Lect. 3. Also, see *In Phys. VIII,* Lect. 8, and *In Met. VII,* lect. 8 and XII, Lect. 7.

9. Cf. above, S{15}.

self,[10] as is any intelligent soul, as will be evident below.[11] For the being of its substance does not consist entirely in its union with corporeal matter, as is the case with the being of a nonsubsisting soul, such as the souls of nonrational animals and plants. So in these latter the above distinction is unnecessary, because the being of such souls is considered simultaneously from the viewpoint of the receiving matter and from the viewpoint of the soul itself.

{38} If we speak, therefore, of a soul abiding steadfastly in itself, namely, any intellectual soul—be it heavenly, if one maintains that the heavenly bodies are animated, as the author of this book supposes, or be it the human soul from the viewpoint of the soul itself—then, according to the basic positions[12] of the Platonists, which the author of this book follows on many points, such a soul results from the impression of an intelligence: for, as was said above in Proposition 3,[13] the Platonists asserted that what is common in anything is caused by one principle, while what is more proper is caused by another principle that is lower. So, according to this, a soul abiding steadfastly in itself has its being from the first cause. But that it is intellectual and that it is a soul result from second causes, which are intelligences. Hence, since it pertains to the nature of the soul to be impressed upon the body, it will follow that it is by an intelligence that this soul is impressed upon the body. But because, as we showed above,[14] the aforementioned position is not true and is contrary to the opinion of Aristotle, we must say that it is from the first cause, from which such a soul has its being, that it is also intellectual and that it is a soul and consequently that it is impressed upon the body. Accordingly,

10. *per se.*
11. Cf. below, S{38}. For St. Thomas the human, or rational, soul is abiding steadfastly *per se* or self-subsistent because, while it is the form of the body, "... the human soul exists by its own act of existing, in which matter in some way shares [though] not wholly comprising it, since the dignity of this form is greater than the capacity of matter ..." and in which the human soul possesses in the intellect a power that transcends the body (*De Unitate Intellectus*, III, n. 84, Zedler trans., p. 58; also see I, nn. 27–28) and is capable of a continued existence apart from the body after death (see *Quaest. Disp. de Anima*, Q. 14).
12. *radices positionum.*
13. Cf. above, S{22}.
14. Cf. above, S{23}.

then, the soul does not result from the impression of an intelligence but from the impression of the first cause.

But if we are speaking about such a soul[15] from the side of the susceptible thing upon which it is impressed, as in the case of a heavenly soul, if the heavens have soul, then the reason would be similar. For the nature of the heavenly bodies is not caused in some way by intelligences but by the first cause, from which they have being. But if we are speaking about the human soul from the side of the susceptible thing [upon which it is impressed], then the human soul does result in a way from the impression of an intelligence, insofar as the human body itself is disposed to being susceptive of such a soul through the power of a heavenly body acting on the seed.[16] For this reason it is said that both a man and the sun generate a man.[17] Furthermore, even doctors of the Christian faith, namely, Augustine and Gregory,[18] {39} asserted that spiritual creatures called angels, or intelligences, or separated intelligences, move heavenly bodies. From this it follows that intelligences do something in the impressing of the human soul upon the body from the side of [the body as something] susceptible [to impression]. In this way it can be said that other souls, which are not abiding steadfastly *per se*, result from the impression of intelligences and heavenly bodies.

The second point, the distinction between souls, remains to be considered next. The author gives the same rationale for the distinction, or multiplication, of souls that he had given for intelligences. For, just as the being of an intelligence is composed of the infinite and the finite insofar as its being is not subsistent but participated by some nature, which is why it can be distinguished into many, so also is it with regard to the being of the soul. And this is what he says: *Souls are multiplied only in the way in which intelligences are multiplied, because the being of the soul likewise has limit, but the part* that *is lower is infinite*. Now he says that the very nature participating being is *lower,* [and this nature] he calls *infinite* because of its power to persist infinitely in being. But the participated being he calls finite, because it is not participated according to the total infinity of

---

15. Reading *de anima huiusmodi* at p. 38.21 with Saffrey's corrected text.
16. *in semine.*
17. Cf. Aristotle, *Physics,* II 2, 194b13.
18. Cf. above, S{25}.

[being's] universality but rather according to the mode of the participating nature. Nevertheless, it should be noted that, because the nature of an intelligence is completely independent[19] of body, the distinction between intelligences is considered according to the gradation[20] of their proper nature without relation to any body. But it is of the nature of the soul to be impressed upon the body. So the distinction between souls is considered in relation to animated bodies. Hence, if animated bodies are of different species, then the souls impressed upon them will differ according to species, which it would likewise be necessary to say if heavenly bodies were animated. But if animated bodies are of one species, then the impressed souls are also of one species, multiplied only numerically, as is clear with regard to human souls.

{40} Next to be considered is the third point, the difference between distinct souls. He asserts three differences, the first of which is taken from the diverse perfection of souls. For he says that *souls*, namely, higher ones, such as those of heavenly bodies, *which follow an intelligence* as immediately ordered after it, *are complete* in the perfection of animated nature. He shows the sign of their perfection when he adds *of slight declination and separation*. For it was said above in Proposition 2[21] that the soul approaches motion to the extent that it is lacking in the completeness of an intelligence. For this reason, the higher and closer to an intelligence souls are, the less motion they have. For lower souls have motion not only inasmuch as they move the body but also inasmuch as they are not always conjoined to their bodies and do not always understand. But higher souls are always conjoined to their bodies and are always understanding, though they do possess motion insofar as they move heavenly bodies. Therefore, he says that *they are of slight declination* because they decline little from the immobility of an intelligence, and *of slight separation* because they are little separated into different things, as when they are found sometimes in this, sometimes in that, with respect only to the local motion of the heavenly bodies. But lower *souls* are lacking *in completeness and* slightness *of declination*, or separation, in relation to *higher souls*.

The second difference is taken up with regard to the infusion of souls upon one another. For, just as he said above that *the first intelligences infuse*

19. *penitus absoluta*.   20. *gradum*.
21. Cf. above, S{15}.

the second intelligences with the goodnesses they receive from the first cause,[22] so he now says that *higher souls infuse lower souls with the goodnesses they receive from an intelligence.* And in both places the reason is the same: it is of the nature of the more imperfect to be perfected by what is more complete, as potency by act.

{41} The third difference is taken up from the viewpoint of the effect. For, just as he said with regard to intelligences that higher [intelligences] impress nobler souls, so he now says with regard to souls that a higher *soul, receiving power* immediately *from an intelligence,* has a *stronger impression* because a higher cause always acts more powerfully, as was said in Proposition 1.[23] Therefore, *what is impressed by* a higher soul is *fixed* upon its body, *abiding steadfastly,* i.e., firm and immobile, and *its motion is regular,* i.e., uniform, and *continuous,* as is evident in a heavenly body. But a lower soul, to which the *power of an intelligence* belongs, with the mediation of a higher soul, has, as a lower cause, a weaker impression upon its body. For this reason what it impresses upon the body, such as life and the like, *is weak,* due to the possibility of the body before an external agent, *evanescent,* changed by an interior principle, *destructible,* because what the soul produces in the body eventually ceases to be in its entirety. And *nevertheless* the body in a sense participates in sempiternity according to species, and this is *through generation.* Here, however, the author of this book, in attributing the corruptibility of human bodies to the weakness of the impression of the soul itself, understood the matter more keenly[24] than did the Platonists, who maintained[25] that even the human soul has a certain incorruptible body always united to it.[26] It is also evident, according to the opinion of this author, that when the human soul shall have been perfected through being conjoined with the first cause, it will be able to impress perpetual life upon its body. In like accord the Catholic faith professes future eternal life not only for souls but also for bodies after the resurrection.

22. Cf. above, S{34}. 23. Cf. above, S{7}.
24. *sensit.* 25. *posuerunt.*
26. Cf. Proclus, Prop. 196 (cited by St. Thomas in *De Subst. sep.*, Cap. 18, n. 111) and Props. 205–210. On the Neoplatonic notion of the astral body as the "first body" (*prōton sōma*) and "vehicle" (*och'amema*) of the soul, see Dodds, pp. 300, 304–9 and 313–21.

Finally, he concludes with what he said in this and the previous proposition. What we have said about the souls of the heavens we have said, not as though asserting them, but as merely reporting the opinions of others.[27]

27. Cf. St. Thomas, *Quaest. Disp. de spir. Creat.*, A. 6.

{42} PROPOSITION 6[1]

The first cause transcends[2] description.[3] Languages fail in describing it only because of the description of its being. For [the first cause] is above every cause and is described only through the second causes which are illumined by the light of the first cause.

This is so because the first cause does not cease to illumine its effect, while it is not illumined by any other light, since it is itself the pure light above which there is no light. As a result, the first cause alone became that for which description fails. This is so only because there is no cause above it, through which it could be known, and[4] every thing is known and described only from its cause. Therefore, when a thing is only a cause and not an effect, it is not known through a first cause and neither is it described, since it transcends description,[5] nor does speech reach[6] it. For description comes about only through speech, and speech through intelligence, and intelligence through thought,[7] and thought through meditation,[8] and meditation through sense. But the first cause is above all things because it is cause of them. Due to this, it happens that it does not fall under sense, meditation, thought, intelligence or speech. Therefore it is not describable.

1. This proposition relates to Prop. 123 in Proclus but in such a way that "all that is divine" (*pan to theion*) relates only to God as the first cause and not to the henads, or gods, of Neoplatonism (as in Proclus, Prop. 162). Cf. Dodds, p. 108.25–34, 110.1–5, 110.8–9. St. Thomas relates this proposition to the negative theology of Pseudo-Dionysius, who was also influenced by Proclus. St. Thomas refers to this proposition in *De Veritate*, Q. 2, A. 1, 11a and *De Potentia*, Q. 8, A. 5, 5a, in which it is stated that God is known by the first effect that He produces, intelligence, but in such a way that "intelligence," since it is an effect, is not the proper definition, or name, of God.

2. *superior est.*

3. *narratione: al-sifah,* "characterization," "description." St. Thomas relates this term to "affirmation." The unknowability of the first cause is ultimately due to the incommunicability of its being, in the tradition of negative theology. See Taylor (1981), pp. 371–73.

4. For *quia* read *et* with the Arabic and Pattin's Latin manuscripts OLPSUV and Aosta.

5. *est superior narratione.* 6. *consequitur.*

7. I.e., discursive thought.

8. *al-wahm.* In this context the translation should have been "imagination" (*imaginatio*) as St. Thomas clearly saw. See S{46}. See Taylor (1981), pp. 372–73.

I say further that a thing either is sensible and falls under sense; or can be meditated upon and falls under meditation; or is fixed and abiding steadfastly in one disposition,[9] and so is intelligible; or is[10] alterable and destructible, falling under generation and corruption and so falling under thought. But the first cause is above intelligible sempiternal things and above destructible things. For this reason, neither sense nor meditation nor thought nor intelligence fall upon it.

The first cause is signified only from a second cause, which is an intelligence and is referred to by the name of its first effect, but only in a higher and better way because the effect has, further, what belongs to the cause, but in a more sublime, better, and nobler way, as we have shown.

COMMENTARY

After dividing higher being in general into three grades, in which the first is above eternity, which belongs to the first cause, the second with eternity, which belongs to an intelligence, and the third below eternity and above time, which belongs to the soul, the author of this book begins here to investigate these three grades, one at a time: (1) the first cause [here]; (2) intelligence in Proposition 7, {43} at: *An intelligence is a substance* etc.; (3) soul in Proposition 14, at: *In every soul* etc.

The most important thing we can know about the first cause is that it surpasses all our knowledge and power of expression. For that one knows God most perfectly who holds that whatever one can think or say about Him is less than what God is. Hence Dionysius says in Chapter 1 of *Mystical Theology*[11] that man "according to the best" of his knowledge is "united" to God as "altogether unknown, because he knows nothing" about Him, "knowing" Him to be "above" every "mind." To show this the author presents this proposition: *The first cause transcends description.*

Now by *description* we should understand "affirmation," because whatever we affirm of God does not belong to Him according to the way in which we signify it. For the names we give [to things] signify according

---

9. The Latin translation omits *la yatasarrafu*, "not varying." See Taylor (1981), pp. 164.
10. Read with the addition of *est* with the Arabic and Pattin's Latin manuscripts LOPUV and Aosta.
11. Pseudo-Dionysius, *Mystical Theology,* I 3; *Dionysiaca,* I, 578; PG 3, 1001 A.

to the way in which we understand, which way divine being transcends.[12] Hence Dionysius says in Chapter 2 of the *Celestial Hierarchy*[13] that "negations in divine things" are "true," while "affirmations are incongruous" or "unsuitable."[14] Proclus also asserts this [in] proposition 123 of his book, in these words: "Every essential being[15] itself, because of its supersubstantial unity, is inexpressible and unknowable by all second [beings]. It can, however, be grasped and known from what participates it, because only the first is entirely unknown as {44} '*amethectum*' being."[16] Now by "essential being" [Proclus] understands, in accord with the Platonists' positions, any ideal form, such as *per se* man, *per se* life and the rest of this

---

12. *transcendit*.

13. Pseudo-Dionysius, *Celestial Hierarchy*, II 3; *Dionysiaca*, II, 758–59; PG 3, 141 A.

14. The expression "incongruous" (*incompactae*) is taken from the version of John Scotus Erigena and the expression "unsuitable" (*inconvenientes*) from the version of John the Saracen (see note at S{43}).

15. *Quod ens*, literally, "what being," i.e. a "whatness," quiddity, or essence. In Dodds the phrase "All that is divine" (*Pan to theion*) is found. Accordingly, Pera, p. 45, n. 162, has *omne divinum* instead of *omne quod ens*, as in Saffrey, p. 43. The meaning, however, is not different, since, as the commentary tells us, the Platonists called any self-subsisting essential being, i.e., ideal form, a "god." Also, see Vansteenkiste, p. 499, where the expression *vel enter ens* as the Latin translation for *ontos on* appears as a gloss for *omne quod ens*. Prop. 161 of the *Elements* explicitly identifies *ontos on* with *theion* and the *theoi*.

16. Proclus, Prop. 123, Dodds, p. 108.25–28. *Amethectum*, Moerbeke's translation of the Greek, *amethekton*, means "unparticipated." In Prop. 24 of the *Elements* Proclus distinguishes between what participates, or the participant (*to metechon*), what is participated (*to metechomenon*), and the first cause, the source (Prop. 23), as the unparticipated (*to amethekton*). What is participated serves as an intermediary, allowing for a distinction between the unparticipated and the participants, the true one and the many: ". . . the first is a unity prior to the many; the participated is within the many, and is one yet not-one; while all that participates is not-one yet one" (Dodds, p. 29). The first, then, is an absolute one and as such unparticipable (see Prop. 116). All else is either a one participated (*to metechomenon*) by a many or a many participating (*to metechon*) a one. The former is higher than the latter as ". . . more nearly akin to the cause of all things . . ." (Dodds, p. 29) because it is the principle that completes and unifies its participants. Nevertheless, what is participated is always a diminishment of the first cause because ". . . it is not the Good, but a good . . ." (Prop. 8; Dodds, p. 11). Cf. Leo Sweeney, S.J., "The Origin of Participant and Participated Perfections in Proclus's *Elements of Theology*," in *Wisdom in Depth: Essays in Honor of Henri Renard, S.J.*, ed. Vincent F. Daves, S.J., et alii (Milwaukee: Bruce, 1966), pp. 235–55.

sort, which they call "gods," as was said above.[17] Furthermore, according to them, things of this sort have supersubstantial unity because they surpass all participating subjects. Thus he says that none of them can be either expressed or known by things below them, but they can be known by things above them. For example, the idea of life can be known by the idea of being. But, although they cannot be perfectly known or expressed by lower things, still they can be grasped and known in some way "from what participates them," i.e., through the things that participate them, just as through those things that participate life something is known about life itself. But what is absolutely first, which, according to the Platonists, is the very essence of goodness, is "entirely unknown" because there is nothing above it that could know it. Such is what Proclus means by *"amethectum,"* i.e., "not existing after" anything.[18]

Since the author of this book does not agree with the Platonists in asserting other separated ideal natures but asserts only one, the first, as was said above,[19] he therefore dismisses those other things, and says about the *first cause* that *it transcends description*. The reason he, like Proclus,

---

17. Cf. above, S{18}. These "gods" are the henads or unities in Prop. 6 of the *Elements* and as *ta metechomena* are participable and in this way differ from the true one (see Props. 24 and 116). But they are like the true one in that they transcend those beings which participate them so that they are above being (*hyperousios*), above life (*hyperzoos*), and above intelligence (*hypernous*) (Prop. 115). While Proclus identifies these henads with the gods of Greek mythology, he conceives of them impersonally. See Dodds, pp. 257–60.

18. In Prop. 99 of his translation of Proclus's *Elements* William of Moerbeke adds a gloss for the word *amethectum*: "i.e., not having after" (*id est non posthabens*) (see Saffrey's note, p. 44). In this gloss Moerbeke seems to be striving to translate the underlying meaning of the Greek verb *metechein* ("to partake," "to have a share of") in terms of its component parts: *meta* ("after") + *echein* ("to have"). St. Thomas himself explains the term *amethectum* with the expression "not existing after" (*non post existens*). Elsewhere, however, St. Thomas relates the idea of participation to having, as in the distinction between "being" (*ens*) and "to be" (*esse*), where "being is spoken of as having 'to be'" (*ens dicitur quasi esse habens*) (*In Met. XII*, Lect. 1).

19. Cf. above, S{20}. Pseudo-Dionysius also rejects these views. See *On the Divine Names*, XI 6. St. Thomas, of course, does not accept the real existence of separated ideal natures either, because ". . . the intellect can perceive a form apart from its individuating principles, though not apart from the matter required by the nature of the form in question. . . . And it was just because the Platonists failed to draw this distinction that they thought that mathematical objects and the essences of things were as separate from matter in reality as they are in the mind" (*In de Anima III*, lect. 8; Foster and Humphries trans., pp. 418–19).

gives for this is its supersubstantiality. So he adds in the proposition: *languages fail in describing it only because of the description of its being.*[20] *For it is above every cause.* He indicates further how it is described as well, adding: *and it is described only through the second causes* that *are illumined by the light of the first cause.* This is identical to what Proclus said: that "it can be grasped and known from what participates it."[21]

{45} Now he proves what he says in the proposition in this way. Something is known in one of three ways: in one way as an effect through a cause, in another way through itself, and in a third way through an effect.

First, then, he shows that the first cause is not known in the first way, namely, through a cause, when he says that the first cause does not cease to illumine its effect, while it is not illumined by any other light because it is itself the pure light above which there is no light. To understand this we should realize that it is through corporeal light that we have sense knowledge of visible things. So we can speak metaphorically of that through which we know something, as if it were a light. Now the Philosopher proves in Book 9 of the *Metaphysics*[22] that every single thing is known through that which is in act. Therefore, the very actuality of a thing is, in a certain way, its light. Since an effect is such that it is in act through its cause, it follows that it is illumined and known through its cause. The first cause, however, is pure act, having no admixture of potentiality. Therefore, it is itself pure light, by which all other things are illumined and rendered knowable. From this the author further concludes that the first cause alone is first in such a way that it cannot be described because it does not have a higher cause through which it could be described, for things are customarily described through their causes.

Because he has proceeded from the process of knowing to description, he subsequently shows that the first cause, since it is above knowledge, must be above description for this reason: because description, i.e., affirmation, comes about through speech, i.e., through some meaningful utterance.[23] But *speech is through intelligence,* because meaningful sounds[24] are signs of things intellected.[25] *Intelligence,* in turn, comes about *through*

---

20. Saffrey's text omits this word.
21. Proclus, Prop. 123, Dodds, 108.26–27. Also, see above, S{43}.
22. Aristotle, *Metaphysics*, IX 9, 1051a29–32.
23. *sermonem significativum.*   24. *voces significativae.*
25. *signa intellectuum.*

thought, i.e., through reasoning—and {46} this is true of human beings who come to the understanding of truth by reasoning[26] *and knowledge through meditation,* i.e., through imagination and the remaining internal sense powers that serve human reason. *And meditation comes about through sense,* because imagination is a movement brought about by a sense in act, as is said in the book *On the Soul.*[27] Thus, since *the first cause is above all things,* it surpasses all of the above. Dionysius asserts this as well in Chapter 1 of *On the Divine Names,*[28] saying: "And there is neither sense of it nor imagination," which our author calls *meditation,* "nor opinion," which he calls *reason,*[29] "nor name," which he calls *speech,* "nor discourse," which he calls *description,* "nor science," which he calls *intelligence.*[30]

Second, he shows that the first cause is not known in the second way, namely, through itself. He proves this through the different ways of knowing. Among things that are known through themselves, some are known by *sense,* such as *sensible things;* others by *meditation,* or imagination, such as imaginable things not present[31] to the senses; others by intellect, such as necessary and immobile things; still others by reasoning, or *thought,* such as generable and corruptible things. With regard to the latter, the Philosopher says in Book 6 of the *Ethics*[32] that we reason over contingent things, which can be otherwise. Hence, since the first cause is above all such things, it cannot be known in any of these ways. Proclus gives this proof as well, except that he uses the word "meditation" in place of *thought* and "opinion" in place of *meditation.*[33]

While it is clear from this argument {47} that the first cause is above sensible, imaginable, and corruptible things, it is not clear that it is

26. See St. Thomas, *ST* I, Q. 79, A. 8, c.
27. Aristotle, *On the Soul,* III 3, 429a1–2.
28. Pseudo-Dionysius, *On the Divine Names,* I 5; *Dionysiaca,* I, 35; PG 3, 593 A.
29. Here St. Thomas ought to have written the word "thought"; see above, S{42} (see Saffrey's note, p. 46).
30. See Pera, pp. 48–49, for tables comparing the terminology of Iamblichus, Proclus, Pseudo-Dionysius, the *Book of Causes* and St. Thomas here.
31. *subjacent.*
32. Aristotle, *Nicomachean Ethics,* VI 1, 1139a12–14.
33. I. e., *dianoia* and *doxa.* See Proclus's exposition of Prop. 123, Dodds, pp. 108–10. The text here requires some explanation by St. Thomas, because *meditatio* is the Latin translation for two different terms, *wahm* in the original Arabic of the *De Causis* and *dianoia* in the Greek of Proclus's *Elements.*

above intelligible sempiternal things. While the author omits any proof of this here, Proclus proves it by saying that "all thought," whether intellectual or rational, is "of beings."[34] For what the intellect first grasps is being.[35] The intellect cannot apprehend that in which the character of being is not found. So, since the first cause is above being, it follows that the first cause is above intelligible sempiternal things. According to the Platonists, however, the first cause is above being inasmuch as the essence of goodness and unity, which is the first cause, also surpasses separated being itself, as was said above.[36] But, according to the truth of the matter, the first cause is above being inasmuch as it is itself infinite "to be."[37] "Being,"[38] however, is called that which finitely participates "to be," and it is this which is proportioned to our intellect, whose object is some "that which is,"[39] as it is said in Book 3 of *On the*

---

34. Proclus, Prop. 123, Dodds, pp. 108–10.
35. This notion of being (*ens*) is being as first known and as transcendental. St. Thomas refers to being in this sense frequently throughout his works. E.g. *De Veritate*, I, Q. 1, A. 1, c.; *ST*, I–II, Q. 94, A. 2, c. Its early formulation in *I Sent.*, Dist. 8, Q. 1, A. 3, c and Dist. 19, Q. 5, A. 1, ad 7 reveals an Arabic influence, especially that of Avicenna. See M.–D. Chenu, "Un vestige du stoicisme," *Revue des sciences philosophiques et théologiques* 27 (1938), pp. 63–68. This notion of *ens* has a wider application than the substantive use of *ens* about which St. Thomas speaks in the next few lines.
36. See above, S{27}
37. *Esse*. Here and thoughout the remainder of this paragraph we have St. Thomas's technical use of the act of "to be," as disitnguised from *ens* as "being."
38. *ens*. The distinction between *ens* and *esse* is a technical one in St. Thomas's metaphysics, one notoriously difficult to render in English without awkwardness. By this substantive use of *ens* St. Thomas means a being composed of essence, which is itself only potential, and existence (*esse*), the act whereby something is or exists. *Esse* is thus the act of existing (*actus essendi*), distinguishable from the essence in all beings except God, whose essence is "to be." For a fuller discussion, see *De Ente et Essentia*, IV, 6–7; *De spirit. Creat.*, I, c; *SCG*, I, 21 and 22; *ST*, I, Q. 3, A. 3 and 4. This distinction is not present in the *Book of Causes*, where *anniyah* (translated *esse*) and *huwiyah* (translated *ens*) seem fully synonymous. On this see, Taylor (1979), p. 506.
39. The Latin expression here, *quod quid est*, is used somewhat interchangeably by St. Thomas with *quod quid* and *quod quid est esse* as equivalent translations of Aristotle's expression *ti estin*. These are also used somewhat interchangeably by St. Thomas with *quod quid erat esse*, the Latin translation of Aristotle's *to ti en einai* (e.g., see *In Met. VII*, Lect. 3–5 and *In post. Anal. II*, Lect. 2–5). For St. Thomas these terms mean "the quiddity, or essence of a thing, which a definition signifies" (*In de. Anima III*, Lect. 8; also, see *De Ente et Essentia*, I, 4). Owens, in *The Doctrine of Being in the Aristotelian Metaphysics* (Toronto: Pontifical Institute of Mediaeval Studies, 1978),

Soul.[40] Hence our intellect can grasp only that which has a quiddity participating "to be." But the quiddity of God is "to be" itself. Thus it is above intellect. In this way Dionysius presents this argument in Chapter 1 of *On the Divine Names*,[41] saying: "If all thoughts are of existing things, and if existing things are limited," namely, inasmuch as they finitely participate "to be," who is[42] above all substance is set apart from all knowledge."

Third, he shows how the first cause is known through the effect. He says that the first cause *is signified* in those things that are said about it *only from a second cause* that *is an intelligence.*[43] For we speak of God in this way, namely as though [speaking of][44] a certain intelligent substance, because an intelligence is its[45] *first effect.* Hence [an intelligence] is most similar to God and through it God can be known in the highest way possible. Nevertheless, God is not sufficiently known through an intelligence, because what an intelligence is {48} is found in the first cause in a *higher way.* So a cause that surpasses its effect cannot be sufficiently known through its effect.

Thus it is evident that *the first cause transcends description,* because it cannot be sufficiently known or expressed either through a cause, through itself, or through an effect.

---

p. 180, argues for a slight difference in the meaning between *ti estin* and *to ti en einai.* But St. Thomas, commenting on this passage from Aristotle, does distinguish between (1) a quiddity that is simply form, in which the form is the entire essence not participated by other beings so that the essence and the individual are identical, as in immaterial substances, such as angels; and (2) a quiddity in which the form exists individuated in matter and participated by many individuals so that the essence and the individual are not identical, as in material substances (see *In de Anima III,* Lect. 8). It is only the latter, the quiddity of material things, that is the proper object of human knowledge (see *ST,* I, Q. 84, A. 7 and Q. 88, A. 1 and 2).

40. Aristotle, *On the Soul,* III 4, 429b10ff.
41. Pseudo-Dionysius, *On the Divine Names* I 4; *Dionysiaca,* I, 34; PG 3, 593 A.
42. *qui est.* This term would have reverberations to the Latin reader of God's name revealed in *Exodus* 3:14 as *Qui est,* "He Who is" (see *ST,* I, Q. 13, A. 11).
43. Here, like Pseudo-Dionysius, the author of the *Book of Causes* departs from Proclus: it is not the highest henads, or gods, but an intelligence which immediately follows upon the first cause as closest to it.
44. *quasi.*
45. I.e, God's.

PROPOSITION 7[1]

An intelligence is an undivided substance.

For, if it has no magnitude, is not a body, and is not in motion, then undoubtedly it is undivided. Furthermore, everything that is divisible is divided only into multiplicity[2] or magnitude or its motion. Therefore, when a thing is in this state it is under time, because it receives division only in time. An intelligence is not in time but rather is with eternity. For this reason it has come to be loftier and more transcendent[3] than every body and every multiplicity. But if multiplicity is found in it, [that multiplicity] is found only as one existing thing.[4] Since, therefore, an intelligence is this way, it is not at all receptive of division.

The indication of this is its reversion upon its essence,[5] because it is not extended along with an extended thing so that one of its extremities is next to[6] another. For, when it wants knowledge of a corporeal thing, it is not[7] extended along with it but

---

1. This proposition relates directly to Prop. 171, which presupposes Prop. 15 in Proclus, as St. Thomas recognizes in his commentary. Cf. Dodds, p. 150.1–14. The author of the *De Causis*, who has already departed from Proclus by removing the henads as what are closest to the One, consequently places the first multiplicity (*multitudo*) or the beginning of plurality in the intelligences, rather than in the henads as Proclus does (see Prop. 171, Dodds, p. 150.10–14). Although an intelligence has multiplicity, it is still one because it is a pure form. The multiplicity in it is from within, in the unity of the knower with the known, and not from without, as in a body, which consists of part outside part. St. Thomas refers to this proposition in *De Potentia*, Q. 6, A. 2 s.c. and *De spir. Creat.*, Q. 1, A. 7 s.c.

2. *multitudo*.

3. *altior et superior*.

4. quasi res existens una. The correct reading of the Arabic, *muwahhada*, "unified" (corresponding to *henotai* in Proclus at Prop. 171, p. 150.6), is preserved in the Ankara Arabic manuscript. The Leiden Arabic, however, has *maujuda*, "existing," corresponding to the Latin translator's *existens*. The correct Arabic text would be rendered, "[this multiplicity] is found unified, as if a single thing."

5. *reditio sui super essentiam suam*.

6. *secunda*. The Latin translator here renders *thaniyan*. The correct version of the Arabic is *na'iyan*, "at a distance," from the Ankara Arabic manuscript. The Arabic then has: "I mean that it is not extended along with the extended thing such that one of two extremities belonging to it is at a distance from the other." Note, however, that St. Thomas understands the text to convey the sense that is more clearly found in the Arabic. See S{52}.

7. The negative, here *non* in the Latin, is not found in the Arabic, nor is it found

*remains fixed according to its own state, since it is a form from which nothing passes.*⁸ *But bodies are not that way.*

A further indication that an intelligence is not a body but that its substance and its activity are undivided is that both are one thing.

An intelligence is indeed many, due to the goodnesses coming to it from the first cause. Although [an intelligence] is a multiplicity in this way, nevertheless, because it is near to the one, it comes to be one and undivided. An intelligence is not receptive of division, because it is the first created [thing] that was created by the first cause, and [so] unity is more worthy of it than division.

Therefore, it has now been verified that an intelligence is a substance that has no magnitude, is not a body, and is not in motion in any of the ways that belong to corporeal motion. For this reason it has come to be above time and with eternity, as we have shown.

COMMENTARY

After having said that the first grade of higher being,⁹ namely, the first cause, is indescribable, [the author] now moves on to the second grade, intelligences. First he determines what an intelligence is {49} with regard to its substance; second with regard to its knowledge, in Proposition 8, at: *Every intelligence knows* etc.

Regarding the first point, we should realize that the things that belong to a higher order cannot be sufficiently known through those things that belong to a lower order, because higher things surpass the way lower

---

in the Aosta Latin or any of the ten Latin manuscripts entirely collated by Pattin for his edition. However, here it must be retained since *non* was contained in the Latin used by St. Thomas, as his quotation of this text indicates. The Arabic has, "For, when it wants knowledge of the corporeal extended thing, it is extended with it while [still] being subsistent and abiding steadfastly in its state, because it is a form from which nothing escapes. Bodies are not like that."

8. *quoniam est forma a qua non pertransit aliquid*. See the previous note regarding the corresponding Arabic. The sense seems to be that the intelligence knows corporeal things without having to be extended with those things and that it is a subsistent, steadfastly abiding substance unaffected in its immaterial act of knowing material things. Neither the Latin nor the Arabic renders this notion clearly. The author's comments here may be reflections on matters raised in Proclus's Prop. 15 and Prop. 167. St. Thomas was well aware of the problem here as his comments indicate. See S{51} and S{52}.

9. *esse*.

things exist and the power that they have. Now, because human knowledge takes its rise from sense, we can know sufficiently those things that present themselves to our senses. But we can arrive at a knowledge of higher things from them only by way of those things that they have in common with the sensible things we know. Moreover, those things that present themselves entirely to our senses are lower bodies, which higher bodies do not agree with either in the species of [their] essence or in the condition of [their] nature.[10] They do, however, agree in the matter[11] of quantity, light, and the things that follow upon these. So, about higher bodies we can attain knowledge of their brightness, by which they are visible to us, the quantity of their magnitude and motion, their shape, and even their genus insofar as they agree in genus with lower bodies. But we are able to know their proper nature with respect to[12] species only through negation, inasmuch as their proper nature transcends[13] that of lower bodies. So Aristotle proves in Book 1 of *On the Heavens*[14] that a heavenly body is neither heavy nor light, nor is it generable or corruptible.

Similarly an intelligence also transcends the entire order of corporeal things. But because its quiddity, or essence, is not its very "to be,"[15] but is a thing that subsists in its "to be" as participated, in a certain way it thus agrees in genus with bodies, which also subsist in their own "to be." So both are placed in the genus of substance according to logical intention.[16] For this reason an intelligence can be made known in a describable or affirmative way with regard to its genus, so that we can call it a substance. But we cannot describe it with regard to its specific difference. Rather, we have to know it through negation {50} inasmuch as it transcends the entire order of corporeal things to which divisibility pertains. And so, making known the essence of an intelligence insofar as we can know it, he proposes this proposition: *An intelligence is an undivided substance*. Now the first cause is not a nature subsisting in its own "to be" as participated. Rather, it is subsisting "to be" itself and so it is super-

---

10. That is, though they too are bodies, they are not the same kind of bodies as are those of the sublunar realm, nor are their natures found in the same conditions.
11. *in ratione.*   12. *secundum rationem.*
13. *transcendit.*
14. Aristotle, *On the Heavens*, I 3, 269b18–270a23.
15. *Esse* here and throughout this paragraph.
16. I.e., an analogy of inequality, where the intention is univocal, but the realities analogous. See *I Sent.*, D. 19, Q. 5, A. 2, ad 1.

substantial and absolutely indescribable. So, Proclus, too, states Proposition 171 in his book in these words: "Every intellect is an impartible substance."[17]

Now the author proves what has been said by division, and, as it appears from the words set down here, he presents a twofold division. The first [kind of division] is on the part of a thing to be divided: a thing that has stable magnitude but changing quantity, as [is the case with something] in time and motion. And this is what he says: *For, if it has no magnitude, is not a body, and is not in motion, then undoubtedly it is undivided.* For when he says, *if it has no magnitude, is not a body,* he excludes stable magnitude, i.e., what has place. And he says, *neither magnitude nor a body,* because a body is a complete magnitude divisible in every dimension, while a surface and a line are incomplete magnitudes, having one or two parts. Or when he says, *if it has no magnitude,* he asserts this in order to exclude those things that are quantified *per accidens*, such as whiteness and the like.

He asserts the other division on the part of division itself[18] and says that *everything* that is divided *is divided* either according to *multiplicity*, i.e., according to discrete quantity, or according to *magnitude*, which is division according to continuous quantity that has place, or according to *motion*, which is the division of a continuous quantity that does not have place. For the division of time and motion is the same, as is proved in Book 6 of the *Physics*.[19] But in the first division he omitted [the consideration] of multiplicity, because the division according to number follows upon the division of a continuum, as is clear in {51} Book 3 of the *Physics*.[20] Therefore, in the things in which there is no division according to magnitude, there is no division according to multiplicity.

Now with these divisions given, he shows that an intelligence is divided in none of these ways. The proof seems to be as follows. Everything that is divided is divided *in time*, for division is a certain motion from unity to multiplicity. But *an intelligence is not in time* but *is* entirely in *eternity*, as

---

17. Proclus, Prop. 171, Dodds, p. 150.1. *Impartibilis* is Moerbeke's translation of Proclus's *ameristos*. We have rendered *impartibilis* literally as "impartible" to distinguish it from *indivisibilis*, which appears throughout the commentary on this proposition.
18. I.e., the possible kinds of division that apply to what is divisible, i.e., a body.
19. Aristotle, *Physics*, VI 1–2, 232a18–233a17.
20. Aristotle, *Physics*, III 1, 200b15–20.

he maintained above in Proposition 2.[21] Therefore, it surpasses all the previously mentioned ways of division. Such is the explanation of this proposition as it appears from the words set down here.

But we should realize that the words set down here are corrupted by a faulty translation, as is apparent from the text of Proclus, which is as follows: "For if" [an intellect] is "without magnitude and is incorporeal and immobile, it is impartible."[22] But Proclus presents what follows, not in terms of another division, but in terms of a proof, for he adds the following: "For everything that is somehow partible is partible either according to multiplicity or magnitude or activities."[23] He immediately proves that it is not partible according to [its] activities, for he adds: "carried out in time,"[24] as if to say: all partible activities are in time. And he adds: "But an intellect is eternal and beyond bodies in all respects, and what is a multiplicity in it is united. Therefore, it is impartible."[25] He shows each of the things asserted above one by one. First he examines incorporeity, saying the following: "An intellect is indeed truly incorporeal, which [its] reversion upon itself makes clear."[26] Now the reversion of the intellect upon itself consists in the fact that it understands itself, "for none of the bodies turns to itself."[27] Proclus had proved this before, when he stated Proposition 15: "Everything able to revert upon itself is incorporeal."[28] He proves this as follows: "For it is not of the nature of any body to revert upon itself. For if something reverts upon anything it is joined {52} to that upon which it reverts. This is clearly the case because all the parts of a body that is turned toward itself will be joined to all [the

---

21. Cf. above, S{14}.
22. Proclus, Prop. 171, Dodds, p. 150.2; Vansteenkiste, p. 516. In Proclus these terms are all expressed negatively: *amegethes* (*sine magnitudine*), *asomatos* (*incorporeus*), *akinetos* (*immobilis*).
23. Proclus, Prop. 171, Dodds, p. 150.3–4; Vansteenkiste, p. 516.
24. Proclus, Prop. 171, Dodds, p. 150.4; Vansteenkiste, p. 516.
25. Proclus, Prop. 171, Dodds, p. 150.5–6; Vansteenkiste, p. 516.
26. Proclus, Prop. 171, Dodds, p. 150.7. Moerbeke translates Proclus's *pros heauton epistrophe*, "reversion upon itself," (Dodds p. 151) as *ad seipsum conversio* (literally "turning around toward itself"). The Latin translation of the *De Causis* gives us *reditio sui super essentiam suam* for the Arabic *ruju'u-hu 'ala dhati-hi*. The terms are technical philosophical jargon in all three languages so we have chosen to render the Latin as "reversion upon itself."
27. Proclus, Prop. 171, Dodds, p. 150.8; Vansteenkiste, p. 516.
28. Proclus, Prop. 15, Dodds, p. 16.30; Vansteenkiste, p. 271.

other parts]."[29] This is "impossible in all things that are partible due to the separation of the parts, some" of them "lying in other places [than others]."[30]

Now we find this proof added here, but confusedly enough, when the author says: *The indication of this,* i.e., that an intelligence is not a body, *is the reversion upon its essence,* i.e., that in understanding itself it reverts upon[31] itself, which is proper to it because it is neither a body nor a magnitude, which have one part distant from another. And this is what he adds: *because it is not extended,* i.e., by the extension of magnitude, *along with an extended thing,* namely, something that has magnitude, *so that one of its extremities is next to another,* i.e., distinct from another in the order of place. And, because someone might conceivably think that an intelligence is extended by understanding bodies, touching them, as it were, he excludes this, adding: *For, when it wants knowledge of a corporeal thing, it is not extended along with it,* so that it would be understanding magnitude by its magnitude, as Empedocles would have it,[32] but *remains fixed according to its own state,* i.e., it is not separated into different parts. He proves this when he adds: *since it is a form from which nothing passes.* For magnitude is only in matter, but an intelligence is an immaterial form from which nothing passes either because one part is not distant from another or because, although it is indivisible, nothing of a thing that has magnitude eludes its knowledge. So he adds: *But bodies are not that way,* from which we can conclude that an intelligence is not a body.

Then, according to what appears from the words set down here, the author introduces another proof to show *that an intelligence is not a body,* because *its substance* as well as *its activity* is indivisible, and each has the unity of indivisibility, which cannot be in bodies. {53} For a body is divided in its substance by the division of magnitude and is divided in its activity by the division of time, neither of which is proper to an intelligence. But Proclus presents this in his book to prove another point, i.e., to show that an intelligence is not divided according to motion, for he says the following: "Furthermore, the identity of its activity with its substance

---

29. Proclus, Prop. 15, Dodds, p. 16.31–34; Vansteenkiste, p. 271.
30. Proclus, Prop. 15. Dodds, p. 18.1–2, 3–4; Vansteenkiste, p. 271.
31. *supra.* In the Latin of the *De Causis* we find *super.*
32. Cf. Aristotle, *On the Soul* I 2, 404b11–15; St. Thomas, *In de Anima I,* Lect. 4, n. 45 and *ST,* I, Q. 50, A. 2.

shows that an intellect is eternal."[33] There is force to this proof because that thing whose activity comes to it accidentally receives variation according to that activity, so that sometimes it acts and sometimes it does not act, or sometimes it acts more and sometimes it acts less. But that thing whose activity belongs to it according to its essence acts without variation. Such is an intelligence, to which an intellectual activity belongs according to the nature of its essence.

Then he shows the third point, that an intelligence is not divided according to multiplicity. To make this clear, he argues that we must assert that there is some multiplicity in an intelligence, for many *goodnesses* accrue *from the first cause*. The reason for this multiplication is that an intelligence cannot attain the simplicity of the unity of the first cause. Therefore, the perfection of goodness, which is united and simple in the first cause, is multiplied into several goodnesses in an intelligence. Nevertheless, although there is a multiplicity of goodnesses in an intelligence, those many cohere to one another indivisibly. For it cannot be that it retain being[34] and lose life or that it retain life and lose knowledge, as happens in these lower things. This is so because, since *an intelligence is the first created thing*, it is nearest to the first cause. Therefore, those things that are in an intelligence belong to it in the noblest way after the first cause. Furthermore, *unity* and indivisibility *are* nobler *than division*. Hence an intelligence {54} possesses indivisibly a multiplicity of goodnesses, which it participates from the first cause. The proof that Proclus offers also reduces to the same thing.[35]

Finally, he concludes with what he had proposed as now proved when he says: *Therefore, it has now been verified* etc.

33. Proclus, Prop. 171, Dodds, p. 150.8–9; Vansteenkiste, p. 516.
34. *esse*.
35. In this proof, however, Proclus places the henads as multiple before the intelligences as multiple for the reason that what is "implicit" (*syneptugmenon*) is before what is "discrete" (*dieremenon*). See Prop. 171, Dodds, p. 150.10–14.

PROPOSITION 8[1]

Every intelligence knows both what is above it and what is below it. It knows what is below it because it is its cause. It knows what is above it because it acquires goodnesses from it.

An intelligence is an intellectual substance. Therefore, it knows according to the mode of its substance both the things it acquires from above and the things of which it is the cause. Therefore, it discerns what is above it and what is below it and knows that what is above it is its cause and that what is below it is caused by it. And it knows its cause and its effect according to the mode that is its cause,[2] namely, according to the mode of its substance.

Likewise, every knower knows a better thing and a lower and meaner thing only according to the mode of its substance and its being, not according to the mode of the things themselves. If this is so, then without doubt the goodnesses that descend upon an intelligence from the first cause are intelligible in it. Likewise, sensible corporeal things are intelligible in an intelligence. This is because the things that are in an intelligence are not the impressions themselves. Rather, they are the causes of the impressions. The indication of this is that an intelligence is itself the cause of the things that are below it [simply] in virtue of its being an intelligence. Therefore, if an intelligence is the cause of things due to the fact that it is an intelligence, then undoubtedly the causes of things in an intelligence are intelligible as well.

Therefore, it is now clear that the things that are either above an intelligence or below it exist through intellectual power. Likewise, corporeal things are intelligible with an intelligence, while intelligible things are intelligible in an intelligence because it is the cause of their cause.[3] Because it apprehends only according to the

---

1. This proposition derives from Prop. 173 in the *Elements*. Cf. Dodds, p. 150.22–152.7. St. Thomas seeks to clarify the way this proposition should be understood, in accord with what Proclus explicitly says in Prop. 173. That an intelligence occupies a "middle rank" in the order of things as both a cause and an effect is frequently referred to in St. Thomas's writings: *ST*, I, Q. 56, A. 2, 2a; Q. 89, A. 2c; I–II, Q. 5, A. 5c; Q. 50, A. 6c; *SCG*, II, 98; *De Veritate*, Q. 2, A. 3c; Q. 8, A. 3c; A. 7c; A. 14, ad 6; Q. 13, A. 2c; *De Potentia*, Q. 3, A. 4, 11a; *Quaest. Disp. de Anima*, Q. 7, A. 8a.
2. The Latin translation *causa eius* reflects the Arabic *'illatu-hu*, instead of the correct reading of the Arabic, *'ilai-hi*, "according to the mode that is proper to it."
3. Saffrey provides Bardenhewer's Latin here, which is *quoniam ipsa est causa esse earum*. Since St. Thomas does not quote the text in his commentary, it is unclear just

mode of its substance and because it is an intelligence, it apprehends things by intellectual apprehension, whether the things be intelligible or corporeal.

COMMENTARY

After having explained[4] an intelligence with respect to its substance, [the author] begins here to clarify its knowledge. First he makes clear how it knows things other than itself; second, how it knows {55} itself in Proposition 13, at: *Every intelligence understands its essence* etc. Regarding the first he does three things: (1) he explains how an intelligence knows both higher and lower things; (2) he shows what is higher than it, in Proposition 9, at: *The stability of every intelligence* etc.; (3) he shows what its nature is[5] in its knowledge of lower things, at: *Every intelligence is full of forms*, in Proposition 10.

So, to make clear the way in which an intelligence knows both higher and lower things, he asserts the following proposition: *Every intelligence knows both what is above it and what is below it. It knows what is below it because it is its cause. It knows what is above it because it acquires goodnesses from it.* On the surface, the meaning[6] of this proposition seems to be that causality is the reason for an intelligence's understanding.[7] But this, if it is considered correctly, is not true, either with regard to that by which an intelligence is caused or with regard to those things that it causes. For [an intelligence] is not caused by its cause through its [own] knowledge, but rather through the knowledge belonging to the cause that causes it. Furthermore, although an intelligence, through its knowledge, causes those

---

what text he had. For his edition Pattin reads *quoniam ipsa est causa causae esse earum.* For our translation we depart from the text printed by Saffrey and read *quoniam ipsa est causa causae earum*, following Pattin, but omitting *esse* with Latin manuscripts ALOPST and Aosta. This latter version corresponds precisely with the Arabic of the Leiden manuscript.

4. *Posita notificatione.*
5. *quomodo se habeat.*
6. <*intellectus*> is added here by Saffrey.
7. *intelligendi.* For St. Thomas, although an intelligence, or angel, understands through its essence, which is a simple form, an intelligence cannot be understood by that either to be essentially intelligence or to be a creative intelligence, both of which belong to God alone (see *ST*, I, Q. 54, A. 2 and 3). An angel knows itself through its essence but receives the species of the other things which it knows from God (see *ST*, I, Q. 55, A. 1 and 2; Q. 56, A. 1 and 2; *SCG*, II, 98).

things that are below it, nevertheless it does not then know them because it causes them. Rather, it causes them because it knows them.

The true meaning of this proposition must be taken as follows. It is clear that in the order of things a cause holds a higher rank[8] than an effect. Therefore, if something is both a cause and an effect, it holds a middle rank between the two. And such is an intelligence, for it is caused by the first cause and is beneath it. But it does in a certain way cause those things that are below it, as was explained in Proposition 3,[9] and so it is above them. Therefore, [the author] wants to say that, according to its rank, by which it is both a cause and an effect, an intelligence occupies a middle mode in understanding. For it understands what is above it in a way lower than that thing is in itself, while it understands the things that are below it in a higher way than they are in themselves. And in this sense, too, Proclus presents {56} the following in Proposition 173 of his book: "Every intellect is intellectually both what is before it and what is after it,"[10] because both higher things and lower things are in an intellect according to its mode, i.e., intellectually.

It is in this sense also that the author introduces this proof. For he says that *an intelligence is an intellectual substance* because to be intellectual belongs to it by reason of its essence. *Therefore, it knows according to the mode of its substance both the things* that *it acquires from above and the things of which it is the cause.* The reason for this is that each thing acts according to the mode of its form, which is the principle of [its] activity; for instance, what is hot heats according to the mode of its heat. Hence every knower must know according to a form, which is the principle of knowledge, namely, according to a likeness of the thing known, which is in the knower according to the mode of the knower's substance. Hence every knower must know whatever it knows according to *the mode of its substance.* Therefore, since an intelligence according to the mode of its substance is both a cause and an effect, it will be, as it were, a kind of boundary, or limit, determining or distinguishing higher things from lower things, so that it knows higher things through the mode of its substance in a lower mode than the higher thing is in itself, while it knows lower things in a higher mode than they are in themselves. We should understand that the mode of

8. *gradum.*
9. Cf. above, S{21}.
10. Proclus, Prop. 173, Dodds, p. 150.22–23; Vansteenkiste, p. 517.

knowledge is taken from the side of the one knowing, because, although the first cause is superintellectual, an intelligence does not know it superintellectually but intellectually. Likewise, although bodies are in themselves material and sensible, nevertheless, an intelligence does not know them sensibly and materially but intellectually. But if the mode of knowledge is taken from the side of the thing known, then it knows each one as it is in itself. For an intelligence knows that the first cause is in itself superintellectually and that corporeal things have in themselves material and sensible being.

From these remarks the meaning of all the things that he says here is evident.

{57} PROPOSITION 9[1]

The stability and essence of every intelligence is through the pure goodness that is the first cause.

The power of the intelligence is of a more powerful unity than the second things, which are after it because they do not receive its knowledge.[2] The intelligence has come to be so only because it is the cause of what is under it. The indication of it is this which we recall: through the divine power that is in it, the intelligence is the ruler of all the things that are under it and through [that divine power] it retains these things because through [that divine power] it is the cause of the things. And it retains all the things that are under it and encompasses them.

This is because everything that is first for things and is the cause of them retains those things and rules them. None of them escapes it because of its exalted[3] power. Therefore, the intelligence is the ruler of all the things that are under it, and it retains them and rules them, just as nature rules the things that are under it through the power of the intelligence. Likewise, the intelligence rules nature through divine power.

The intelligence has come to retain things that are after it and to rule them and to suspend[4] its power over them only because they are not substantial power for it. Rather, it is the power of substantial powers because it is the cause of them. The intelligence encompasses generated things, nature and the horizon of nature,[5]

---

1. This proposition, like Proposition 22(21) and a substantial portion of Props. 4 and 5(4), does not have the *Elements of Theology* of Proclus as its source. Rather, it derives ultimately from the *Enneades* of Plotinus. Cf. *Enneades* V, 5, 9 = PA *Epistola* nos. 194–202, Lewis p. 353; *Enn.* V, 1, 7.18–20, 7.25–26 = PA *Dicta* pp. 185.4–9, Lewis, p. 281, nos. 10–16; *Enn.* VI, 7, 17.40–43 = PA *Dicta* pp. 188.2–198.12, Lewis pp. 475–6, nos. 32–46; and *Enn.* V 1 title. Also see V 1, 15–16 = PA *Theologia* p. 109.10, Lewis, p. 267, no. 107. Here St. Thomas relates this proposition to Prop. 12 in Proclus. He cites it in *De Ente et Essentia*, IV and V; *SCG*, I, 26; *De Potentia*, Q. 5, A. 1, 4 s.c.; *De Veritate*, Q. 21, A. 5c; *Quodlibet. II*, Q. 2, A. 3 s.c.

2. That is, they do not attain its level of cognition.

3. For Saffrey's *alteram* we read *altam* with Bardenhewer, Pattin, and the Arabic (*al-'aliya*).

4. *suspendens*.

5. The Latin translator's Arabic manuscript had the corrupt reading, *ufuqa al-tabi'a, horizontem naturae*, instead of *ma fauqa al-tabi'a*, "what is above nature," which is found in all the extant Arabic manuscripts.

namely, the soul, for it is above nature. This is because nature contains generation, while soul contains nature, and intelligence contains soul. Therefore, the intelligence contains all things. And the intelligence came to be so only because of the first cause, which is supereminent to all things because it is the cause for intelligence, soul, nature, and the rest of things.

The first cause is not intelligence, soul, or nature. Rather, it is above intelligence, soul, and nature because it creates all things. But it creates intelligence without a medium, while it creates soul, nature, and the rest of things with the mediation of an intelligence.

Divine knowledge is not like intellectual knowledge, nor is it like the soul's knowledge. Rather, it is above an intelligence's knowledge and the soul's knowledge because it creates the various kinds of knowledge.[6] The divine power is above all intellectual, animated, and natural power because it is the cause for every power. The intelligence has yliatim[7] *because it is being and form. Likewise, soul has yliatim, and nature has yliatim. But the first cause does not have yliatim, because it is being alone.[8]*

But if someone should say: the first cause must have[9] yliatim, we will say: its yliatim is infinite being and its individuality[10] is the pure goodness that infuses the intelligence with all goodnesses and, with the mediation of the intelligence, [also infuses] the rest of things.

COMMENTARY

After stating how an intelligence knows what is above it and what is under it, [the author] shows here what is above {58} it, introducing this proposition to show that an intelligence depends on the first cause: *The*

---

6. *scientias*.

7. *yliatim* reflects the Latin manuscript tradition's corruption of *helyatin*, a transliteration of the indefinite singular genitive of the Arabic *hilya*, "form" or "shape." For further discussion of this and St. Thomas's interpretation of the transliterated term in his commentary on this proposition, see Taylor, "St. Thomas and the *Liber de causis* on the Hylomorphic Composition of Separate Substances," *Mediaeval Studies* 41 (1979), pp. 506–13.

8. *esse tantum*.

9. Bardenhewer's text is modified by Saffrey to read *necesse est ut sit <habens> yliatim*. Pattin reads the text as Bardenhewer without *<habens>*. We read *necesse est ut sit ei yliathim*. The word *ei* found in Latin manuscripts OPS and Aosta is a literal translation of *la-ha* found in the Arabic manuscripts.

10. *individuum suum*.

stability and essence of every intelligence is through the pure goodness that is through[11] *the first cause.* Proclus also states this proposition, but more universally, saying in Proposition 12 of his book: "The principle of all beings and their first cause is the good."[12] The author means the same thing by "pure goodness" in his proposition that Proclus means by "the good" in his proposition. For pure goodness is said to be, not a participated goodness, but the very subsisting essence of goodness, which the Platonists called the "good itself." What is essentially, purely, and primarily good must be the first cause of all things because, as Proclus proves, a cause is always "better"[13] than its effect. So what is the first cause must be the best. But this is what the very essence of goodness is. Hence it must be that what is essentially "good is the first cause of all things."[14]

And this is what Dionysius says in Chapter 1 of *On the Divine Names*: "But because" God is the very "essence of goodness through" his "very being, he is the cause of all existing things."[15] So, too, must intelligences, which have participated being and participated goodness, depend on pure goodness as an effect does on its cause. And this is what [the author] says: *The stability and essence of an intelligence exists through pure goodness* because an intelligence has from the first goodness stable being, i.e., it endures without motion.[16]

He proves this in two ways. First through the effect of an intelligence itself. The force of his proof consists in this: if the proper activity of any thing is found in another thing, then that thing must of necessity possess this {59} activity from a participation of the other thing as an effect possesses something from [its] cause. For example, if fired iron performs the proper activity of fire by burning, it is necessary to say that iron possesses this from fire as an effect from [its] cause. But the proper activity of God himself is that he is the universal ruling cause of all things, as was held in Proposition 3.[17] Hence something can achieve this activity only insofar as it participates it from the first cause as its effect. But, because the first

---

11. *per.* This quotation of the beginning of the proposition differs from the proposition by the addition of this word. Whether the word was found in the text of the *De Causis* used by St. Thomas is uncertain.
12. Proclus, Prop. 12, Dodds, p. 14.1–2; Vansteenkiste, p. 269.
13. *melior.*
14. Proclus, Prop. 12, Dodds, p. 14.23; Vansteenkiste, pp. 270 and 271.
15. Pseudo-Dionysius, *On the Divine Names* I 5; *Dionysiaca* I, 41; PG 3, 593 C.
16. *est immobiliter permanens.* 17. Cf. above, S{18} and S{21}.

cause is one to the highest degree,[18] the more simple and one anything is, the closer it is to the first cause and the more it participates its proper activity. Furthermore, *intelligences* are of greater *unity* and simplicity *than lower things*. A sign of this is that whatever is below an intelligence and has the power to know cannot arrive at the knowledge of the substance of an intelligence, because an intelligence's simplicity surpasses it. For the same reason, corporeal sense also lacks the knowledge of any intelligible thing. That an intelligence is simpler is shown by the fact that it is a *cause* of lower things in the way spoken of before in Proposition 3.[19] [The author] shows this through what immediately follows: *an intelligence rules all the things* that *are under it through the divine power that is in it*. We are to understand by "rule" the ordering and movement of lower things toward an end, *and through* such divine power existing in it *it retains*, i.e., conserves, *things* from the impediments to its rule—for these two, namely, to rule and to retain, are proper to a cause in relation to its effect. Therefore, *an intelligence rules things and retains them through divine power because, through* it, *it is the cause of things*. He shows how it retains lower things when he adds that *it retains all* causes that *are under it and contains them*, namely, by impressing its power upon them. For it is not the cause of all lower things immediately, but with the mediation of lower causes. {60}

He subsequently proves what he had said through this: *everything that is first* in *things and is a cause of them retains those things and rules them*, as was said.[20] And none of the things that are under any cause can be exempt from the rule and retention of its cause through any extraneous power. So, since an *intelligence* is first with respect to lower things and consequently is their cause in the way stated, it follows that with respect to lower things an intelligence has, as it were, the office of *ruler* in *retaining* and *ruling* [them]. For thus we see that even those things that are below an intelligence have ruling power *through the power of an intelligence, just as* through *nature*, which is the principle of motion in natural things, those things that *are under* nature *are ruled* and retained. So *likewise, an intelligence rules nature* and the other things that are under it *through divine power*. In this way he has therefore proved from higher things that as a *ruler* an intelligence rules and retains lower things through the power of a higher

---

18. *maxime.*
19. Cf. above, S{21}.
20. Cf. above, S{59}.

cause and that this is so because it is their *cause*. That it is a cause proceeds from the fact that it is *of a more powerful unity.*

But he has not yet proved how it follows from the fact that an intelligence is a cause that it retains and rules the effects. So he adds the proof of it: *The intelligence has come to retain the things that are after it and to rule them and to suspend its power over them only because* they *are not substantial power for it. Rather, it is the power of substantial powers because it is a cause of them.* The force of this proof is that everything is ruled and conserved by some power belonging to it, through which it performs some activity for an end and resists impediments. But the power of an effect depends on the power of the cause, and not the converse. For, since power is the principle of acting in each thing, the source of a thing's having the principle of acting must be the power of its power. It was said in Proposition 1[21] that a lower cause acts through the power of a higher cause. Hence the power of the higher cause is the power of the power of the lower cause. It is in this sense that {**61**} he says that the power of an intelligence is *the power of substantial powers,* i.e., of the powers proper to the substances of lower things. Thus, it is evident that an intelligence rules and retains lower things, extending its power over them, from the fact that it is their cause.

He shows what the lower things that it rules are, adding that *an intelligence encompasses generated things,* i.e., it contains generable and corruptible things under it as effects that it rules and retains, *and nature,* which is the principle of motion in them and is found first in the first of bodies. *It* also *encompasses the horizon of nature, namely, the soul*—for it was said in Proposition 2[22] that the soul is on the horizon of eternity and time, existing below eternity and above time—because *it is above nature,* which is the principle of motion, which is measured by time. He proves that an intelligence encompasses all the above through the fact that *nature contains generation,* i.e., generated things, existing as the principle of generation: the particular nature for a particular generation, while the universal nature that is in a heavenly body universally encompasses all generation as its effect. Furthermore, *soul contains nature* because, according to the opinion of those who hold that heavenly bodies are animated, which the author of this book supposes, soul is the principle of the motion of the first body and consequently of all natural motions, as was held in Prop-

---

21. Cf. above, S{7}.   22. Cf. above, S{16}.

osition 3.[23] *And* again *intelligence contains soul* because the soul participates intellectual activity from an intelligence, as was said in the same proposition.[24] Hence he concludes that *an intelligence contains all things* because whatever is contained by something contained is contained by the thing containing it. He reiterates the reason why this belongs to an intelligence: *because of* the power *of the first cause*, to which it is proper to be *supereminent to all things*, not through the power of another thing, but through [its] proper power. For through its divine power it *is the cause of intelligence*, {62} *soul, nature, and the rest of things*, namely, generable and corruptible things. In this way he has therefore shown that an intelligence depends on the first cause, because from it an intelligence possesses the universal power of containing lower things.

Then, when he says, *The first cause* etc., he shows the same thing from the position of the first cause by a demonstration, as it were, showing the "reason why," for the previous proof was more through a sign.[25] First he lays down the proof; second he excludes an objection, at: *But if someone should say* etc. So he says first, proposing, as it were, what he intends to prove, that *the first cause is* not *intelligence, soul, or nature* but *is above* all these as their creator [acting] with a certain order, for *it creates intelligence immediately, but soul, nature, and the rest of things with the mediation of an intelligence*. We should understand this to mean, as we said before in Proposition 3, not that their being[26] has been created by an intelligence, but that these things have been created in their essence by the first cause alone,

---

23. Cf. above, S(24).   24. Cf. above, S{21}.

25. The contrast here is between a *propter quid* demonstration, in which the effect is known through a knowledge of the cause, giving the "reason why," and a *quia* demonstration, which knows something about the cause from the effect as a "sign" of the cause. The argument through a sign (*syllogismos dia semeiou*) is referred to by Aristotle, *Posterior Analytics*, 75a34. St. Thomas remarks on this passage: "He [Aristotle] further shows that even if the premises were always both necessary and true but not per se, one would not know the cause why [propter quid] of the conclusion. This is clear in syllogisms which prove through signs, for although the conclusion be per se, one does not know it per se nor propter quid. For example, if someone were to prove that every element is corruptible on the ground that it is seen to grow old. This would be a proof through a sign but neither per se nor propter quid, because to know propter quid one must know through the cause" (*In post. Anal. I*, Lect. 14; Larcher trans., p. 49).

26. *Esse* here and throughout the rest of the commentary on this proposition, except where otherwise indicated.

while they receive certain superadded perfections through an intelligence.[27]

Now he begins to prove that the first cause creates all the above-mentioned things at: *Divine knowledge* etc. To understand this proof, we should realize that, of the perfections coming to things from the first cause, there is something that reaches all things, even down to generable and corruptible things, namely, being. But there is something that does not reach effects insofar as they are effects but only causes insofar as they are causes, namely, power. Hence the participation of power reaches as far as nature, which has {63} the character of a principle. But there is something that reaches as far as the intellectual soul, namely, knowledge, which, however, is in a soul in a way lower than it is in an intelligence. For it belongs to an intelligence [to know] without motion, inasmuch as it apprehends truth immediately, while it belongs to the soul [to know] with a certain motion, as the soul proceeds from one thing to another [in knowing].[28] Thus, both an intelligence and the soul attain being, power, and knowledge; nature [attains] being and power; generated things [attain] only being. So, if the first cause is the cause of all knowledge, power, and the totality of being, then it follows that all things are created by it. Furthermore, he proves that it is the cause of all these things through the fact that what is first and most excellent in each order is the cause of all the things that follow in that order. But the first cause has knowledge more excellent than all knowledge, and power more excellent than all power, and being more excellent than all being.[29] Therefore, it is the cause of all knowledge, power, and being. From this it follows that it is the creator[30] of intelligence, soul, nature, and the rest [of things].

So [the author] first shows this concerning knowledge and says that *divine knowledge is not like intellectual knowledge*, because the knowledge of an intelligence is through a participation of the thing understood.[31] Much less is it *like the soul's knowledge*, which is not only through a participation of the thing understood but also through a participation of the intellectual

---

27. Cf. above, S{22}.
28. That is, the soul knows discursively. See *ST* I, Q. 54–58 on angelic knowledge and QQ. 79 and 84–89 on human knowledge.
29. *Ens* here, contrasted with *esse*, which latter term is used throughout this paragraph.
30. *creatrix*.
31. See *ST* I, Q. 55, AA. 1 and 2.

light from an intelligence, possessing knowledge only by means of motion.[32] *Rather divine knowledge is above an intelligence's knowledge and above the soul's knowledge* because it has essential knowledge without motion and without any participation of intellectual light or of the thing understood, knowing things through its essence.[33] This is so because it is the creator[34] of all knowledge. Hence it must be higher than all knowledge.

Now he proceeds in the same way with power and says that *divine power is above all intellectual,* {64} *animated, and natural power* because intelligence, soul, and nature have power participated from another, as the power of a second cause is participated from the power of the first cause, which is not participated from another, but *is* itself *the cause of all power.*[35]

He also proceeds in similar fashion with being, showing that the first cause has being in a higher way than all other things. For *intelligence has yliatim,* i.e., something material or in a condition like matter,[36] for *yliatim* is derived from *yle,* which means "matter." How this is so he explains, adding: *because it is being and form.* For the quiddity and substance of an intelligence itself is a certain subsisting immaterial form. However, because it is not its own being but subsists in participated being, the subsisting form itself is compared to participated being as potency to act or matter to form. *Likewise the soul has yliatim* as well, [having] not only a subsisting form but also a body, whose form it is. Likewise *nature has yliatim* as well because a natural body is truly composed of matter and form. But *the first cause* in no way has *yliatim,* because it does not have participated being but *is* itself pure *being* and consequently pure goodness because everything, inasmuch as it is a being,[37] is good. But everything that is participated must be derived from what subsists purely through its

---

32. *mobiliter se habens circa scientiam.* For St. Thomas, the human intellect knows through a "motion," or change, of some kind inasmuch as (1) it moves from potency to act in the acquisition of knowledge through the formation of concepts; (2) its knows things only through one concept at a time and thus reasons, moving in its consideration from one thing to another as the expression of thinking (*cogitatio*) and inquiry (*inquisitio*). These two features characterize rational intellect in distinction to angelic and divine intellect. (3) To know and to be are not the same for the human intellect, or angelic intellect. See *In Ioan. I,* Lect. 1.
33. See *ST* I, Q. 14, on God's knowledge.
34. *creatrix.*
35. See *ST* I, Q. 25, on the power of God.
36. *aliquid materiale vel ad modum materiae.*
37. *ens.*

essence. Hence, the essence of an intelligence and of all beings is from the pure goodness of the first cause. So the reason is evident why he said above[38] that *the first cause is not intelligence, soul, or nature,* since its knowledge surpasses the knowledge of an intelligence and the soul, while its power surpasses all power, and its being all being.

Then, when he says: *But if anyone should say* etc., he removes a certain objection. For someone could say that, if the first cause is only being, then it seems that it is common being, which is predicated of all things, {65} and that it is not something that is an individual being, distinct from others.[39] For what is common is individuated only by being received in something. But the first cause is something individual, distinct from all others. Otherwise, it would not have any activity. For it does not belong to universals either to act or to be acted upon. Therefore, it seems that it is *necessary* to say that the first cause has *yliatim,* i.e., something that receives being. But to this he responds that the *infinity* of divine *being,* inasmuch as it is not limited through some recipient, takes in the first cause the place of the *yliatim* that is in other things. This is so because, just as in other things the individuation of a commonly received thing comes about through what the recipient is, so divine *goodness,* as well as being, is individuated by its very own purity through the fact that it is not received in anything.[40] Due to the fact that it is thus individuated by its own purity, it has the ability to *infuse the intelligence and other things with goodnesses.*

In evidence of this we should consider that something is said to be an "individual" because it is not of its nature[41] to be in many things, for it is of the nature of a universal to be in many things. Now that it is not of the nature of something to be in many things can happen in two ways. In one way through the fact that it is determined to some one thing in

38. Cf. above, S{62}.
39. *aliquid individualiter ens ab aliis distinctum.*
40. In *ST* I, Q. 29, A. 3, ad 4, St. Thomas replies to the objection that the term "individual" cannot be predicated of God because the term implies matter as the principle of individuation by saying, "But God cannot be called an *individual* in the sense that His individuality comes from matter; but only in the sense which implies incommunicability. *Substance* can be applied to God in the sense of signifying self-subsistence. . . . *Person* in God is *the incommunicable existence of the divine nature*" (Benzinger trans., vol. I, p. 158).
41. *natum est.*

which it is, such as, it is of the nature of whiteness by reason of its species to be in many things. But the whiteness received in this subject can only be in this subject. But this cannot proceed into infinity, because there is no proceeding into infinity in formal and material causes, as is proved in Book 2 of the *Metaphysics*.[42] Hence we must arrive at something whose nature is not to be received in anything else, and from this it has individuation, as, for instance, does as prime matter in corporeal things, which is the principle of singularity. Hence everything whose {66} nature is not to be in something else must by this very fact be an individual. This is the second way in which it is not of the nature of something to be in many things because it is not of its nature to be in something else, as, for instance, if whiteness were separate, existing without a subject, then it would in this way be an individual. It is in this way that individuation exists in separate substances, which are forms having being, and in the first cause itself, which is subsistent being itself.[43]

42. Aristotle, *Metaphysics*, II 2, 994a20ff and 994b17ff.
43. See *ST* I, Q. 3, A. 3 and 4.

PROPOSITION 10[1]

Every intelligence is full of forms. Among intelligences, however, there are some that contain more universal forms and others that contain less universal forms.

This is because the forms that are in the second, lower universal intelligences in the mode of particulars are in the first intelligences in the mode of universals. And the forms that are in the first intelligences in the mode of universals are in the second intelligences in the mode of particulars.

The first intelligences have[2] great power because [these intelligences] possess a more powerful unity than the second, lower intelligences. The second, lower intelligences have[3] powers that are weak because [these intelligences] possess less unity and more multiplicity. This is because the intelligences near the true pure one possess less quantity[4] and greater power, while the intelligences that are more distant from the pure one possess greater quantity and weaker power. Because the intelligences near the true pure one possess less quantity,[5] it so happens that the forms that proceed from the first intelligences proceed by a universal procession that is united. We abbreviate and say that the forms that come from the first to the second intelligences are of a weaker procession and are more powerfully separated[6] from one

---

1. This proposition relates to Prop. 177 in Proclus. Cf. Dodds, p. 156.1–9, 156.16–20. It presupposes the principle articulated in Prop. 173: what is received by something is received according to the mode of the recipient. St. Thomas frequently quotes this proposition's assertion that an intelligence is "full of forms" (*ST* I, Q. 83, A. 3, ad 1; *SCG*, II, 98; *De Veritate*, Q. 8, A. 5, 3 s.c.; A. 8, 1 s.c.; A. 14, 9a; A. 15c; *Quaest. Disp. de Anima*, Q. 7, ad 1 and Q. 18c); that the higher intelligences possess forms which are more universal (*ST* I, Q. 55, A. 3 s.c.; *SCG*,II, 98; *De Veritate*, Q. 8, A. 10, 2 s.c.; *Quodlibet VII*, Q. 7, A. 3c; *Quaest. Disp. de Anima*, Q. 7, ad 5); and that the higher or more transcendent something is, the more it extends itself to other things (*ST* II–II, Q. 45, A. 3, ad 1; *SCG*, III, 74; *Quodlibet. III*, Q. 3, A. 1c.

2. Pattin reads *in primis intelligentiis* following Bardenhewer, whose text Saffrey reprints here. We read *primus intelligentiis*, in the dative, found in Latin manuscripts LOSTUV and Aosta, which corresponds precisely to the Arabic text.

3. Again we read *primis intelligentiis* instead of *in primis intelligentiis*. See the previous note.

4. *quantitatis*. St. Thomas interprets this to mean "composition." Cf. below, S{71}.

5. With Latin manuscripts LOPSUV[s] and Aosta as well as the Arabic, we omit *et maioris virtutis* found in Bardenhewer and Pattin.

6. That is, distinguished.

another.[7] *For that reason it comes about that the second intelligences cast their gaze upon the universal form that is in the universal intelligences, dividing and separating it, because they can receive those forms in their unity and truth*[8] *only through the mode according to which they can receive them, namely, through separation and division. Likewise, any thing receives what is above it only through the mode according to which it can receive it, not through the mode according to which the received thing [itself] is.*

COMMENTARY

{67} After the author of this book has shown how [an intelligence] knows what is above it and below it and [has shown] what is above it, he begins now to show how it understands things other than itself besides the first cause. First, he shows how in general it knows all things other than itself; second, how in particular it knows eternal things, in Proposition 11, at: *Every intelligence* etc. So, first he presents the following proposition: *Every intelligence is full of forms. Among intelligences, however, there are some that contain more universal forms and others that contain less universal forms.* This we also find in Proposition 177 in the book of Proclus in these words: "Every intellect is a plenitude of species. But one contains more universal species, while another contains more particular species."[9] Now we must consider two things about this proposition: first, what is common to all intelligences, or separate intellects, namely, the plenitude of forms, or intelligible species; second, the difference between the universality and the particularity in them.

So, with regard to the first point, we should consider, as we already said before,[10] that the Platonists, because they hold that the forms of things are separate, maintained that the order of intellects depends upon the order of these forms. For, since all knowledge comes about through

7. Literally, "and are of a more powerful separation."
8. *certitudinem.*
9. Proclus, Prop. 177, Dodds, p. 156.1–2. *Species* is the translation given by Moerbeke for Proclus's *eidos.* While *eidos* means "form" according to the Platonic usage of the term, a sense easily carried by *species,* there seems to be an advantage in transliterating it here as "species" to help convey the notion that what is being talked about in this context is a form as known. *Plenitudo* ("plenitude") is Moerbeke's rendition of *pleroma.*
10. Cf. above, S{18}.

the assimilation of the intellect to the thing understood, it was necessary that the separate intellects participate abstract forms in order to understand. The kind of participations of forms [meant] are the very forms, or intelligible species, spoken of here. But following the view of Aristotle, which on this score is more consonant with the Christian faith, we assert that there are no separate forms above the order of intellects other than the separate good itself, to which the whole universe is ordered as to an extrinsic good, as is said in {68} Book 12 of the *Metaphysics*.[11] We must say then that, just as the Platonists said that the separate intellects obtain diverse intelligible species from participation in diverse separate forms, so we should say that they obtain such intelligible species from participation in the first separate form, which is pure goodness, namely, God. For God himself is goodness itself and "to be"[12] itself, encompassing virtually in himself the perfections of all beings. For he himself alone knows all things through his essence without the participation of any other form. But lower intellects, since their substances are finite, cannot know all things through their essence. In order to have a knowledge of things, they must understand things by means of the intelligible species that they receive from a participation in the first cause. Hence Dionysius says in Chapter 7 of *On the Divine Names*, that "from" the Divine Wisdom "itself the intelligent and intellectual powers of the angelic <minds> have simple and blessed intellects."[13]

We should also consider, as Augustine says in Book 2 of *On Genesis Literally Interpreted*[14] that, just as forms proceed from the word of God into corporeal matter in the constitution of things, so, too, from the same thing, namely, the word, a knowledge of things comes about in angels through the reception of such intelligible species.[15] The Platonists also held that it is due to the participation of ideas both that separate intellects

---

11. Aristotle, *Metaphysics*, XII, 1075a13–15.
12. *esse*.
13. Pseudo-Dionysius, *On the Divine Names*, VII 2; *Dionysiaca* I, 388; PG 3, 868 B.
14. St. Augustine, *Super Genesim ad Litteram*, II 8; PL 34, 269; CSEL XXVII 44, 5–23.
15. I.e., the word (*verbum*) is an intelligible emanation from God, expressive both of the diverse forms of created things and the intelligible species of these same things as that by which an angelic intellect knows them *a priori*, i.e., by God providing them with the corresponding species. See *ST* I, Q. 15 on the ideas in God, Q. 55 on angelic knowledge and QQ. 56 and 57 on the angel's knowledge of immaterial and material things. Also, see *SCG*, II, 96–100.

know things and that corporeal matter becomes varied according to diverse species. But we should realize that the same diversity of participation is found both in intellects and in corporeal matter. For the matter of lower bodies participates some form for its specific being. {69} Yet, the potency of matter, which still extends itself to other forms, is not exhausted[16] by that form. But the matter of heavenly bodies is exhausted by the form that it participates, because no potency remains in it for another form. Likewise, human intellects, which are lower, are not filled[17] by intelligible species. Rather, from the beginning the human possible intellect is like a tablet upon which nothing is written, as is said in Book 3 of *On the Soul*.[18] Later, however, it receives species in a certain order. Nevertheless, it is not filled in this life. But separate intellects from the very beginning are immediately filled with intelligible species for knowing all the things to which their natural faculty extends itself. Hence Dionysius says in Chapter 4 of *On The Divine Names* that "intellects understand supermundanely and are illuminated" according to "the ideas of existing things."[19] And this is what [our author] says, that *an intelligence is full of forms*, or, as Proclus says more expressly,[20] is a "plenitude" of forms because intellectuality itself belongs to the proper nature of an intelligence, or separate intellect.

Regarding the difference between the universality and the particularity of intelligible species, we should first note what both the author says here and Proclus says in his book: that the higher [intelligences] have more *universal forms*, while the lower ones *less universal*.[21] Dionysius says this as well in Chapter 12 of *The Celestial Hierarchy*, where he remarks that "the order of cherubim participates higher wisdom and cognition,"[22] while the lower substances "participate more particular wisdom and knowledge."[23] This universality {70} and particularity ought not to be re-

16. *repletur.* 17. *repletur.*
18. Aristotle, *On the Soul*, III 4, 430a1.
19. Pseudo-Dionysius, *On the Divine Names*, IV 1; *Dionysiaca* I, 148–49; PG 3, 693 C. We translate *rationes* here as "ideas." *Supermundane* ("supermundanely") is the Latin for *hyperkosmios* in Pseudo-Dionysius.
20. Proclus, Prop. 177, Dodds, p. 156.1; Vansteenkiste, p. 519.
21. See St. Thomas, *ST* I, Q. 55, A. 3; *SCG*, II, 98; *De Veritate*, Q. 8, A. 10.
22. *cognitione.*
23. *scientia.* Pseudo-Dionysius, *The Celestial Hierarchy*, XII 2; *Dionysiaca* II, 936; PG 3, 292 D.

ferred to the things known, as some have poorly understood, surmising that God knows only the universal nature of a being.[24] The consequence of that would be that, among the lower intellects, to the extent that each was higher, its knowledge would rest to a greater extent in the universal. For instance, that one intellect would know only the nature of substance, while a lower one the nature of body, and so on down to the individual species. But this way of thinking clearly contains a falsity. For the knowledge by which something is known only in the universal is imperfect knowledge, while the knowledge by which something is known in its proper species is perfect knowledge. For a knowledge of the species includes a knowledge of the genus, but not the converse. It would thus follow that the higher an intellect was, the more imperfect its knowledge would be. Therefore, the difference between universality and particularity concerns only that by which an intellect understands. For the higher an intellect is, the more universal is that by which it understands, so that its knowledge is extended by that universal to knowing even proper things much more so than the knowledge of a lower intellect, which knows through something more particular. We also observe this among ourselves by experience. For we see that those who possess a more excellent intellect comprehend the whole truth of some question or state of affairs from fewer things heard or known, which others of coarser intelligence cannot apprehend unless the matter be shown to them point by point, for which reason it is necessary to give examples frequently.[25] Therefore, God, whose intellect is most excellent, comprehends all things by one reality alone, namely, his essence. But among the other separate intellects, the

---

24. *ens*. See St. Thomas, *ST* I, Q. 14, A. 6. In *I Sent.*, D. 35, Q. 1, A. 3, St. Thomas attributes this view to Averroes. In *De Veritate*, Q. 2, A. 5, he discusses it with reference to Averroes and Avicenna. In speaking of this position in *De Subst. sep.*, 14, St. Thomas presumably has in mind contemporary Latin Averroists at the University of Paris, who referred to Aristotle's remarks about God in Book 12 of the *Metaphysics* (XII 7, 1072b22–23 and XII 9, 1074b15–1075a10) to argue that God does not know singulars. St. Thomas concludes his interpretation of these passages in Aristotle by saying, "It is therefore apparent to anyone who considers carefully the above words of the Philosopher, that it is not his intention to exclude absolutely from God a knowledge of other things, but rather, that God does not understand other things through themselves as participating in them in order that He then may become understanding through them; as happens in the case of any intellect whose substance is not its understanding" (Lescoe trans., pp. 85–86).

25. *frequentes inducere*.

more one has knowledge of things by fewer species that extend themselves to more things, the higher it is. Thus the human intellect, which is the lowest, cannot have knowledge of things unless it knows the natures of various things by means of various species,[26] while corporeal matter {71} and corporeal sense are found to lack universal participation in species altogether.

Now both the author and Proclus[27] give the same proof of this difference between the universality and the particularity of species, which they take from the effect.[28] For, just as intelligences know through intelligible forms, so, too, do they produce their effects through intelligible forms, because every intellect acts by understanding, as will be said later.[29] But *the greater powers* belong to the higher intelligences. This is so because they are more simple and of *less quantity,* i.e., composition, as being *nearer* the first *one.*[30] Therefore, their active powers must extend themselves to more things. Yet, the powers themselves are more simple. From this it appears that the forms of the higher intelligences are more universal.

Now he shows subsequently how forms that are united in the higher intelligences are multiplied in second intelligences, ascribing the reason for this, like Proclus, to the lower intelligences. For lower intelligences obtain their intelligible species from the higher intelligences by looking toward them in a sense, because just as an intelligence does everything that it does by understanding, so it receives everything that it receives in an intellectual way, namely according to the mode of its proper nature. And because the nature of a lower intelligence is not of such a simplicity and unity as the nature of a higher intelligence, so neither are the intelligible forms received in a lower intelligence in that unity in which they

---

26. I.e., the human intellect knows the universally intelligible aspects of a nature, which the individuals sharing that nature concretely possess, only through a species, or concept, abstracted from the sense experience of an individual of that nature. See *ST,* I, QQ. 84 and 85 for St. Thomas's explanation of how and what the human intellect knows.
27. Proclus, Prop. 177, Dodds, p. 156.5–15; Vansteenkiste, p. 519.
28. I.e., *a posteriori.*
29. Cf. the following paragraph.
30. I.e., composed of fewer species by which more, and not less, is understood: "Thus the higher the angel is, by so much the fewer species will he be able to apprehend the whole mass of intelligibile objects. Therefore his forms must be more universal; each one of them, as it were, extending to more things" (*ST* I, Q. 55, A. 3c; Benzinger trans., vol. 1, p. 279).

exist in higher intelligences. For this reason, intelligible forms are more multiplied in lower intelligences than in the higher [intelligences], so that those things that are understood by a higher intelligence through one intelligible species, a lower intelligence understands through many. But because, as was [just] said, whatever an intelligence does, it does by understanding, {72} just as it receives what it receives by understanding; therefore, the reason for this multiplication of species can be due, not only to the receiving intelligence, but also to the impressing intelligence, by whose provision species are multiplied in a lower intelligence according to its capacity. Hence Dionysius says in Chapter 15 of *The Celestial Hierarchy*: "By provident power each intellectual essence divides the uniform intelligence given to it by a more divine [intelligence] and multiplies [it] according to a proportion[31] that leads to a lower [intelligence],"[32] i.e., according to the proportion of a lower substance.

31. *analogiam*.
32. Pseudo-Dionysius, *The Celestial Hierarchy*, XV 3; *Dionysiaca*, 1006–1007; PG 3, 332 B.

PROPOSITION 11[1]

Every intelligence understands sempiternal things, which are not destroyed and do not fall under time.

This is because, if an intelligence is always that which is immobile, then it is itself the cause of sempiternal things, which are not destroyed and do not fall under generation and corruption. An intelligence is so only because it understands[2] a thing through its being, and its being is a sempiternal one that is not corrupted.

Therefore, since this is so, we say that[3] things are destructible due to corporeity, i.e., due to a temporal corporeal cause, not due to an eternal intellectual cause.

COMMENTARY

After showing how an intelligence understands things other than itself because [it understands] through intelligible forms with which it is full, [the author] treats here in particular of the knowledge by which an intelligence knows eternal things. First, he shows that it knows eternal, or incorruptible, things; second, he shows how it knows them, at: *All of the*

---

1. This proposition is primarily derived from Prop. 172 in Proclus's *Elements*. Cf. Dodds, p. 150.15–21. However, in his assertion that it is a conflation of Prop. 172 and Prop. 174, St. Thomas was not without substantial reason, especially in the Latin text. The Arabic is very close to Prop. 172 except in the opening line, where the author has *ya'qilu, intelligit*, "understands," for Proclus's *hypostates*, "is directly constitutive of" (Dodds pp. 150.16 and 151). While it is possible that the extant Arabic here is itself a corruption, there is no clear manuscript evidence for this. Thus it would seem, as St. Thomas points out, that the author had Prop. 174 in mind while basing his text primarily on Prop. 172. St. Thomas cites this proposition in *ST* I, Q. 56, A. 2, sc and in the *De Veritate*, Q. 8, A. 7, 1, sc.

2. The Latin *intelligit* reflects a corrupt reading in the translator's Arabic manuscript, *ya'qilu*, which is also found in the Leiden Arabic manuscript. The correct reading of the Arabic is *yaf'alu*, "it effects," found in the other Arabic manuscripts. This latter is a translation of *paragei* (Prop. 172, Dodds p. 150.19), which Dodds renders "gives rise to" (p. 151).

3. Omissions here in the Latin translator's Arabic caused the translator to render the Latin quite differently from what we find in the Arabic: "If this is then so, we say: the cause of things subject to change and falling under generation and corruption is from corporeity, i.e., from a corporeal, temporal cause, not from an intellectual, perpetual cause."

first things are etc.⁴ With regard to the first point, he proposes the following proposition: *Every intelligence {73} understands sempiternal things, which are not destroyed and do not fall under time.* He understands by *sempiternal things* those things that are above time and motion, as he explained in Proposition 2.⁵ Now, he expressly says *which are not destroyed and do not fall under time,* for certain things fall under time that are nevertheless not destroyed, such as the motion of the heavens, which, while measured by time, will neither be destroyed nor cease, according to the position of the philosophers.

On the surface it seems that the meaning of this proposition is that an intelligence does not know things that are corruptible and fall under time, but [knows] only incorruptible things that exist above time. But that this is not the meaning of the proposition is evident from the proof that is added, in which he proves, not that an intelligence knows sempiternal and incorruptible things, but that it immediately causes only sempiternal things. Hence we need to explain what is meant by: *every intelligence understands,* i.e., how by understanding it causes sempiternal things. This is clear from Proclus's book, where he presents two propositions on this point. One of these is 172: "Every intellect is proximately constitutive⁶ of things perpetual and unchangeable in substance."⁷ The other is 174: "Every intellect by understanding establishes the things that are after it."⁸ The author of this book has conflated these two propositions into one, and, while he sought brevity, he introduced obscurity.⁹ Nonetheless, in this sense,¹⁰ he proves the proposition in the same way as Proclus. In this proof he does two things. First, he shows that an intelligence does not immediately produce things that are corruptible or fall under time, but only sempiternal things; second, [he shows] the source of corruptibility in things.

4. Cf. Prop. 12., S{77}.
5. Cf. above, S{12}.
6. *substitutor.* Literally, "the underlying cause" as Moerbeke renders Proclus's *hypostates* according to the literal sense of the parts of the word.
7. Proclus, Prop. 172, Dodds, p. 150.15–16; Vansteenkiste, p. 517.
8. Proclus, Prop. 174, Dodds, p. 152.8; Vansteenkiste, p. 517.
9. Cf. Horace, *Poet.* 25. Also, see St. Thomas, *In Boeth. de Trin.*, Prooemium.
10. I.e., with the understanding that "he does not prove that an intelligence knows sempiternal and incorruptible things, but that it causes only sempiternal things immediately."

{74} He shows the first in this way. An intelligence produces its effect according to its being.[11] This is so because its understanding is connatural and essential to it, for it produces something only by understanding, as we have shown above.[12] Hence whatever it produces, it produces through its own being. But the being of an intelligence is incorruptible and above time, equal to eternity, as was said in Proposition 2.[13] Therefore, the immediate effect of an intelligence is sempiternal, not falling under corruption or time. He makes the second point clear, saying that, since an intelligence does not immediately cause corruptible things, it does follow that corruptible things are not immediately from an intelligence but are from some *temporal corporeal cause.* For corruption and generation in these lower things are caused through the motion of the heavens, while the motion itself of the heavens is not immediately from an intelligence but from a soul, as he said above in Proposition 3.[14]

Now, if someone wanted to reduce this process to the meaning that appears superficially from the proposition, one could further say that an intelligence knows corruptible things as sempiternal, for, although they are in themselves material, they are not in an intelligence materially, and thus not temporally, but sempiternally. This is made evident through the effect, since the immediate effect of an intelligence is sempiternal. For that by which an intelligence knows is the productive principle[15] in it, just as an artist acts through the form of an art. But the proof given here, even though it is granted by some philosophers, does not have necessity. For, if this proof were granted, many of the foundations of the Catholic faith would be removed, for it would then follow that angels would be able to do nothing new in lower things immediately, and much less God, who is not only {75} eternal but before eternity, as was said above.[16] Furthermore, it would follow that the world always was.

For this seems to be the most effective reason for those who maintain that the world is eternal, taking as their reason the unchangeableness of the maker. For they do not see how it could be possible for some agent, if it existed altogether unchangeably, to begin now to act when originally it had not acted, unless perhaps some exterior change is presupposed. For,

---

11. *Esse* here and throughout this paragraph.
12. Cf. above, S{71}.
13. Cf. above, S{15}.
14. Cf. above, S{24}.
15. *principium factivum.*
16. Cf. above, S{14}.

as Averroes argues in his commentary on Book 8 of the *Physics*,[17] if some voluntary agent wants to make something after and not before, he must imagine at least time, which is the number of motion. So he concludes that it is impossible for a new effect to come about from an unchangeable and eternal will, unless some motion is presupposed. Because this seems to be the more effective argument used to prove the eternity of the world, we must pay careful attention to an analysis of its argumentation.[18]

Now we should note that there is one way of speaking about an agent that produces something in time, and another way about an agent that produces time together with the thing that is produced in time. For when something is produced in time, it is necessary to accept some proportion to time, either with regard only to what is produced, or also with regard to the producer itself. For sometimes the action is in time, not only on the part of what is acted upon, but also on the part of the agent, for something is in time insofar as it is in motion, whose number is time. So when some change is found on the part of what is acted upon and on the part of the agent, then the action with regard to both is in time. For instance, when somebody becomes cold, it occurs anew[19] to him to light a fire to ward off the cold. But this is not {76} always what happens, for something exists whose substance is not in time, but whose activity is in time, as he will say below.[20] An agent of this kind, without any change in itself, produces an effect in time that did not exist before. In this way God, too, can produce something in time that is new[21] and did not exist previously, according to a defined[22] proportion of this effect to this time, as happens in all miraculous effects produced immediately by God. Nor is this opposed

---

17. Averroes, *In Phys*, VIII 1, 252 a 10–b 6, text. 15. Also, cf. St. Thomas, *In Phys. VIII*, Lect. 2 and *In Met. XII*, Lect. 5.

18. For further discussion on the question of whether the world is eternal or temporal, see *ST* I, Q. 46; *SCG*, II, Cap. 32 and 35; *Quodlibet.*, III, Q. 14, A. 2 and XII, Q. 6, A. 1; *De Aeternitate Mundi contra Murmurantes*. Briefly, for St. Thomas that the world is eternal can be neither proved nor disproved. He takes the argument given by Aristotle for the eternity of the world as only probable. In the *De Aeternitate Mundi contra Murmurantes*, St. Thomas argues against John Pecham, a contemporary at the University of Paris, who claimed that it could be proved that the world is not eternal; see Ignatius Brady, "John Pecham and the Background to the De aeternitate mundi of St. Thomas Aquinas," *St. Thomas Aquinas Commemorative Studies* (Toronto: PIMS, 1974). The creation of the world as temporal is thus a matter of faith, according to Aquinas.

19. *de novo.*
20. Cf. Prop. 31, S{140}.
21. *de novo.*
22. *certam.*

to saying that God produces through his being,[23] because his being is his understanding. Just as his being is one, yet he understands many things and because of this can produce many things, even though his understanding remains one and simple, so too, though his being is eternal and unchangeable, he can nevertheless understand any temporal and changeable being. And so, although his understanding is sempiternal, he can nevertheless through it produce a new effect in time. An indication of this appears in some measure[24] in us, for a man can, with his will remaining unchanged, defer his work to the future, so that he does it at a predetermined time.[25]

But if someone should say that as often as this happens one must presuppose[26] another prior motion, at least that very course of time that cannot be understood without motion, from which it could happen that something that was not appropriate to be made earlier, is indicated afterwards as appropriate to be made, we will say this is quite true in God's particular effects, which he brings about in time. For that he raised up Lazarus on the fourth day but not before, he did with respect to some preceding change of circumstances.[27] But this is irrelevant to the production of the universe because time and the whole totality of motion come to be at once with the world. Thus there is no other preceding time or motion to which it would be necessary that the newness of this effect be proportioned. {77} [Rather, the newness of this effect need be proportioned] only to the reason of the maker inasmuch as he understood and willed that this effect will not have been from eternity but that it begin to be after not being. For thus time is the measure of activity or motion, just as dimension is the measure of corporeal magnitude. So, if we should ask about some particular body, for example, earth, "Why is it forced within these limits of magnitude and not extended further?" the reason for this can be [taken] from its proportion to the world as a whole. But if we should ask further why the whole universe of bodies does not surpass the boundaries of such a determined magnitude, the reason for this cannot be from its proportion to some other magnitude. Either we must say that corporeal magnitude is infinite, as the ancient natural philosophers

---

23. *Esse* here and throughout the remainder of the paragraph.
24. *aliqualiter.*
25. *determinato tempore.*
26. *praeintelligere.*
27. *rerum.*

held, or we must say that the reason for such a determined magnitude is due solely to the intelligence and will of the maker. Therefore, just as the infinite God could produce a finite universe according to the plan[28] of his wisdom, so the eternal God could produce a new world according to the same plan of wisdom.

28. *Rationem* here and in the next line.

PROPOSITION 12[1]

All of the first things[2] are in one another in the mode appropriate for one of them to be in another.

This is because life and intelligence are in being,[3] and being and intelligence are in life, and being and life are in intelligence. Nevertheless, being and life in intelligence are two intelligences, and being and intelligence in life are two lives, and intelligence and life in being are two beings.

This is so only because each one of the first things is either a cause or an effect. An effect is in a cause in the mode belonging to the cause, and a cause is in the effect in the mode belonging to the effect. We abbreviate and say that a thing acting in a thing[4] in the mode belonging to a cause is in it only in the mode that is its cause,[5] as sense is in soul in an animate mode, soul is in intelligence in an intellectual mode, intelligence is in being in an essential mode, the first being is in an intelligence in an intellectual mode, intelligence is in soul in an animate mode, and soul is in sense in a sensible mode. Let us return[6] and say that sense is in the soul and intelligence in the first cause in their own modes, as we have shown.

COMMENTARY

{78} After showing that an intelligence understands sempiternal things, [the author] here introduces a proposition in order to show how intelligences, which are sempiternal things, mutually understand one another.

1. This proposition relates to Prop. 103 in Proclus's *Elements*. Cf. Dodds, p. 92.13–18. There Proclus speaks of the first triad of hypotheses, being (*on*), life (*zoe*) and intelligence (*nous*) and the three basic relations to which they give rise: causal (*kat' aitian*), essential (*kath' huparchin*) and participative (*kata methexin*). St. Thomas refers to Prop. 12 in *ST* II–II, Q. 23, A. 6, ad 1; *SCG* II, Cap. 73; *De Veritate*, Q. 24, A. 8, 6a; *De Potentia*, Q. 3, A. 3, 1a; *Quodlibet. IX*, Q. 4, A. 1c.

2. I.e., primary principles.

3. *esse* here and throughout the proposition and St. Thomas's commentary on it.

4. In place of *in rem* read by Bardenhewer and Pattin, we read *in re* with nine (BCLOPSTUV) of the ten manuscripts entirely collated by Pattin and with the Aosta Latin. Our reading is consistent with the corresponding Arabic as well.

5. The Latin translator read *huwa 'ilatu-hu* here. The correct reading of the Arabic is *huwa 'alai-hi*, "which is appropriate to it."

6. *redeamus*.

Something is understood because it is in the being that understands, and so he shows in this proposition how one higher being[7] is in another. The proposition is as follows: *All of the first things are in one another in the mode appropriate for one of them to be in another.* Proclus also sets forth this proposition [as] 103 in his book in these words: "All things are in all things, but properly in each."[8] Moreover, what Proclus says, "but properly in each," and what is said here, *in the mode appropriate for one of them to be in another,* are the same thing. For in both places what is meant is that one is in the other according to the mode appropriate to that in which it is.

But Proclus introduces this proposition according to the positions of the Platonists by which they assert separate subsistent forms among which, as was said above,[9] each one is higher to the degree that it is more universal and extends its participation to more things. Accordingly, being itself is higher than life itself and the latter higher than intellect itself. And so, establishing this, Proclus adds in his proposition, "For life and intellect are in being, and being and understanding are in life, and being and living are in intellect."[10] The author of this book also seems to speak in the same way, calling such separate things "first things." For he adds, explaining as it were, *This is so because life and intelligence are in being, and being and intelligence are in life, and being and life are in intelligence,* which is identical with the words of Proclus.

In his proposition Proclus adds an explanation of the way in which one of these is in the other, saying, "But all beings are in one place intellectually, and in another vitally, and in another beingly[11] (i.e. after the mode of being)." It is as if he said that {79} all three of the above are in intellect intellectually, in life vitally, and in being essentially. But in this book what is asserted in place of this seems to be corrupted and badly understood. For it goes on to say, *Nevertheless, being and life in intelligence are two intelligences.* But we should understand that these two, namely, being and life, are in an intelligence intellectually; *and being and intelligence in life are two lives,* that is, both are in life vitally; *and intelligence and life <in being> are two beings,* that is, both are in being itself essentially. But,

7. *unum de entibus superioribus.*
8. Proclus, Prop. 103, Dodds, p. 92.13; Vansteenkiste, p. 492.
9. Cf. above , S{18}.
10. Proclus, Prop. 103, Dodds, p. 92.13–15; Vansteenkiste, p. 492.
11. *enter.*

if we understand his words literally, this is false. For to live for a living being is its very being,[12] as is said in Book II of *On the Soul*,[13] and to understand for the first intelligence[14] is itself its life and its being, as Book XII of the *Metaphysics* says.[15] So too, Proclus, excluding this misunderstanding, says that "the being of an intellect is knowing and" its "life" is "knowledge."[16] Otherwise, the incongruity that Aristotle describes in Book III of the *Metaphysics*[17] against the Platonists would follow, namely, that Socrates would be three animals, because he himself is an animal, and the idea of animal in general in which he participates is also predicated of him, and likewise the idea of man, which is also an animal. So it would follow that each one of these three would not be one but many.

But Proclus gives a clear proof of what we have been discussing when he distinguishes how one thing is said of another in three ways: in one way, causally, as heat is said of the sun; in another way essentially, or naturally, as heat is said of fire; and in a third way "according to" a certain "having after,"[18] i.e., consecutiveness[19] or participation, namely, when something is had not fully but in a posterior way and particularly, as heat is not found in bodies composed of elements {80} in the fullness with which it is in fire. Thus, what is essentially in the first is in the second and in the third by participation; while what is essentially in the second is causally in the first and in the last by participation; and what is essentially in the third is causally in the first and the second.[20] In this way all things are in all things.

But because the author of this book does not seem to posit separate forms, when he says here that being, life, and intelligence are in one another, we should understand him to mean this only insofar as they are found in things having being, living, and understanding. For living and

12. *vivere enim viventis est ipsum esse eius.*
13. Aristotle, *De Anima*, II 4, 415b13.
14. *intelligentis.*
15. Aristotle, *Metaphysics*, XII 7, 1072b24ff.
16. Proclus, Prop. 103, Dodds, p. 92.28–29; Vansteenkiste, p. 492.
17. Aristotle, *Metaphysics*, III 6, 1003a11ff. and above, S{23}.
18. *Posthabitio* is Moerbeke's translation here for *methexis*, apparently emphasizing the component parts "to have" (*echein*) and "after" (*meta*) of the Greek word, since otherwise Moerbeke translates this term as *participatio*.
19. *consecutionem.*
20. Cf. Proclus, Prop. 103, Dodds, p. 92.17–20, and Prop. 65, Dodds, p. 62.13–14; Vansteenkiste, pp. 492 and 289–90.

understanding are found causally in being itself according to its proper character,[21] in the way in which it was said[22] in Proposition 1 that being is the first cause, while living and understanding are posterior causes. But we should not understand literally that *intelligence and life are in being itself two beings*, but that these two, insofar as they are in being itself, are not other than being. Similarly, being, insofar as it is in life, is life itself, since life adds nothing to being except a determined mode of existing,[23] or the determined nature of a being.[24] The same should be understood in the other comparisons according to which one of these is said to be in the other.

But because, according to the understanding of this author, these three are not certain subsisting things, as was said,[25] he subsequently applies this proposition to things that subsist per se, which are: first being, which is God, intelligence, the intellectual soul and the sensitive soul. He states that in this way the cause is in the effect and conversely, insofar as the cause acts on the effect and the effect receives the action of the cause. Moreover, the cause acts on the effect in the mode belonging to the cause itself, but the effect receives the action of the cause in its own mode. So it is necessary that *the cause* be *in* the effect *in the mode* belonging to the effect {81} and that the effect be in the cause in *the mode belonging to the cause*. Thus, those things that are in the senses sensibly are in an intellectual soul in the mode appropriate to it, and those things that are in the soul in an animate mode are in the intellect in its proper mode, and the things that are in an intelligence intelligibly are in the first cause essentially according to its mode. Conversely, prior things are in posterior things according to the mode of posterior things. From this we can grasp how intelligences understand one another and the first cause. For each one understands the other insofar as the other is in it in the mode of that in which it is, because lower things are also in higher things according to certain more excellent likenesses, or species, while higher[26] things are in lower things according to certain more deficient likenesses and species.

21. *rationem.*
22. Cf. preceding paragraph.
23. *essendi.*
24. *entis.*
25. Cf. above, S{5}.
26. *superiores.*

PROPOSITION 13[1]

Every intelligence understands its essence.

This is because it is simultaneously what understands and what is understood.[2] Therefore, since an intelligence is both what understands and what is understood, then it undoubtedly sees its essence. And when it sees its essence, it knows that it understands its essence through intelligence.[3] And when it knows its essence, it knows the rest of the things that are under it, because they are from it. But they are in it in an intelligibile mode. Therefore, an intelligence and the things understood are one. This is because, if the things understood and an intelligence are one, and an intelligence knows its own being, then undoubtedly, when it knows its essence, it knows the rest of the things. And when it knows the rest of the things, it knows its essence, and[4] when it knows things, it knows them only because they are what is understood. Therefore, an intelligence simultaneously knows its essence and the things understood, as we have shown.

COMMENTARY

After showing how an intelligence understands other things, [the author] now introduces this proposition to show how it understands itself. This proposition is also found as 167 in Proclus's book in these words: "Every intellect understands itself."[5] But we must take the mean-

---

1. This proposition is based on Prop. 167 as well as 168 and 169 in Proclus's *Elements.* Cf. Dodds, p. 144.22; p. 146.26–27; p. 146.19–21, 146.23. The author departs from Proclus on the question of the existence of an ideal intellect, as St. Thomas notes. St. Thomas refers to this proposition in *ST* I, Q. 94, A. 2, 3a and I–II, Q. 50, A. 6c.
2. I.e., it is both knower and known.
3. *et, quando videt essentiam suam, scit quod intelligit per intelligentiam essentiam suam.* Like the Leiden Arabic manuscript, the Latin translator's Arabic text here suffered from homeoteleuton and misplaced or missing diacritical marks. The proper Arabic text has, "When it sees its essence, it knows that it is an intelligence in act. When it knows that it is an intelligence in act, it knows that it is an intelligence that understands its essence."
4. We read *et* for *quia* with Pattin's Latin manuscripts LOSUV and Aosta and in accord with the corresponding Arabic.
5. Proclus, Prop. 167, Dodds, p. 144.22; Vansteenkiste, p. 514.

ing of this proposition and {82} its proof from the things that Proclus says.

For, as was said above, according to the opinions of the Platonists, the order of intellects is placed under the order of separate forms, from whose participation they come to be actually understanding. Hence separate forms are compared to them as the intelligible to the intellect. Furthermore, just as the Platonists asserted certain ideas for other things, so too [they asserted an idea] for intellects themselves, which they called the "first intellect."[6] This ideal intellect understands inasmuch as it is intellect and is a form understood inasmuch as it is an ideal form. Thus intellect and thing understood are entirely united in it. Through this [union] [the first intellect] understands itself completely, because its essence as a whole is [something] intelligible, [and] not just [something] that understands. Furthermore, according to the Platonists, every intellect has a participated intellect. But the higher intellects participate intellect itself more perfectly. Hence they participate it not only in order to be intellect but also in order to be intelligible and, in a certain sense, formal intellects. Thus a being that understands and a thing that is understood are in a certain sense conjoined in [higher intellects] according to their substance. Therefore, they also understand their essence, but differently from the way that the first intellect does. For the first ideal intellect does not participate some prior form of intellectuality but is itself the first form of intellectuality. Hence its intelligible [object] is not other than itself. Posterior intellects do have something of the form of intellectuality in their substance, but in such a way that it is derived from the higher ideal intellect. Thus in this way they understand their own essence because they also {83} understand the higher intellect that they participate. And this is what Proclus adds in his proposition: "But the first [intellect understands] only itself, and in it intellect and the intelligible thing are numerically one. But each subsequent intellect [understands] itself and those things that are prior to it simultaneously in such a way that the intelligible thing for it is both what it is and that by which it is.[7]

But because, according to the opinion of Aristotle (which in this agrees more with Catholic doctrine), we do not maintain that there are many forms above intellects but only one, which is the first cause, we must say

6. Cf. Proclus, Prop. 21, Dodds, p. 24.27–29.
7. Proclus, Prop. 167, Dodds, p. 144.21–25; Vansteenkiste, pp. 514–15.

that, just as the first cause is being itself, so is it life itself and first intellect itself. Hence, Aristotle also proves in Book 10 of the *Metaphysics*[8] that the first cause understands only itself, not because it lacks knowledge of other things, but because in understanding its intellect is not informed by any intelligible species other than itself. Thus in this way the higher separate intellects, inasmuch as they are close to the first cause, understand themselves both through their essence and through participation in a higher nature.

So, to prove this proposition, the author first states here that in separate intellects *what understands and what is understood are simultaneously* [one thing] inasmuch as they are not only intellects according to their substance but also intelligible as what most closely participate first intellect. So he concludes that *an intelligence understands its essence*. Because its essence is the essence of something that understands, it follows that, by understanding its essence, it understands that it understands its essence. Furthermore, he shows subsequently how it understands other things as well, through the fact that it understands its essence. For it results from the proposition given that all other things *are in* an intelligence {**84**} *in an intelligible mode,* and so *an intelligence and the things understood are one* insofar as they are in an intelligence. Therefore, *when* it understands *its essence,* it understands other *things.* For the same reason, whenever an intelligence understands other *things,* it understands itself. But we shall consider below whether these things are applicable to the intellectual soul.[9]

8. Aristotle, *Metaphysics,* XII 9, 1074b30ff.
9. Cf. Prop. 15., S{88}.

PROPOSITION 14[1]

Sensible things are in every soul because it is their example,[2] and intelligible things are in it because it knows them.[3]

The soul came to be so only because it extends between intellectual things, which are not in motion, and sensible things, which are in motion. Because the soul is such, it comes to impress corporeal things. For this reason it came to be the cause of bodies and the effect of the intelligence that is before it. Therefore, things that are impressed by the soul are in the soul in the sense[4] of an example, because sensible things are exemplified according to the example of the soul, while things that are located above the soul are in the soul in an acquired manner.

Therefore, since this is so, let us return and say that all sensible things are in the soul in the manner of a cause, except that[5] the soul is an exemplary cause. And I understand by "soul" the power acting upon sensible things.[6] But the efficient power in the soul is not material, and the corporeal power in the soul is spiritual, and the power that impresses things that have dimensions is without dimension. Furthermore, intelligible things are in the soul in an accidental manner because undivided intelligible things are in the soul in a divisible manner, while united intelligible things are in the soul in a multiplied manner, and immobile intelligible things are in the soul in the manner of motion.

Therefore, we have already shown that intelligible and sensible things are in the soul. But sensible, corporeal, mobile things are in the soul in an animated, spiritual, united manner, while intelligible, united, quiescent things are in the soul in a manner that is multiplied, mobile.

---

1. This proposition is derived from Prop. 195 in Proclus's *Elements*. Cf. Dodds, p. 179.4–15. St. Thomas quotes it in *Quaest. Disp. de Anima*, Q. 19, 10a.
2. *exemplum*. I.e., an exemplar, as St. Thomas explains below.
3. The Latin differs from the Arabic because of a misreading by the translator or because of a faulty manuscript. The Arabic has "because it is a sign of them."
4. *intentionem*.
5. *praeter quod* corresponds precisely to the Arabic *min ghaira an*.
6. *virtutem agentem res sensibles*. The Latin verb *ago* does not quite carry the sense found in the Arabic, which has "the power effecting sensible things."

COMMENTARY

{85} After determining what the first cause is and what an intelligence is, he determines here what the soul is. First, he determines what it is in its relationship to other things. Second, he determines what it is in itself, at: *Every knower* etc.[7] With regard to the first he asserts the following proposition: *Sensible things are in every soul because it is their example, and intelligible things are in it because it knows them.* But to understand this proposition, let us see what Proclus writes in his book concerning this. There Proposition 195 states the following: "Every soul is all things, sensible things exemplarily, but intelligible things *yconice.*"[8] He says, "*yconice,*" i.e., in the manner of an image, for an image is something made in the likeness of another, as an exemplar is that in whose likeness something else is made.

Now, this proposition is proved both here and in Proclus's book in this way. The soul, as was held in Proposition 2,[9] *is* midway *between intellectual things, which* are altogether separate from motion, and in this are made equal to[10] eternity, *and sensible things, which are in motion* and fall under time. And because prior things are the cause of posterior things, it follows that *the soul is the cause of bodies* and an intelligence is the cause of the soul in the manner previously explained.[11] Furthermore, it is clear that it is necessary for effects to preexist in causes by way of exemplarity, because causes produce effects according to their likeness. Conversely, *effects have the image of their causes,* as Dionysius also says in Chapter II of *On the Divine Names.*[12] Thus sensible *things,* which are caused *by the soul, are in it in* the manner *of an example,* so that {86} those things that are below the soul are caused according to the example and likeness of the soul. But *things that are above the soul are in the soul in an acquired manner,* i.e., through a certain participation, so that they are related to the soul as exemplars, while the soul is related to them as in a certain sense an image. Thus it is evident that sensible things preexist in the soul as in a cause, which is in a certain sense the exemplar of its effects.

---

7. Cf. below, Prop. 15, p.
8. Proclus, Prop. 195, Dodds, p. 170.4–5; Vansteenkiste, p. 525. Moerbeke renders Proclus's *paradeigmatikos* by *exemplariter* ("exemplarily") and *eikonikos* by *yconice.*
9. Cf. above, S{15}.
10. *parificantur.*
11. Cf. above, S{22}.
12. Pseudo-Dionysius, *On the Divine Names* II, 8; *Dionysiaca* I, 99; PG 3, 645 C.

Further, he subsequently explains what the soul understands, saying: *I understand by "soul" the power acting upon sensible things.* For, according to those who maintain that the heavenly bodies are animated, the soul of the heavens is the cause of all sensible bodies, just as each of the lower souls is the cause of its own body. Therefore, no lower soul has universal causality over sensible things. And so, sensible things are not in it in the manner of a cause but only in the soul of the heavens, which has universal causality over sensible things. Here he calls this, *the power acting upon sensible things.* Each of the souls that exists here has causality over its own body. But it does not cause that body either through sense or through intellect. Hence it does not pre-possess the intelligible and exemplary characteristics[13] of its body. Rather, it causes that body through natural power. So, too, in Book II of *On the Soul*[14] it is said that the soul is the efficient cause of the body. But such an agent does not act through some exemplary character properly understood, unless we call the very nature through which it acts the exemplar of the effect that is produced in some way in its likeness. {87} In this manner all the sensible parts of its body preexist virtually in the nature of the soul, for they are adapted to the potencies of the soul, which proceed from its nature.

Even though sensible things are in the soul, which is their cause, they are not, however, in it in the manner in which they are in themselves. For *the power* of the soul *is immaterial,* even though it is the cause of material things, *and is spiritual,* even though it is the cause of bodies, and *is without* corporeal *dimension,* even though it is the cause *of things that have dimension.* Because effects are in a cause according to the power of the cause, it is necessary that sensible bodies exist indivisibly, immaterially and incorporeally in the soul. Just as things lower than the soul are in it in a manner higher than in themselves, so higher things, namely, intelligences, are in the soul in a mode lower than in themselves, namely, *yconice,* or in the manner of an image, as Proclus says. In place of this [term] the author says here, *in an accidental manner,* i.e., through a certain lower mode of participation, so that intelligible things, which are in themselves undivided, united, and immobile, are in the soul in a divisible, multiple, and mobile way in relation to the intelligence—for they are proportioned to be the causes of the multiplicity, division, and motion of sensible things.

13. *rationes.*
14. Aristotle, *On the Soul,* II 4, 415b8.

Or he says that immobile *things <are in the soul> in the manner of motion* because, according to the Platonists, it is proper to the soul that it move itself, but, according to Aristotle, the soul is the principle of the motion of a thing that moves itself.[15]

Finally, in the epilogue he concludes to what he had proposed, which is clear from his premises. From what he has said, it can be made clear how the higher souls of the heavens, if the heavens are animated, can know sensible and intelligible things, for they know them insofar as these things are in them.

15. Cf. above, S{15}.

{88} PROPOSITION 15[1]

Every knower knows its essence. Therefore, it reverts to its essence with a complete reversion.

This is because knowledge is nothing but an intellectual action. So, when a knower knows its essence, it then reverts through its intellectual activity to its essence. And this is so only because the knower and the known are one thing, since the knower's knowledge is its essence from itself and toward itself.[2] It is from itself because it is a knower, and toward itself because it is the known. This is because, due to the fact that knowledge is the knowledge of the knower and the knower knows its essence, its activity is a reversion to its essence. Therefore, its substance again reverts to its essence.

And by the reversion of a substance to its essence I mean nothing other than that it is abiding steadfastly,[3] fixed per se, *not needing in its fixity and its essence anything else to raise it up,[4] since it is a simple, self-sufficient substance.[5]*

---

1. This proposition is derived from Proclus's *Elements*, Proposition 83. Cf. Dodds, pp. 76.29–30, 76.33–78.1, 76.31–78.4. St. Thomas relates it to six propositions in Proclus: Props. 15, 16, 43, 44, 83, and 186. St. Thomas quotes this proposition in *ST* I, Q. 14, A. 2, 1a and ad 1, where he applies it preeminently to God; *De Veritate*, Q. 1, A. 9c; Q. 2, A. 2, 2a and ad 2, where he refers to it as metaphorical, since there is no motion, properly speaking, in intellectual knowing; Q. 8, A. 6, 5 s.c.

2. St. Thomas, as his interpretation of Aristotle in *On the Soul*, III 4, 430a1–9, shows, would understand what is said here to apply only to separate substances, not the human intellect (see *In de Anima III*, Lect. 9). What the human intellect as the lowest of intellects knows is the quiddity of material things, so that the human intellect becomes one with what it knows intentionally, not physically (see *ST* I, Q. 84, A. 2). But we can know what the intellect is indirectly through an act of reflection (see *ST* I, Q. 87, A. 1 and 3; *De Veritate*, Q. 10, A. 8).

3. *stans.*

4. *erigente.* The Arabic expresses this notion more clearly: "not needing in its stability any other thing to make it subsist."

5. This position is Neoplatonic with important Platonic foundations. The knower, be it an intellect or higher soul, is a self-sufficient substance existing and knowing through its own essence. For St. Thomas intellectual beings subsistent in their own essences can exist without matter, though they depend on God for the actuality of existence (*esse*). As mentioned above, intelligences or angels have knowledge only from their essences or from divine illumination. In contrast, for St. Thomas, following

COMMENTARY

After showing how the soul relates to other things, [the author] shows here how the soul relates to itself. He proposes the following proposition: *Every knower knows its essence. Therefore, it reverts to its essence with a complete reversion.* To understand this proposition we ought to consider certain propositions given in Proclus's book.

One of these is Proposition 15 in his book, which is as follows: "Everything that is able to turn upon itself is incorporeal."[6] The author clarified this proposition before, in Proposition 7 of this book.[7]

Let us take as the second Proposition 16 in Proclus's book, which is as follows: "Everything able to turn upon itself has a substance separable from every body."[8] The proof of this is that, since a body cannot turn upon itself, as {89} is held in the stated proposition, it follows that turning upon itself is an activity separated from a body. Furthermore, a substance whose activity is separable from a body must also be separable. Hence everything that can turn upon itself is separable from a body.

Let us take as the third Proposition 43 of Proclus's book, which is as follows: "Everything that is able to turn to itself is *authypostaton*,"[9] i.e., is *per se* subsistent.[10] This is proved by the fact that every thing turns [back] upon that through which it is made a substance. Hence, if anything turns upon itself according to its being, it must subsist in itself.

Let us take as the fourth Proposition 44 of Proclus's book: "Everything that is able to turn upon itself according to its activity is also able to turn

---

Aristotle, the senses, both external and internal, are required as an objective instrumental cause for any human knowledge, since the human is not a simple substance but a substance composed of body and soul (see *ST* I, Q. 84, A. 6.).

6. Proclus, Prop. 15, Dodds, p. 16.30; Vansteenkiste, p. 271. Proclus's term *epistreptikon* is rendered by Moerbeke as *conversivum ad*, which we translate literally as "able to turn upon." Corresponding to this are the *reditio* ("reversion") of which the author of the *De Causis* speaks and the *conversio* ("conversion," "turning") and *reditus* ("return") of which St. Thomas speaks.

7. Cf. above, S{51}.

8. Proclus, Prop. 16, Dodds, p. 18.6–7; Vansteenkiste, p. 271.

9. Proclus, Prop. 43, Dodds, p. 44.25; Vansteenkiste, p. 282.

10. This is a gloss added to Prop. 40 by William of Moerbeke. The Latin *De Causis* expresses Proclus's term *authypostaton* by *stans, fixa per se* ("abiding steadfastly, fixed *per se*") while the Arabic has *qa'imun bi-dhati-hi* with the same sense.

upon itself according to its substance."[11] This is proved through the fact that, since to turn upon itself is [a mark] of perfection, if what turns [upon itself] according to activity were not to turn upon itself according to substance, it would follow that the activity would be better and more perfect than the substance.[12]

Let us take as the fifth Proposition 83 of Proclus's book, which is as follows: "Everything that knows its very self is in every way able to turn upon itself."[13] The proof of this is that what knows itself turns to itself through its activity and consequently through its substance, as is evident from the stated proposition. {90}

We shall take as the sixth Proposition 186 of Proclus's book, which is as follows: "Every soul is an incorporeal substance, separable from a body."[14] This is proved in this way, according to what has [already] been stated: The soul knows itself. Therefore, it turns upon itself in every way. Therefore, it is incorporeal and separable from a body.

Now having seen these propositions, we should consider that three things are asserted in this book [regarding this matter]. The first of them is that the soul *knows its essence,* for what is said here ought to be understood with respect to the soul. The second is what he concludes from this, that *it reverts to its essence with a complete reversion.* And this is the same as what Proclus said in his proposition: "Everything that knows its very self is in every way able to turn upon itself."[15] The complete reversion or conversion is understood both according to substance and according to activity, as was said.[16]

Now, he proves that the second point follows from the first in this way. When I say that *a knower knows its essence,* "to know" itself signifies an

---

11. Proclus, Prop. 44, Dodds, p. 46.1–2; Vansteenkiste, p. 282.
12. St. Thomas's own position with regard to the human intellect is given in *ST* I, Q. 87, A. 1: "But as in this life our intellect has material and sensible things for its proper natural object, as stated above (Q. 87, A. 7), it understands itself according as it is made actual by the species abstracted from sensible things, through the light of the active intellect, which not only actuates the intelligible things themselves, but also, by their instrumentality, actuates the passive intellect. Therefore, the intellect knows itself not by its essence, but by its act" (Benzinger trans.). Hence for St. Thomas what Proclus says here applies only to separate substances (see ibid., ad 2 and 3).
13. Proclus, Prop. 83, Dodds, p. 76.29–30; Vansteenkiste, p. 296.
14. Proclus, Prop. 186, Dodds, p. 162.13–14; Vansteenkiste, p. 521.
15. Proclus, Prop. 83, Dodds, p. 76.29–30; Vansteenkiste, p. 296.
16. Cf. above, S{89}.

intellectual activity. Therefore, it is evident that, due to the fact that *the knower knows its essence, it returns*, i.e., it turns, *to its essence through its intellectual activity* by understanding it. That this ought to be called "reversion" or "conversion" he shows through the fact that *the knower and the known are one thing*, since the soul knows its essence. Thus *the knowledge by which it knows its essence*, i.e., the intellectual activity itself, *is from itself because it is a knower and is toward itself because it is the known*. Thus there is a certain circular motion which is conveyed by the word "reversion" or "conversion." Furthermore, from the fact that it reverts to its essence according to its activity, he concludes further that even according to its *substance it reverts to its essence*. {**91**} Thus the return is made complete according to activity and substance.

He explains subsequently what it means *to revert* according to substance *to its essence*. For those things are said to turn upon themselves according to substance that subsist through themselves, having fixity such that they do not turn upon anything else that sustains them, as is the [case with] the conversion of accidents to subjects.[17] Now this pertains to the soul and to everything else that knows itself, because every such thing *is a simple substance, self-sufficient through itself*, not needing, as it were, material support. And this can [serve as] the third point, namely, that "the soul is separable from a body," as Proclus proposes in his proposition.[18]

Now the first of these [three points], namely, that the soul knows its essence, is not proved here. But Proclus proves it in his book in this way: "But that it knows itself" is "clear," "for, if it knows what is above it, then all the more is its nature to know itself, as knowing itself from causes that" are "before it."[19] Here we ought to consider carefully that before, when [the author] treated of the knowledge of intellects, he said that the first intellect knows itself alone, as he said in Proposition 13,[20] because

---

17. I.e., accidents inhere in their subjects and so have their being through them and not through themselves. See *Quodlibet. IX.* Q. 3, A. 5, 2m.
18. I.e., Prop. 16. Cf. S{88}.
19. Proclus, Prop. 186, Dodds, p. 162.21–23; Vansteenkiste, p. 522. But such knowing for the intellectual soul would not involve a complete identification between the knower and the known, as the *De Causis* seems to suggest, but Proclus does not. By returning to Prop. 13 of the *De Causis*, St. Thomas will suggest an interpretation that allows for the distinction found in Proclus to be also made for the author of the *De Causis*.
20. Cf. above, S{82}.

it is itself the ideal intelligible form. But other intellects as close to it participate both the form of intelligibility and the power of intellectuality from the first intellect, just as Dionysius says in Chapter IV {92} of *On the Divine Names*, that the supreme intellectual "substances" are both "intelligible and intellectual."[21] Hence each of them knows both itself and what is above it, which it participates. But because an intellectual soul participates the first intellect in a lower way, it has in its substance only the power[22] of intellectuality. Hence it knows its substance, not through its essence, but, according to the Platonists, through the higher things that it participates;[23] and according to Aristotle in Book III of *On the Soul*,[24] through the intelligible species, which are made to be in a certain sense forms, inasmuch as through them it comes to be in act.[25]

   21. Pseudo-Dionysius, *On the Divine Names*, IV 1; *Dionysiaca* I, 147; PG 3, 683 B.
   22. *vim.*
   23. But see *ST* I, Q. 84, especially A. 1, 3, 4 and 6, where St. Thomas rejects this view.
   24. Aristotle, *On the Soul*, III 4, 430a1-2.
   25. This is, of course, St. Thomas's position. Following Aristotle, for St. Thomas the human intellect does not already contain forms but is like a blank tablet, a pure potentiality (*ST* I, Q. 84, A. 3). Since the object of the human intellect is the quiddity of material things (see *ST* I, Q. 84, A. 7), the human intellect must first turn to the phantasms to have any knowledge (see ibid.). The return of the human intellect to itself first requires an act of judgment by which the intellect judges that a thing corresponds to the form which the intellect has produced and apprehends so that the intellect knows that it knows (see *ST* I, Q. 16, A. 2). But this does not mean that the human intellect comes to know itself directly by such a judgment. What is further required, in a path of indirection, is that the intellect move in its reflection from the objects which it knows (the quiddity of material things) to the acts whereby such objects are constituted and thereby to the knowledge of the kind of power required to produce such objects and acts, which power must be immaterial (see *ST* I, Q. 87, A. 1 and 3). The object of the human intellect's knowledge and the indirect way the human intellect returns to itself must be sharply distinguished, then, from that of separate intellects, which know their essence directly through themselves without having to turn to other things because what they are and that by which they know are the same (see ibid.).

PROPOSITION 16[1]

All the unlimited powers[2] are dependent upon the first infinite, which is the power of powers, not because they are acquired,[3] but rather [because] they are a power belonging to things having stability.[4]

But if someone should say that the first created being, namely, an intelligence, is unlimited power, we say that created being is not power [itself] but rather a certain power. And its power came to be infinite only with respect to the lower, not with respect to the higher, because this[5] is not the pure power, which is power only because it is power[6] and which is the thing that is limited neither with respect to the lower

---

1. This proposition relates to Props. 92 and 93 in Proclus's *Elements*. Cf. Dodds, p. 82.23–28; p. 84.5–6; p. 82.28–35. The author, in his monotheism, departs from Proclus by identifying the first infinite power with God instead of understanding it to be a Platonic idea that occupies an intermediary position between the one and good, which transcends it, and being, which is below it. St. Thomas refers to this proposition in *ST* I Q. 50, A. 2, ad 4; *De Potentia*, Q. 6, A. 3, 9a; *De Ente et Essentia*, 5; *De Natura Materiae*, 3.

2. Literally, "All the powers for which there is no limit."

3. *non quia* ipsae *sunt acquisitae, stantes in rebus* entibus. The words in roman type are present in Bardenhewer's Latin but not reproduced by Saffrey. These omissions seem to be typographical errors, since St. Thomas quotes this text using just these words in his commentary. The corresponding Arabic as well as Latin manuscripts O and Aosta support this text. The reading proposed by Pattin (Pattin, 129.72–73) is not found complete in any of the manuscripts he collated.

4. *immo sunt virtus rebus habentibus fixionem*. Here Saffrey refrains from reproducing *entibus* (. . . *rebus entibus, habentibus* . . .) found in Bardenhewer's text, since St. Thomas omits this in his quotation. The Latin text of this entire opening sentence seems to be based on a misunderstanding of the Arabic text on the part of the translator. The Arabic has "All the infinite powers are dependent upon the first infinity, which is the power of powers, not in that it is acquired or stable and subsistent in things having being but in that it is a power belonging to things having being and possessing stability." The Arabic more clearly evidences its dependence upon the opening text of Proclus's Proposition 92: "The whole multitude of infinite potencies is dependent upon one principle, the First Infinity, which is not potency in the sense that it is participated or exists in things that are potent, but is Potency-in-itself, not the potency of an individual but the cause of all that is." St. Thomas is well aware of the textual problems here and even rightly suggests that the text should read the singular where the Latin has the plural. Cf. below, S{93–94}.

5. *ipsa*.

6. I.e., it is not power *qua* power or power *per se*.

nor with respect to the higher. But the first created being, namely, an intelligence, has limit and its power has limit, according to which its cause remains.[7]

The first creating being is the first pure infinite. This is because, if for powerful[8] beings there is no limit, due to their acquisition [of infinity] from the first pure infinite, due to which they are beings, and if the first being itself is that which determines[9] things for which there is no limit, then without doubt it is above the infinite. But the first created being, namely, an intelligence, is not the infinite, but rather it is called what is infinite and is not called what is itself that which is not finite.[10]

Therefore, the first being is the measure of first intellectual beings and of second sensible beings because it is that which has created beings and measured them with a measure appropriate to every being.

Let us, therefore, return and say that {93} the first creating being is above the infinite, while second created being is infinite, and what is between the first creating being and second being is not finite. And the remaining simple goodnesses, such as life, light and their like, are the causes of all things that have goodnesses, because the infinite is from the first cause. And the first created [being] is the cause of all life and similarly of the remaining goodnesses, which descend from the first cause upon the first created [being], and [this] is an intelligence. Then,[11] they descend upon the remaining intelligible and corporeal effects with the mediation of an intelligence.

COMMENTARY

After distinguishing higher causes and after elaborating the individual parts of his division, he begins here to show how [higher causes] relate to one another. In regard to this he does three things. First, he shows how

---

7. *et virtuti eius est finis secundum quem remanet causa eius.* This passage was clearly problematic to its Latin readers, as St. Thomas's understanding of it indicates. The problem lies with the particular Arabic manuscript used by the translator or with the translation itself. The Arabic text is much more clear here: "and its power is also finite so long as its cause continues to be."

8. *fortibus.*

9. *ponit.*

10. Again the Arabic is considerably clearer: "And the first originated being (*al-huwiyah*), i.e., the intelligence, is not infinite, but rather one says that it is without limit and one does not say that it is what is infinity itself."

11. I.e., the first created intelligence.

lower things depend upon higher things. Second, he shows how higher things infuse lower things, in Proposition 20, at: *The first cause rules* etc. Third, he shows how in different ways lower things receive the infusion of the first infusing [cause], in Proposition 24, at: *The first cause exists* etc. In regard to the first he does two things. First, he shows how lower things depend upon higher things according to power. Second, how they are dependent [upon them] according to their substance and nature, in Proposition 18, at: *All things have an essence*. In regard to the first he does two things. First, he shows that all infinite powers depend upon the first infinite power. Second, he shows that they are assimilated to it to greater or lesser degrees, in Proposition 17, at: *Every united power* etc.

In regard to the first he asserts this proposition: *All the unlimited powers are dependent upon the first infinite, which is the power of powers, not because they are*[12] *acquired, fixed, abiding steadfastly in things having being, but rather [because] they are a power belonging to things having stability.* But the second part of this proposition seems to be corrupted in all the books. For it ought to be said in the singular: "not because it is acquired, fixed, abiding steadfastly {94} in things having being, but rather because it is the power" etc., so that it refers to *the power of powers*. This is clear from Proclus's book, which says in Proposition 92: "Every multitude of infinite potencies has originated from one first infinity, which neither exists as a participated potency nor subsists in those things with potencies but [subsists] according to itself, being not a potency belonging to some [particular] participant but [a potency] belonging to all caused beings."[13]

In the first place we should consider here that "infinite potency" is said of whatever always exists, as was said above in Proposition 4,[14] inasmuch as we see that those things that can last longer have greater power of being. Hence those things that can last infinitely have infinite potency in this respect. Now, according to the positions of the Platonists, anything that is found in many things must be reduced to something first, which is such through its essence, from which the others are said to be such

---

12. Here St. Thomas has *sint* in place of *sunt* found in Bardenhewer.
13. Proclus, Prop. 92, Dodds, p. 82.23–26. The actual conclusion of Proclus's text reads, "but the cause of all beings" (*alla panton aitia ton onton*), instead of what Moerbeke gives, "but for all caused beings" (*sed omnium causatorum entium*). As Vansteenkiste points out (p. 299, Prop. 92, n. 1), Moerbeke apparently read *aitia ton* as the single word *aitiaton*.
14. Cf. above, S{30}.

through participation. So, according to them, infinite powers are reduced to something first that is essentially the infinity of power, not because it is a power participated in some subsisting thing but because it subsists through itself. But this, according to the Platonists, is not the very idea of being, because such separate being has infinite potency. But with this it also has finitude, as maintained before in Proposition 4.[15] Hence it remains that it is not the first potency that is essentially infinity itself. Nor did the Platonists maintain that this idea of infinity is the first simply, because infinity itself participates unity and goodness. Hence the one and good is the first simply. But this ideal infinite, upon which all infinite powers depend, is a "medium between" the one and good, which is the "first" simply, "and being." This is how Proclus explains his proposition.[16]

{95} But the author of this book does not maintain that there is a real diversity between such abstract ideal forms, which are said to be through their essence, but attributes all things to the one first, which is God, as was also clear above from the words of Dionysius.[17] Consequently, according to the intention of this author, this first infinite, upon which *all* infinite *powers* depend, is the first simply, which is God. Now, by *the being* that is below *the infinite,* which Proclus also mentions, he does not mean the idea of being[18] but rather *the first created being,* which is *an intelligence.* What Proclus proves about the idea of being he proves here about the first created being, which is an intelligence. So he says: *If anyone* would wish to say that *the first created being,* which is *an intelligence,* is infinite *power,* it will not therefore be necessary to say *that* it is essentially *power; rather it is* what has power. Hence it is not that *first infinite* upon which *all* infinite *powers* depend. That it is not the first infinite power is made clear through the fact that it is not infinite in every way and in every respect, but is *infinite* only *with respect to the lower, not with respect to the higher.* He says that the power of an intelligence is infinite *with respect to the lower* because it is not comprehended by those things that are below it. However, it is not infinite *with respect to the higher* because it is surpassed by what is higher than it, by whose comprehension it is limited. So Proclus also says in

15. Cf. above, S{30}.
16. Cf. Proclus, Prop. 92, Dodds, p. 82.34–35; Vansteenkiste, p. 299.
17. Cf. above, S{20} and S{30}.
18. *ens.*

Proposition 93: "Every infinite in beings is infinite neither with respect to the things situated above it nor with respect to itself"[19] because, as he himself proves in the same place, each thing is circumscribed and limited both by itself and by higher things. Nor can it be circumscribed or limited by lower things. Therefore, the power of an intelligence is not infinite with respect to all things, because *it does not* have *pure power,* {96} i.e., it is not essentially power so as to be subsisting power. For such *a thing* that is essentially power *is limited neither with respect to the lower nor with respect to the higher,* for it does not have anything prior by which it could be circumscribed. But *an intelligence* that is *the first created being has limit, and its limit is that according to which it remains,* i.e., [its limit is] according to [the degree to which] it falls short of what is above it, remaining after it, as it were, without the force to equal it.

Next he shows what that *first infinite* is, upon which *all* infinite *powers* depend. He understands here that *the first creating being,* namely, God, is *the first pure infinite,* as the essentially existing infinite power. He proves this *because* intelligences, which he calls here knowing[20] and *powerful* due to the greatness of power that they have, are infinite *due to their acquisition* [of infinity] *from,* i.e., participation in, *the first,* which is the pure infinite, i.e., essentially, from which they have not only infinity but also being. *And if the first* creating *being is what* by its participation makes *things* to be infinite, *then* it is necessary that it be above the infinite. According to what he says here, we should understand [him to mean] that the first being is above the participated and created infinite. But in Proclus this is said of the idea of the one and good, which is above the idea of the infinite, according to the Platonists. So, explaining what he had said, that *the first being* is *above the infinite,* he adds that *the intelligence is infinite,* namely, participatively, but not essentially, so *that it is itself* that *which is infinite.*

Therefore, he concludes from the premises that, since *the first being* gives {97} being and infinity to intelligences, it *is the measure of first beings,* namely, *of intelligible things,* and consequently *of second beings,* namely, *of sensible things,* inasmuch as the first in each genus is the measure of that genus insofar as, by approaching it or receding from it, something is known to be more perfect or less perfect in that genus. But he explains

---

19. Proclus, Prop. 93, Dodds, p. 84.1–2; Vansteenkiste, p. 299.
20. The term, "knowing" (*scientes*), does not appear in the Latin text of the *De Causis* here. St. Thomas imports this idea into this proposition's explanation.

that *the first being* is *the measure of* all *beings because it has created* all *beings with the* due *measure* appropriate to each thing according to the mode of its nature. For the fact that some things approach it more or less is due to the arrangement of the first being.[21]

Finally, then, in summing up, as it were, he gathers from his premises what he principally intended and says *that the first creating being is above the infinite,* namely, what is infinite by participation. But the second being, which is *created,* namely, an intelligence, *is infinite* participatively. Furthermore, that *which is* mediate *between the first* created *being,* which is an intelligence, *and second created being,* which is a corruptible body, *is infinite,* namely, a celestial body. But Proclus asserts this as if the idea of the infinite were mediate between the idea of the good and the idea of being. Now, having established the order of things with regard to the infinite, [the author] continues in a similar vein with respect to the other things and says that all the other *simple goodnesses,* namely, *life, light, and the like, are the causes of things that have such goodnesses.* For just as the first cause is the infinite itself, and all other things have infinity from it, so also is the first cause life itself and light itself, and from it the first created [being], namely, an intelligence, has life and intellectual light. *And likewise* {98} also other *goodnesses descend from the first cause,* first *upon the first created* [being], which *is an intelligence,* and *then upon* the others *with the mediation of an intelligence,* whether these others are understood to be intellectual souls or spiritual things.

21. *ex eius dispositione.*

PROPOSITION 17[1]

Every united power is more infinite than a multiplied power.

This is because the first infinite, which is an intelligence, is close to the pure true one. So, for this reason it has happened that infinity is more in every power close to the true one than in a power distant from it. This is because when a power begins to be multiplied, its unity is then destroyed. And when its unity is destroyed, its infinity is then destroyed. And its infinity is destroyed only because it is divided.

The indication of this is divided power and the fact that the more [that power][2] is concentrated and united, [the more] it is magnified and becomes more powerful and effects wondrous activities. And the more it is partitioned and divided, [the more] it is lessened and weakened and effects base activities.

Therefore, it is now clear and plain that the more a power approximates the pure true one, the more powerful its unity becomes. And the more powerful its unity becomes, the more apparent and more manifest is the infinity in it, and its activities are great, wondrous, and noble activities.

COMMENTARY

After showing in the preceding proposition that all infinite powers depend upon the first infinite power, [the author] subsequently shows in this proposition how one power more approaches the first infinity than another. And he says that: *Every united power is more infinite than a multiplied power.* Proclus asserts this same proposition [as Proposition] 95 in his book, in these words: "Every potency that exists more unitedly is more infinite than a [potency] made plural."[3] Now, this is proved in two ways in both places.

{99} First, through an argument, [which proceeds] in this way. As is

---

1. This proposition, which follows from the preceding proposition, relates to Prop. 95 in Proclus's *Elements*. Cf. Dodds, p. 84.28–32, 84.34–35. St. Thomas quotes this proposition and its explanation frequently. Some examples are: *ST* I, Q. 77, A. 2, 2a; II–II, Q. 37, A. 2, ad 3 and Q. 52, A. 2, 2a; *SCG*, II, Cap. 20; *De Veritate*, Q. 3, A. 2, 3a and Q. 5, A. 2, 3a; *De Potentia*, Q. 5, A. 10, 6a; Q. 6, A. 3, 10a; Q. 7, A 8c; *Quaest. Disp. de Anima*, Q. 13, 9a.

2. *ipsa*.

3. Proclus, Prop. 95, Dodds, p. 84.16–17; Vansteenkiste, p. 300.

known from the previous proposition, all infinite powers depend upon the first infinite, which is the power of powers. So, to the degree a power has been closer to that first power, to that degree it necessarily participates its infinity. Now, that first power is essentially one. So, to the degree that something is more one, to that degree it necessarily has more infinite power. And so it is that the power of an intelligence, which is first among the infinite created powers, is infinite to the greatest degree as closer to the first one. But powers that are multiplied, by this very fact, fall away from unity and so their potency[4] is lessened. An example of this appears in knowing powers, for the intellect, which is not divided into many potencies, is more efficacious in knowing than sense, which is diversified into many potencies. For the same reason the knowing power of an intelligence, which is not divided by the sensitive and the intellectual, is stronger than the human knowing power both with regard to knowing singular sensible things and with regard to knowing intelligible things.

Second, this is proved through a sign.[5] For we see in corporeal things, which are divisble into parts,[6] that, when many are brought together and united, their power becomes stronger.[7] From this, wondrous activities follow, as is evident in many men simultaneously dragging a ship, who individually[8] would be unable to drag either it or its proportional parts. And the more the power of a corporeal thing is divided, the weaker it becomes and it performs baser activities, just as an entire house burns by a great fire that has gathered together, which could not happen if the fire were separated[9] throughout different parts of the house.

From these two propositions [the author] concludes to what he had proposed, as is evident in the text.

4. *posse.*
6. *partibilibus.*
8. *divisim.*

5. I.e., through experience.
7. *vehementior.*
9. *dividatur.*

{100} PROPOSITION 18[1]

All things have essence[2] through the first being, while all living things move themselves[3] through their essence due to the first life, and all intellectual things have knowledge due to the first intelligence.

This is because, if every cause gives something to what it causes, then undoubtedly the first being gives being to everything it causes. Likewise, life gives motion to its effect, because[4] life is [both] a procession from the first being, [which is] at rest and sempiternal, and the first motion. Likewise, an intelligence gives knowledge to its effect, which is because all true knowledge is intelligence[5] alone, and an intelligence is the first knower that there is, and it infuses knowledge upon the rest of knowers.[6]

Now, let us repeat and say that the first being is at rest and the cause of causes. If it gives being to all things, then it gives [it] to them by way of creation. And the first life gives life to those which are under it, not by way of creation, but by way of form. Likewise, an intelligence gives knowledge and the remaining things to those which are under it only by way of form.

1. This proposition relates to Prop. 102 in Proclus's *Elements*. Cf. Dodds, p. 92.5–8, 92.10–12. The author of the *De Causis* introduces a distinction here with regard to being, life, and intelligence foreign to Proclus, for whom the above three are impersonal hypostases. The first is "by way of creation," the other two "by way of form." St. Thomas, following Aristotle and Pseudo-Dionysius, understands all three to be one and the same as God. St. Thomas quotes this proposition in *De Potentia*, Q. 3, A. 1c and presupposes it in *Quodlibet. III*, Q. 3, A. 1c. Throughout this proposition and St. Thomas's commentary on it *esse* and *ens* appear regularly. They can usually be distinguished by the context, where *esse* appears as "being without qualification and *ens* as "being" qualified by an article or in the plural.
2. *habent essentiam*. Though this reading was in the manuscript used by St. Thomas and is common in the Latin tradition, it is a corruption of the original translation, *habent entia*. The latter is found in Latin manuscripts T and Aosta and corresponds precisely with the Arabic *dhawatu huwiyat*.
3. *sunt motae*.
4. We read *quoniam* for *quia* as corrected by Saffrey.
5. *intelligentia*. While this reading is found quoted by St Thomas, the original translation had *in intelligentia*, "in the intelligence," which is found in Latin manuscripts L, S, and Aosta and in two of the Arabic manuscripts.
6. *scientia*.

COMMENTARY

After showing that all things depend on the first [being] for[7] their power, [the author] shows here that all things depend on the first [being] for their nature. With regard to this he does two things. First, he shows the universal dependence of things on the first [being] for all the things that pertain to their nature or substance. Second, he shows the different grades of closeness to the first [being], upon which they depend, just as he had spoken about the dependence of [their] power. [He treats] this in Proposition 19, at: *Among intelligences there is* etc. Thus first he asserts the following proposition: *All things have essence through the first being, while all living things move themselves through their essence due to the first life, and all intellectual things have knowledge due to the first intelligence.* Proclus says the same thing in his book in Proposition 102 in these words: {101} "All beings whatsoever consist of a limit and the infinite due to the primal being.[8] Furthermore, all living things move themselves due to the first life. And all knowing things participate knowledge due to the first intellect."[9] Now he says that "all things consist of a limit and the infinite due to the primal being," since, <as> was stated before in Proposition 4, *created being is composed of the finite and the infinite*.[10]

Now to understand this proposition we should first note that all the grades of things seem to reduce to three: being, living, and knowing.[11] This is so because every thing can be considered in a threefold way. First, in itself, and thus being is proper to it. Second, insofar as it tends to something else, and thus to move itself[12] is proper to it. Third, insofar as it has other things in itself, and thus to know is proper to it, since knowledge is accomplished because the known is in the knower, not materially, but formally. Furthermore, just as to have something formally and not materially in oneself, in which the nature of knowledge consists, is the noblest way of having or containing something, so to be self-moved is the noblest kind of mobility. In this consists the nature of life, for we call those

---

7. *secundum*.
8. *Prime ens* renders *to protos on*, which Dodds translates, "the primal Being." Dodds, p. 93.
9. Proclus, Prop. 102, Dodds, p. 92.1–4; Vansteenkiste, p. 491.
10. Cf. above, S{30}.
11. *intelligere*.
12. *moveri*.

things living which in some way move themselves. Therefore, being, which is first, is common to all things, but not all things attain the perfection of moving themselves. Hence not all things are living, but [only] certain things that are more perfect among beings. Again, among those things that are able to move[13] themselves or others, not all are able to move by way of knowledge, but [some move] through some material principle, as happens with plants. *Further,* not all living things attain {102} the level[14] of knowledge, but only those things in which the principle of motion is something formal without matter, for sense itself is able to receive[15] the species of sensible things without matter, as is said in Book II of *On the Soul.*[16]

Second, we should note that in every genus the cause is what is first in that genus, by which all the things that belong to that genus are constituted in that genus, such as among the elementary bodies, fire is the first hot thing, from which all things obtain heat. Now, one does not proceed into infinity in any order of things. So in the order of beings something must be first, which gives being to all. And this is what he says, that *all things have essence through the first being.* Likewise, in the genus of living things something must be first, and from this all living things have life. And because it is proper to a living thing that it be able to move itself, he therefore says that *all living things are in motion through their essence,* i.e., move themselves, *due to the first life.* So, too, Proclus says in his book, "All living things that are able to move themselves are due to the first life."[17] And [the author] proves that to move oneself proceeds from the first life, adding: *because life is a procession proceeding from the first being, [which is] at rest and sempiternal.* To understand this we should realize that [a thing] is first something in itself before being moved toward another. Hence, to be moved presupposes being. But, if being itself is, as it were, what underlies motion, it will be necessary again for some principle of motion to be presupposed, and so on, until some immobile being is arrived at which is the principle of self-motion for all things. And this is the first life. Hence it is clear that life in all living things is a certain *procession proceeding* from a certain *first being, [which is] at rest and sempiternal,* i.e., subject to no mo-

---

13. *motiva.*
14. *gradum.*
15. *susceptivus.*
16. Aristotle, *On the Soul,* II 12, 424a18–19.
17. Proclus, Prop. 102, Dodds, p. 92.2–3.

tion. Likewise, in the order of knowers as well, {103} something must be first. It is clear that in the order of perfection and nature intellectual knowledge is prior to sensible [knowledge] because it is more immaterial. Hence we judge about sensible knowledge through the intellect as of the lower through the higher.[18] Moreover, in intellectual knowledge itself it is clear that rational inquiry proceeds from principles known per se, of which we have intuitive understanding.[19] Hence reasoning follows intuitive understanding. Therefore, the first in the order of knowers is an intellect, and so *all intellectual things*, i.e., knowing things, must *have knowledge*,[20] that is, knowledge[21] *due to the first intellect*. Hence Proclus says in his book that "all knowing beings participate knowledge due to the first intellect."[22] And [the author] assigns the reason for this: because *all knowledge* at root *is intelligence alone*, for intelligence is a certain "summit," as Proclus says,[23] of all knowledge. Hence *an intelligence is the first* knower *and it infuses* knowledge *upon all things that know*.

But, as we said before,[24] according to the Platonists, the first being, which is the idea of being,[25] is something above the first life, i.e., above the idea of life, and the first life is something above the first ideal intellect. But, according to Dionysius, the first being, the first life, and the first intellect are one and the same, which is God. So, too, in Book XII of the *Metaphysics*[26] Aristotle says of[27] the first principle that it is intellect and that its understanding is life, and due to this all things have being, life, and understanding[28] from it.

{104} Third, we should note that these three are caused in different ways in things, whether by different principles, according to the Platonists, or by the same principle, according to the teaching of faith and of Aristotle. For there is a twofold way of causing [something]. One is the way by which something is made with something else being presupposed. By this way something is said to be made through imparting form;[29] because what arrives later is related to what was presupposed by way of

18. *superius.*
19. *intellectus.*
20. *scientiam.*
21. *cognitionem.*
22. Proclus, Prop. 102, Dodds, p. 92.3–4; Vansteenkiste, p. 491.
23. Proclus, Prop. 102, Dodds, p. 92.11; Vansteenkiste, p. 492.
24. Cf. above, S{78}.
25. *ens.*
26. Aristotle, *Metaphysics*, XII 7, 1072b24ff. Also, cf. above, S{24}.
27. *attribuit.*
28. *intelligere.*
29. *informationis.*

form. By another way something is caused without anything presupposed. By this way something is said to be made through creation. So, while understanding presupposes living and living presupposes being, being does not presuppose anything else prior [to it]. So it is that *the first being gives being to all things by way of creation*. But *the first life*, whatever that might be, *does not give* life *by way of creation* but *by way of form*, i.e., by imparting form. The same must be said of an intelligence. From this it is evident that, when [the author] said before[30] that an intelligence is the cause of a soul, he did not understand [an intelligence] to be [the soul's] cause by way of creation but only by way of imparting form, as we explained above.

30. Cf. above, S{22}.

PROPOSITION 19[1]

Among intelligences there is that which is a divine intelligence because it receives from the first goodnesses, which proceed from the first cause through a multiple reception; and among them there is that which is merely an intelligence, because it receives from the first goodnesses only with an intelligence mediating. Among souls there is what is an intellectual soul because it depends upon an intelligence; also among them there is what is only soul. Among natural bodies there is what has soul ruling and directing it; and among them there are what are only natural bodies that do not have a soul.

This comes about only because it[2] is not totally intellectual,[3] or totally animated, or totally corporeal, nor does it depend upon a cause that is above it unless what from it is complete [and] entire and what depends upon a cause that is above it. For not every intelligence depends upon {105} the goodnesses of the first cause, but only that intelligence among them which is especially complete [and] entire. For it is able to receive the goodnesses that descend from the first cause and to depend upon them, so that its unity is made powerful.[4] Likewise, again, not every soul depends upon an intelligence, but only that [soul] among them which is complete, entire, and more powerfully at one with intelligence because it depends upon an intelli-

---

1. This proposition relates to Prop. 111 in Proclus's *Elements*. Cf. Dodds, p. 98.18–32. It expresses a theme common to Neoplatonism and medieval thought: the interconnectedness of all things in reality through a downward participation devoid of gaps.

2. Because of an omission in this sentence (see next note), it appears that the referent of *ipsa* would be quite unclear to Latin readers. St. Thomas does not cite this passage or discuss it in literal detail.

3. *Et hoc non fit ita nisi quoniam est ipsa* < . . . > *neque intelligibilis tota*. While Bardenhewer's Latin text (without the ellipsis) seems to reflect what St. Thomas had before him, the original Latin translation had the word *expositio*. This rendering of the Arabic *al-sharh*, "series," is rare in the Latin tradition but preserved in S and Aosta. Corresponding to this text and the next few lines, the Arabic has "This came to be so only because neither the whole intellectual series, nor the whole [series] of souls, nor the whole corporeal [series] is linked with the cause that is above it; rather, only that part of [each] which is complete and perfect, so that it is what is linked to the cause that is above it."

4. *vehemens*.

gence, and [this] is a complete intelligence. Likewise, again, not every natural body has a soul, but only that among them which is complete [and] entire, as if it were rational. And the remaining intelligible orders follow this arrangement.

COMMENTARY

After showing in the preceding proposition that all things depend upon the first [being] for their nature, [the author] shows here how certain things diversely approach it according to [their] participation of natural perfection. He asserts the following proposition: *Among intelligences there is that which is a divine intelligence because it receives from the first goodnesses, which proceed from the first cause through a multiple reception; and among them there is also that which is merely intelligence, because it receives from the first goodnesses only with an intelligence mediating. Among souls there is what is an intellectual soul because it depends upon an intelligence; and among them there is also what is only soul. Among natural bodies there is what has soul ruling and directing it; and among these there are what are only natural bodies, which do not have a soul.* This proposition is found in Proclus's book [as Proposition] 111 in these words: "In every intellectual series (i.e., order)[5] there are divine intellects receiving the after-possessions[6] (i.e., participations) of the gods, and there are intellects only; and in every [series] of souls[7] there are intellectual souls dependent upon their proper intellects, and there are {106} souls only; and in every corporeal nature some have souls present[8] from above, and some are natures only, lacking the presence of souls."[9]

In evidence of this we should realize that, according to the Platonists, a fourfold order is found in things. The first is the order of the gods, i.e., of the ideal forms, which have among themselves an order corresponding to the order of the universality of forms, as was said before.[10] Beneath this order is the order of separate intellects. Beneath that is the order of souls. Again, beneath that is the order of bodies. These three lower orders are understood to correspond to the three things that were touched upon in

---

5. *ordinationis.*
6. *posthabitiones.* See Prop. 12, note 383.
7. *animalis.* Literally, "animated [series]."
8. *astantes.*
9. Proclus, Prop. 111. Dodds, p. 98.18–23; Vansteenkiste, p. 495.
10. Cf. above, S{18}.

the previous proposition. For bodies participate being only, while souls according to their proper nature participate further being and living, and intellects participate being, living, and understanding. But the causality of these things belongs to the divine order, whether we assert that there are many gods ordered under the one, according to the Platonists, or only one [God], possessing all things, according to us, for the universality of causality is proper to God.

Such orders, since they proceed from the first one, have a certain continuity with one another, so that the order of bodies touches the order of souls and the order of souls touches the order of intellects, which touches the divine order. Moreover, wherever diverse orders are joined together one under the other, what is the highest of a lower order must participate something of the perfection of the higher order due to [its] closeness to the higher order. We see this clearly in natural things, for certain animals participate some likeness of reason and certain plants participate something of the distinction of sex, which is proper {107} to the genus of animals. So, too, Dionysius says in Chapter VII of *On the Divine Names* that through divine wisdom "the ends of the first are conjoined to the beginnings of the second."[11] Thus, those which are the highest in the order of intellects or intelligences depend more closely upon God through a certain more perfect participation, and they participate more his goodnesses and his universal causality. Thus, they are called divine intellects or divine intelligences, just as Dionysius, too, says that the highest angels are, as it were, placed together "in the vestibule" of the deity.[12] Lower intellects that do not reach such a degree of excellence in participation of the divine likeness are intellects only, not having that divine dignity. The same reasoning applies to souls with respect to intellects, for the highest[13] souls are intellectual insofar as they are close to the order of intellects. But the other lower souls are not intellectual, having only what belongs to the soul, namely, to be life-giving, as is most evident in the case of the souls of animals and plants. The same reasoning applies to the order of bodies with respect to souls, for more noble bodies, which

---

11. Pseudo-Dionysius, *On the Divine Names*, VII 3; *Dionysiaca* I, 407; PG 3, 872 B.
12. Cf. Pseudo-Dionysius, *Celestial Hierarchy*, VII 2; *Dionysiaca* II, 844; PG 3, 208 A.
13. Or, *most transcendent*.

are constituted of a more perfect nature, are animated but the other bodies are inanimate. And the same reasoning applies to all the other orders into which the previously mentioned general orders are distinguished, because there are diverse orders among bodies, and likewise among souls and intellects.

{108} PROPOSITION 20[1]

The first cause rules all created things without being mixed with them.

This is because rule does not weaken its unity, exalted over every thing, and does not destroy it, nor does the essence of its unity, separated from other things, prevent it from ruling things.[2]

This is because the first cause is fixed, ever abiding steadfastly with its pure unity. And it rules all created things and infuses them with the power of life and [with] goodnesses according to the mode of their powers[3] to receive[4] and their possibility. For the first goodness infuses all things with goodnesses in one infusion. But each thing receives that infusion according to the mode of its power and its being.

The first goodness infuses all things with goodnesses only through one mode because it is goodness only through its existence, being[5] and power, so that it is goodness, and both goodness and being are one thing. So, as the first being and goodness are therefore one thing, it happens that it infuses things with goodnesses with one common infusion. And goodnesses and gifts are diversified due to the concurrence of the recipient. This is because recipients[6] do not receive goodnesses equally, rather some of them receive more than others. [All] this is due to the greatness of its largesse.

Therefore, let us return and say that every agent that acts through its being alone is neither a connecting link nor another mediating thing.[7] The connecting

---

1. This proposition relates to Prop. 122 in Proclus's *Elements*. Cf. Dodds, p. 108.1–15, 108.11–12, 108.15–16. The author of the *De Causis* reserves providence to the first cause alone rather than to "every divine thing," as in Proclus. St. Thomas refers to this proposition in *ST* I, Q. 3, A. 8s.c.; Q. 5, A. 1, 2a; *De Potentia*, Q. 7, A. 2; *De Veritate*, Q. 21, A. 1, 7c.

2. Bardenhewer gives *eas* here, while St. Thomas has *res* in his quotation of this passage. *Res*, which corresponds preciesly with the Arabic, is preserved in Latin manuscripts OST and Aosta.

3. We read *virtutum* for Bardenhewer's *virtutis*, with Latin manuscripts LOPSUV and Aosta and with the Arabic.

4. *receptibilium*.

5. *suum esse et suum ens*.

6. The Arabic has "recipients of goodnesses."

7. St. Thomas explains the meaning of these two terms when he comments on Proclus's Prop. 122. Cf. below, S{111}. *Continuator*, "connecting link," corresponds to *wuslatun* in the Arabic.

link between an agent and its effect is nothing but an addition to being, as when an agent and its effect are through an instrument and [the agent] does not act through its being, and they are things that are composed.[8] For this reason what receives receives through a continuous connection[9] between itself and its maker, and then the agent is separated from its effect. But an agent [in which] there is no connecting link at all between itself and its effect is a true agent and a true ruler, making things for the sake of beauty, after which it is not possible for there to be some other beauty, and it rules its effect through the ultimate of rule.[10] This is because it rules things through the mode in which it acts, and it acts only through its being. Therefore, its being will also be its rule. For this reason, it happens that it rules and acts through ultimate beauty and rule in which there are neither diversity nor deviation.[11] And activities and rule due to first causes are diversified only according to the merit of the recipient.

COMMENTARY

After showing how lower things depend upon higher[12] things, [the author] shows here how higher things infuse lower things through their rule. In this regard he does two things. First, he treats of the universal rule of the first cause. Second, of the rule of an intelligence, in {**109**} Proposition 23, at: *Every divine intelligence* etc. With regard to the first he does two things. First, he shows the manner of the first cause's universal rule. Second, he shows the appropriateness of the first cause to rule, in Proposition 21, at: *The first is rich* etc.

Regarding the first he asserts the following proposition: *The first cause rules all created things without being mixed together with them.* In evidence of this we should note that in human rule we see it happen that the one who has charge of ruling a number of things must be drawn from his own rule to many things. But he who is free from the charge of ruling others is

---

8. The Arabic has "and its being is composed."
9. *continuationem*.
10. The Latin text here omits parts of the Arabic and carries different nuances. "As for the agent that is such that between it and its act there is no connecting link at all, this agent is a true agent and a true dispenser of providence which effects things with the utmost and ultimate of thoroughness and which directs its act with the utmost of providence."
11. *tortuositas*.
12. *superioribus*, i.e., transcendent.

more able to preserve uniformity in himself. Hence the Epicurean philosophers asserted that in order to conserve divine quiet and uniformity the gods could have charge of no rule. Instead, they are entirely at leisure, caring about nothing, so that in this way they are seen to be happy.[13] And so, against this [the author] begins in this proposition by saying that these two things are not contrary in the first cause and that the universal rule of things and the supreme unity, by which God is exalted above all things, do not impede one another. So he immediately asserts at the beginning of his explanation: *This is because rule does not weaken its unity, exalted over every thing, and does not destroy it* because neither in whole nor in part is anything taken away from divine unity by universal rule. Conversely, he adds: *Nor does the essence of its unity, separated from things, prevent it from ruling things.* Proclus asserts all this in Proposition 122 in these words: "Every divine thing both provides for secondary things and is separated from those things for which it provides; and providence does not subvert its unmixed and united excellence, nor does separated unity destroy providence."[14]

{110} Now, to make this proposition clear [the author] introduces three things. For, first, he shows the different manner of receiving the infusions of the first cause on the part of the recipients. Second, he shows the unity on the part of the first cause which infuses, at: *And the first goodness* etc. Third, from these two he concludes to what he proposed, namely, that the rule of the first cause stands above[15] without being mixed with things, at: *Therefore, let us return and say.*

So, he says in the first place that all goodnesses that are found in things flow from the first cause. Each thing receives such goodnesses according to the manner and proper character[16] of its substance and power—for there are different natures and powers for different things—and so it is that, although the first cause infuses all things with one infusion, its infusion is nevertheless received differently in different things. A clear example of this is in light, which proceeds from a luminous body in one

---

13. Cf. Augustine, *City of God*, XVIII, Cap. 41; PL 41, 601. Also, see Dodds's commentary on Prop. 122 of Proclus's *Elements*, p. 264.
14. Proclus, Prop. 122, Dodds, p. 108.1–4; Vansteenkiste, p. 499.
15. *exstat*, in place of Saffrey's *extat*.
16. *proprietatem*.

way, but according to the way that different rays pass through variously colored glass, the rays produce a different appearance.

Next he shows that the first cause infuses all things with a single infusion, for it infuses things under the aspect[17] of the good. For it has the goodness that makes things good, i.e., that which is the principle of goodness in all things. But the goodness of the first cause is its very being and essence because the first cause is the very essence of goodness. Hence, since its essence is one to the greatest degree, because the first principle is the one and good in itself, it follows that the first cause for its part acts on things and infuses them in one way. But things receive its infusion in different ways, some more and others less, each according to its proper character.

He then concludes from the premises to the first cause's lack of mixture with other things. A full understanding of this conclusion can be had if we take the words of Proclus's explanation,[18] who thus says, {111} "Therefore, the ones who provide (namely, the gods) do not receive a relation to those things for which provision is made, for through the being that they are they make all things good. Furthermore, what acts upon all things through being acts without relation, for relation is an addition to being, due to which it is outside [its] nature."[19] Now, he means by "relation" some disposition through which an agent is adapted or rendered proportionate to a patient, or a recipient. And because [an agent] acts thus in different things it must have different dispositions by which it is adapted to diverse things. In this way a certain multitude[20] occurs in a thing of this sort, that is, one that acts in different ways upon different things according to its different dispositions, which are outside its nature, or essence, which is one. Thus, such a thing, that is, one that acts according to different dispositions, is mixed with the things upon which it acts according to a certain adaptation to them. But the first cause acts

17. *secundum rationem.*
18. *commento.*
19. Proclus, Prop. 122, Dodds, p. 102.13–17; Vansteenkiste, p. 499. Proclus's term *schesis* is translated by Moerbeke as *habitudo* ("relation") and St. Thomas relates it to *dispositio* ("disposition"). In similar fashion St. Thomas says in *ST* I, Q. 13, A. 7 and Q. 45, A. 3, that creation places a real relation in the creature only and not in God.
20. That is, a certain plurality.

through its being, as was proved.[21] Hence it does not act through any additional relation or disposition through which it would be adapted to and mixed with things. And such a "relation" is called here a *connecting link* or mediating thing because through such a disposition or relation an agent is adapted to a recipient, and is in a certain sense a mediating thing between the essence of the agent and the patient itself. So, because the first cause acts through its being, it must rule things in one manner, for it rules things according to the way that it acts. Hence it is clear that its rule is the best and the most beautiful. For every ruler of a multitude tends to reduce the many whom he rules into one. And this is found to the greatest degree in divine rule, which is one in itself and diversified in effects only according to the diversity of the things subject [to it] according to [their] diverse merits, as it were.

21. Cf. above, S{110}.

{112} PROPOSITION 21[1]

The first is rich owing to itself and it is more rich.[2]

The indication of this is its unity, not because its unity is dispersed in it.[3] *Rather, its unity is pure because it is simple in the extreme of simplicity. If anyone wishes to know that the first cause is rich, let him cast his mind over composite things and inquire about them with close scrutiny. For he will find that every composite thing is diminished,*[4] *needing either another or the things from which it is composed. Furthermore, the one simple thing which is goodness is one, and its unity is goodness, and its goodness is one thing.*[5] *That thing is more rich which infuses, while no infusion upon it occurs in any way.*[6] *But the rest of things, whether they are intellectual or corporeal,*[7] *are not rich in themselves. Rather, they need the true one infusing them with goodnesses and all graces.*

COMMENTARY

After determining the manner of divine rule, [the author] shows here the sufficiency of God to rule. He attends to this in two ways: first, ac-

---

1. This proposition relates to Prop. 127 in Proclus's *Elements*. Cf. Dodds, p. 112.25–32. For the author of the *De Causis* only God as the first cause is self-sufficient, in contrast to Proclus, who distinguishes self-sufficiency from the one, or good (see *Elements*, Prop. 10).

2. The Arabic has, "The First Cause is sufficient in itself and is the most (self)sufficient." See Taylor (1981), p. 229.

3. The Arabic has, "[it is] not the case that it is a unity that has been established (*mathbutah*) in it," i.e. by something external.

4. *diminutum* for the Arabic *naqisan*. The notion of diminished or deficient being is also found in both Avicenna and Averroes, though with a different sense than what is found here.

5. The Latin translator's Arabic manuscript apparently omitted *a'ni* and *al-wahid* in this sentence, as do the Ankara and Istanbul Arabic manuscripts. The corresponding Arabic text has quite a different sense: "But the simple thing, i.e., the One which is good (*khairun*), is one and its unity is good, and the good and the one are a single thing."

6. That is, what is only a cause of the infusion of goodnesses and itself does not receive any infusion from another is more rich in goodnesses than what is below it and a recipient of its beneficence.

7. *Reliquae autem res intellectibiles* sint *aut corporae*. In agreement with the Arabic we add *sint* here following Latin manuscripts S and Aosta.

cording to the abundance of God; second, according to his superexcellence,[8] and this at: *The first cause* etc.[9] For these two things are necessary for a ruler. The first is that he have an abundance of good things from which he is able to provide for those subject [to him]. So, too, Dionysius says in Chapter XII of *On the Divine Names*[10] that "domination is the entire perfect possession of beautiful and good things," and "rule is the distribution of every end, law and order." Now, to show the abundant sufficiency in God he proposes this proposition: *The first is rich owing to itself and is more rich*. In evidence of this let us take Proposition 127 from Proclus, which is the following: "Every divine thing is simple in the first and greatest degree, and because of this it is self-sufficient in the greatest degree."[11]

{113} Now, he proves that God is simple in the first and greatest degree by reason of unity, for God is in the greatest degree one, since he is the first unity, just as he is the first goodness. But simplicity pertains to the notion[12] of unity—for something is said to be simple that is one, not gathered together from many. Hence, to the extent that God is one in the first and greatest degree, to that extent he is also simple in the first and greatest degree. From this he proceeds further to show the second part of his proposition, namely, that God is self-sufficient to the greatest degree because self-sufficiency follows upon simplicity. For every composite thing requires many things from which its goodness is constituted. Not only does it need those things from which it is composed as from parts, but it also needs something else that causes and conserves the composition, as is obvious in compound bodies, for different things would not come together into one except through some cause uniting them. Therefore, since God is simple in the first and greatest degree as having his whole goodness in a oneness that is most perfect,[13] it follows that God is self-sufficient in the first and greatest degree.

8. *superexcellentiam.*
9. Cf. Prop. 22, S{123}.
10. Pseudo-Dionysius, *On the Divine Names*, XII 2; *Dionysiaca* I, 529; PG 3, 969 B.
11. Proclus, Prop. 127, Dodds, p. 112.25–26. The term "self-sufficient in the greatest degree" (*maxime per se sufficiens*) in Proclus is *autarkestaton*, which he applies to "all that is divine" but not to the good, which transcends the divine. See *Elements*, Prop. 10.
12. *rationem.*
13. *in uno perfectissimo.*

But the author of this book bypasses the first part of the proposition, which is about simplicity, presupposing it, as it were, and speaks only of self-sufficiency, which he signifies by the word "riches." In place of what Proclus says in his proposition, that God is "self-sufficient," [the author] says that *the first is rich owing to itself.* For in every genus the first is that which is owing to itself, for what is in itself is prior to what is through another. Furthermore, in place of what [Proclus] says there, that "it is to the greatest degree sufficient," [the author] says here that *it is more rich than all other things.* But the proof for what is proposed is identical in both places. For [the author] first says that the divine *unity,* which is not dispersed into many parts but *is pure unity,* is *the sign* that God is *in the extreme of simplicity,* i.e., is simple in the greatest degree. From this he proves further that God is self-sufficient in the greatest degree by the lack of what is found in *composite* things, as he already said.[14] {**114**} But because by the word "riches" not only sufficiency but also the abundance that is able to redound upon others is understood, to show that God is rich he continues on about the infusion of things with his goodness, since due to the abundance of his goodness he infuses other things, while there is nothing which infuses him. But all other *things,* whether they be *intellectual,* such as intelligences and souls, or in a body, *are not rich in themselves,* as if they had an abundance of goodness from themselves, but *they need* to participate goodness from the first true *one, which infuses them* freely with all goodnesses and perfections, without anything being added to him thereby.

14. Cf. the preceding paragraph.

PROPOSITION 22[1]

The first cause is above every name by which it is named, because[2] neither diminution nor mere completeness belong to it.

[This is] because what is diminished is not complete and cannot effect a complete activity when[3] it is diminished.[4] And what is complete among us, although it is self-sufficient, nevertheless cannot create anything else, nor [can it] infuse anything from itself at all. Therefore, if this is so among us, then we say[5] that the first is neither diminished nor merely complete. Rather, it is above the complete[6] because it creates things and infuses them with goodnesses with a complete infusion, because it is goodness without limit or dimensions. Therefore, the first goodness fills all worlds with goodnesses. But every world receives that goodness only according to the mode of its potency.

Therefore, we have already shown and made clear that the first cause is above every name by which it is named, and higher and loftier than it.

1. This proposition, like 9(8) and 4 and 5(4) above, does not have Proclus's *Elements* as its source. Though the *Enneades* of Plotinus are not directly quoted, it is clear that this work is the ultimate source for the thought of this proposition, as is the case for 9(8) and 4 and 5(4). Regarding the teaching that the First is above mere perfection, cf. *Enneades* V 2, 1.1–18 = PA *Theologia*, pp. 134.1–137.5, Lewis, pp. 291–92, nos. 1–12. For the doctrine of the First Cause being above every name, cf. *Enneades* V 3, 13.4–14.19 = PA *Epistola*, nos. 121–138, Lewis, p. 323. St. Thomas finds Proclus's Prop. 115 as a possible source but seems to be aware that the correspondence between that proposition and the *De Causis* text here is far from precise. St. Thomas quotes this proposition in *De Veritate*, Q. 2, A. 1, 3a.

2. *quoniam*. The Latin translator's Arabic had *li-anna-hu* (as do two of the Arabic manuscripts) rather than the correct reading, *wa-dhalika anna-hu*, "for."

3. *quando*. The Latin translator's Arabic had *idha* instead of the correct reading, *idh*, "since."

4. The Latin requires this translation. However, the Arabic has a different sense: "The First Cause is above every name by which it is named. For neither deficiency nor mere perfection is appropriate to it, because the deficient is imperfect and unable to effect a perfect act since it is deficient."

5. Two Arabic manuscripts (Ankara and Istanbul) agree with the Latin and have *'inda-na*, "among us" or "in our view." The correct reading, however, is *'adna*, "we resume," found in the Leiden Arabic manuscript. Thus the Arabic text has, "Therefore, if this is so, we resume and say . . ."

6. We read *supra completum* with Bardenhewer, in place of Saffrey's revision *super-completum*.

COMMENTARY

After showing the abundance of the divine goodness, [the author] shows here its excellence, saying: *The first cause is above every name by which it is named.* To understand this proposition we should note that what [the author] gathers together here into one [proof], Proclus distinguishes in his book {115} into several [proofs]. Proposition 115 of his book is this: "Every god is supersubstantial, supervital, and superintelligent."[7]

Proclus proves this in a twofold way. First, by a general proof, which is as follows. God is a "unity perfect in itself." "But each one" of the other things that are below God is "not unity" itself "but" is something that participates unity. Therefore, it is clear that "God is beyond all" such "things."[8] Second, he proves it by a special proof, namely, it is not the same for a substance to be, to be a substance, and to be one. But any subsisting substance participates being and oneness.[9] Hence it remains that God, who is oneness itself[10] and being in itself, is above substance, and consequently above life and intellect, which presuppose substance,[11] as is also clear in this book from Proposition 18 presented above.[12]

But because the author of this book presents the proposition in general, he is content with a general proof alone. For in all things that are below the first cause, we find some things existing perfectly, or complete, [while] others things [are] imperfect or diminished. The perfect seem to be those things that are self-subsistent in nature, which we signify through concrete terms, such as "man," "sage," and the like. But the imperfect are those things that are not self-subsistent, such as the forms "humanity," "wisdom," and the like, which we signify through abstract terms.[13] The difference between these two is that what is *not complete* can-

---

7. Proclus, Prop. 115, Dodds, p. 100.28; Vansteenkiste, p. 496. The respective terms in Proclus are: *huperousios, huperzoos, hupernous*.
8. Proclus, Prop. 115, Dodds, p. 100.29–33; Vansteenkiste, p.496.
9. *esse et uno*.
10. *ipsum unum*.
11. Proclus, Prop. 115, Dodds, p. 100.34–102.12; Vansteenkiste, p. 496.
12. Cf. above, S{100}.
13. St. Thomas's explanation here is Aristotelian rather than Platonic. For Aristotle, and St. Thomas following him, universal forms do not subsist in themselves, as the Platonists held, but are abstracted by the human intellect from the particular and concrete existing things that have these forms, whether substantially or accidentally.

not effect a perfect *activity*, for heat does not make hot, but a hot thing does, and wisdom does not think wisely, but a sage does. Now, what is *complete among us, although it is* self-subsistent, is in some sense *sufficient unto itself*, in that it does not need another in which to inhere as in a subject. *Nevertheless*, since the form, which is the principle of action, is, in [what is complete among us], limited and participated, *it cannot* act by way of creation or {116} infusion, as does what is totally form, which in itself is totally productive of other things by a participation in itself. Since, therefore, *it is so among us* in those things that are diminished and concrete, it follows that God is neither *diminished* nor *complete* simply, but rather *above the complete*. For his action is not lacking as if it were something diminished, and he acts by way of creating and infusing, which those things that are complete among us cannot do. And this is what he adds: because *it creates things and infuses them with goodnesses with a complete infusion*. And this is so *because* he *is* subsistent *goodness without limit*, i.e., he is not goodness limited to some participative incorporeal nature, as is the goodness of an intelligence. And he is *without dimensions* to which he would be limited, as is the case for corporeal goodness. From this he concludes further that, because the first cause is unlimited goodness itself, it follows that it is *the first goodness* and that it fills *all worlds*, i.e., all distinctions of things and of times, with its goodnesses, although not all things receive its goodness in the same mode and equally, but each one *according to the mode of its potency*, as was stated before in Proposition 20.[14]

Therefore, the entire force of this proof goes back to what Proclus briefly touched upon, namely, that "God is unity" itself, "not" something "united," such as the complete things found among us, and yet [this unity] is "perfect in itself," from which the diminished things, i.e., the nonsubsistent forms that are among us, fall short. From this he here concludes further that the first cause is *higher* than any name we impose, since every name we impose either signifies after the manner of a complete thing that participates, such as concrete terms, or signifies after the manner of a diminished thing and of the formal part, such as abstract terms. Hence no term we impose is worthy of the divine excellence.

14. Cf. above, S{110}.

{117} PROPOSITION 23[1]

Every divine intelligence knows things inasmuch as it is an intelligence and rules them inasmuch as it is divine.

This is because knowledge is the characteristic proper to an intelligence, and its completeness and fullness[2] are only in its being a knower. Therefore, God, who is blessed and sublime, rules because he fills things with goodnesses. And an intelligence is the first created thing and is more similar to God, who is sublime. Due to that it rules things that are under it. Just as God, who is blessed and sublime, infuses things with goodness, similarly an intelligence infuses the things that are under it with knowledge. But, although an intelligence rules the things that are under it, nevertheless God, who is blessed and sublime, precedes an intelligence in ruling. And he rules things by rule more sublime and of a higher order than is the rule of an intelligence, because [his rule] is what gives rule to an intelligence.

The indication of this is that things that receive[3] an intelligence's rule receive the rule of the creator of the intelligence. This is because nothing whatsoever escapes his rule, since he wills to make all things receive his goodness at once. This is because it is not the case that everything desires intelligence or desires to receive it, but all things do desire goodness from the first[4] and desire very much to receive it. There is no one who doubts that.

COMMENTARY

After relating the manner of divine rule and showing the sufficiency of God to rule, [the author] treats here of the rule of the second cause, namely, an intelligence, whose rule comes from the power of the first cause. He asserts this proposition: *Every divine intelligence knows things in-*

---

1. This proposition relates to Prop. 134 in Proclus's *Elements.* Cf. Dodds, p. 118. 20–32. St. Thomas interprets rule here in light of the Aristotelian notion of the good as end.
2. *integritas.*
3. Pattin follows the Arabic and reads <*non*> *recipiunt.* However, there is no evidence for *non* in the Latin tradition. Consequently, we translate Bardenhewer's Latin as found in Saffrey without the negation.
4. *bonitatem ex primo.* The translator's Arabic manuscript apparently had, *al-khair min al-awwal,* instead of the correct reading, *al-khair al-awwal,* "the First Good."

asmuch as it is an intelligence and rules them inasmuch as it is divine. A similar proposition, 134, is found in Proclus's book, in these words, "Every divine intellect understands as an intellect, but it provides as a god."[5]

In evidence of this we should note what he said before in Proposition 19. Among intelligences some are divine, others are not.[6] He calls the highest intellects, or intelligences, {118} "divine" because of their abundant participation of the divine goodness from [their] closeness to God. Now, whatever abundantly participates a characteristic proper to some thing becomes like[7] it not only in form but also in action. This is clear with the things the sun illuminates. Some participate the sun's light only to the extent that they are seen, but some to the extent that they illuminate other things, which is the proper action of the sun, as is clear of the moon. Because form is the principle of action, everything that acquires its action from an abundant participation of the infusion of a higher agent must have two actions: one according to its proper form, another according to a form participated from the higher agent, as a heated knife cuts according to its proper form but burns insofar as it is heated. Thus, each of the highest[8] intelligences that is called "divine" has a double action: one insofar as it abundantly participates the divine goodness, and another according to its proper nature. Now, it is proper for an intelligence, inasmuch as it is such a thing, to know things, and so a divine intelligence, inasmuch as it is an intelligence, is able to know[9] things. But it is proper to God, who is the very essence of goodness, to communicate himself to other things. We see that everything, insofar as it is perfect and a being in act, transmits its likeness to other things. Hence what is essentially act and goodness, namely, God, essentially and originally[10] communicates his goodness to things. This belongs to his rule, for it is proper for a ruler to lead those that are ruled to their appropriate[11] end, which is the good. Thus, to the extent that it abundantly participates the divine goodness, a divine intelligence is itself made capable of ruling things.[12]

Now, it is clear that whatever performs some action according to its proper and natural form performs that action more powerfully and more

---

5. Proclus, Prop. 134, Dodds, p. 118.20; Vansteenkiste, p. 503.
6. Cf. above, S{105}.
7. *assimilatur.*
8. *supremorum.*
9. *cognoscitiva.*
10. *primordaliter.*
11. *debitum.*
12. *fit regitiva rerum.*

perfectly than what performs it {119} by participation of the power of a higher agent, as fire heats more intensely than a heated body, and the sun illuminates more than does the moon. So, the rule of God, which is his action according to his essential goodness, must be higher and more efficacious than an intelligence's rule, which belongs to it according to a participation of the divine goodness. And so it is that the rule of the first cause, which is according to the essence of goodness, extends to all things. A sign of this is that all things desire the good with an appetite that is either intellectual, animate, or natural. But the rule of an intelligence, which is proper to it, does not extend to all things, for it does not diffuse intellectual goodness in all things, but only in those things whose nature is to understand. So, all things seek, not the intellectual good, but only the good simply.

PROPOSITION 24[1]

The first cause exists[2] in all things according to one disposition, but all things do not exist in the first cause according to one disposition.

This is because, although the first cause exists in all things, each thing, nevertheless, receives it according to the mode of its potency. This is because among things there are some that receive the first cause by a united reception while others receive it by a multiple reception, and among them there are some that receive it by an eternal reception while others receive it by a temporal reception, and among them there are some that receive it by a spiritual reception while others receive it by a corporeal reception.

And the diversity of reception is due not to the first cause but to the recipient. This is because the recipient[3] is also diversified.[4] Because of that, what is received is therefore diversified. But the infusion, existing as an undiversified one, infuses all things with goodnesses equally, for goodness from the first cause equally infuses all things. So, the things are the cause of the diversity of the infusion of the things

---

1. This proposition relates to Prop. 142 in Proclus's *Elements.* Cf. Dodds, pp. 124.27–126.7. However, the clarity found in Proclus is far from evident here, due to the infelicitous rendering of the Greek *pareinai* with a dative object by the Arabic *maujudathun fi* or other forms of the root *w-j-d.* While the Greek has the sense of "to be present to," the Arabic can have the sense of "to be found," and "to exist." Both of these fail at times to translate the corresponding Greek. Moreover, the Latin translator uses both senses of the Arabic in different passages, sometimes perferring forms of *existo* and other times preferring forms of *invenio* in the passive. For his interpretation, St. Thomas relies on both the clearer sense found in Moerbeke's translation of Proclus and his own understanding of what the *De Causis* text should mean here. St. Thomas refers to this proposition in *De Veritate,* Q. 1, A. 4, 6 s.c and Q. 5, A. 2, 9a.

2. *existit.* Some confusion arises here because of the translation of the forms of the Arabic root *w-j-d* in this proposition. Here *maujudatun* is rendered as *existat,* while later *tujadu* is rendered as *inveniuntur,* "are ... found." Both senses of the Arabic are possible, but in this context the rendering needs to be consistent. Regarding the root *w-j-d,* see A.-M. Goichon, *Lexique de la langue philosophique d'Ibn Sina (Avicenne)* (Paris, 1938), pp. 418–23.

3. *suscipiens.*

4. In place of *est diversificatum* we read *etiam diversificatur,* following Latin manuscripts OS Aosta and the Arabic.

with goodness. Therefore, without doubt all things are not found in the first cause through one mode.

Therefore, it has already been shown that the first cause is found in all things through one mode, while all things are not found in it through one mode. {120}

Thus, the degree[5] of closeness to the first cause[6] and the way[7] in which a thing is able to receive the first cause [determine] the extent of its reception and enjoyment of the first cause.[8] This is because a thing receives from the first cause and enjoys it only through the mode of its being. And I understand by ''being'' only being and knowledge,[9] for a thing receives from it [the first cause] according to the mode in which a thing knows the first creating cause and according to that extent it enjoys it [the first cause], as we have shown.

COMMENTARY

After showing the manner of divine rule and its sufficiency to rule, [the author] begins to show here how the divine rule is participated in diverse ways by diverse things. First, he clarifies this in general. Second, he proceeds in particular concerning the diversity of things that are under divine rule, in Proposition 25, at: *United substances* etc. Regarding the first, he asserts the following proposition: *The first cause exists in all things according to one disposition, but all things do not exist in the first cause according to one disposition.*

In evidence of this we should note that something is said to be in another in several ways: in one way really, in another way according to the relation of action and passion. Now, according to the first way, all things must be said to be in the first cause in one way, because that by which all things are in the first cause is one and the same thing, namely, divine

---

5. *modum.*
6. The Latin translator's Arabic manuscript apparently had *fa-s-sabab al-awwal 'ala nahwa qurbahu,* instead of the correct reading, *al-ilah al-ula <yaqdiru ash-shai'u 'ala qubuli-ha> 'ala nahwa quwati-hi,* ''<The thing is able to receive> the first cause in accordance with its potentiality. . . .''
7. *modum.*
8. *delectari per eam.*
9. For *per esse nisi cognitionem* we read *per esse nisi esse et cognitionem,* following Latin manuscripts ABCOPSTUV Aosta and the Arabic of the Ankara and Istanbul manuscripts.

power, for effects are virtually in their cause. But according to this mode the first cause is in things in diverse ways because the first cause is in the things caused inasmuch as it imprints its likeness on them, while diverse things receive the likeness of the first cause in diverse ways. But in the second way the opposite is the case. For *the first cause* acts upon all things according to one mode and so [the author] says it is *in all things according to one disposition*. But all things do not receive the action of the first cause in the same way, and so he says that *all things do not exist in the first cause according to one disposition*. To clarify this proposition, three things follow. First, he clarifies the proposition. Second, he proves it, at: *And the diversity* etc. Third, he draws a certain corollary, at: *Thus, according to the mode* etc.

{121} He says first, then, that *all things* are said *not* to be *in the first cause according to one disposition* because, although *the first cause exists in all things* insofar as it touches all things through the effect of its action, *each thing, nevertheless, receives* its action *according to the mode of its power*. He gives an example of this according to the first three kinds of diversity[10] found in things. The first of them is according to the diversity of unity and multiplicity; this diversity belongs to substances themselves. For those things whose substance is simple *receive* the action of the first cause in a united way, while those whose substance is composed *receive it in a multiple way*, namely, according to the mode of their substance. The second [kind of] diversity is taken from the duration of things in their being, for some *receive* the action of the first cause *by an eternal reception*, namely, those whose being is not subject to motion. Hence the duration of these in their being does not vary according to before and after. But others, namely, those whose being is subject to motion, *receive* the action of the first cause *by a temporal reception* and consequently their duration is continuous according to the succession of before and after. He states a third [kind of] diversity due to the very species, or form, of a thing insofar as certain things are incorporeal according to their species, and these *receive* the infusion of the first cause spiritually. But others are corporeal according to their species, and such *receive* the infusion of the first cause *by a corporeal reception*.

But Proposition 142 in Proclus's book contains everything that has been said above. It states the following: "The gods are present to all in

---

10. *diversitates*.

the same way, but not all things are present to the gods in the same way. Rather, each assumes their presence according to its order and potency: some unitarily, others in a multiplied way; some perpetually, {122} others in time; some incorporeally, others corporeally."[11]

Then, when he says, *And the diversity* etc., he proves what he premised in this way. For diversity of reception can come about for two reasons: sometimes due to the agent, or the one that infuses; but at other times due to the recipient. For, because the diversity of the cause produces diversity in the effects, if the agent is diverse and the recipient is one, the diversity of the reception must be caused by the agent, and not by the recipient—for instance, water, which is frozen by cold and melted by heat. Conversely, if the agent should be one and the recipient diverse, the diversity of reception will be due to the recipient and not the agent, as is clear with the sun, which hardens mud and melts wax. Now, it is clear that the first cause is one, without diversity. But those things that receive the infusion of the first cause are diverse. Therefore, the diversity of reception is not due to the first cause, which is pure goodness infusing all things with goodness, but is because of the diversity of the recipients. Thus, it is clear that *the first cause is found in all things through one mode*, but not conversely. We should keep in mind that the action of the first cause is twofold: one inasmuch as it establishes things, which is called creation; another inasmuch as it rules things already established. Therefore, what he says here has no place in the first action because, if all diversity of effects must reduce to the diversity of the recipients, it will be necessary to say that there would be some recipients that are not from the first cause, which is contrary to what he said before[12] in Proposition 18: *All things have essence through the first cause*. So, it is necessary to say that the first diversity of things, according to which they have diverse natures and powers, is not due to some diversity of the recipients but is due to the first cause, not because there is some diversity in it, but because it knows diversity, for it is an agent according to {123} its knowledge. Therefore, it produces the diverse grades of things for the completeness of the universe. But in the action of ruling, which we are treating now, the diversity of reception is according to the diversity of the recipients.

Finally, when he says, *Thus, according to the mode* etc., he infers a certain

---

11. Proclus, Prop. 142, Dodds, p. 124.26–31; Vansteenkiste, p. 506.
12. Cf. above, S{100}.

corollary from what he previously said. For, if the diversity of reception of what the first cause infuses comes about in things according to the diverse power of the recipients, it follows that, since those closer to the first cause have greater power, they receive the first cause and its infusion more perfectly. And because every knowing substance, insofar as it has being more perfectly, knows both the first cause and the infusion of its goodness more perfectly, and the more it both receives and knows this the more it takes delight in it, it follows that the closer something is to the first cause the more it takes delight in it.

PROPOSITION 25[1]

United intellectual substances are not generated from another thing, and every substance that is abiding steadfastly in its essence is not generated from another thing.

But if someone says, it is possible for it to be generated from another thing, we shall say, if it is possible for a substance that is abiding steadfastly in its essence to be generated from another thing, then undoubtedly that substance is diminished, needing that from which it is generated to complete it. The indication of this is generation itself. This is because generation is only a pathway from diminution to completeness. For, if a thing is found needing nothing other than itself for its generation, i.e., for its form and formation, and it is itself the cause of its formation and its completeness, then it is forever complete and entire.

And it comes to be forever the cause of its own formation and its completeness only because of its relation to its cause. Therefore, that relation[2] is its formation and its completeness simultaneously.

Therefore, it has already been made clear that every substance that is abiding steadfastly in its essence is not generated from another thing.

COMMENTARY

{124} The author said above[3] that creatures receive the rule of the first cause in diverse ways according to a threefold diversity: that of unity and multiplicity, which concerns simplicity and composition; that of eternity and time; and that of the spiritual and the corporeal—for corruption happens to what is corporeal and incorruptibility [characterizes] what is <spiritual>. So, here he begins to pursue the above-mentioned kinds of diversity in things. First, the difference between the corruptible <and the

---

1. This proposition relates to Prop. 45 in Proclus's *Elements*. Cf. Dodds, p. 46.12–19. Following Proclus closely, the author asserts that intellectual substances in which the essence and the substance are nothing but the form itself are self-caused and self-complete. As St. Thomas notes, however, the author also holds that this does not preclude the dependence of these pure forms on a higher cause.
2. *comparatio*.
3. Cf. above, S{121}.

incorruptible>; second, the difference between the simple and the composed, in Proposition 28, at: *Every substance that is abiding steadfastly in its essence is simple* etc.; third, the difference between eternity and time, in Proposition 30, at: *Every substance created in time*. Regarding the first he does two things. First, he shows that certain substances are ingenerable. Second, he treats of their incorruptibility,[4] in Proposition 26, at: *Every substance that is abiding steadfastly in itself does not fall* etc.

Regarding the first, he asserts two propositions, the first of which is the following: *United intellectual substances are not generated from another thing*. He calls simple substances *united substances* because every composed thing contains some multiplicity within itself. But, he calls those whose nature is to understand *intellectual substances*, which, since they are immaterial, are also intellectual in act. Now, when he says that they *are not generated from another thing*, this can be understood to mean either "from matter," insofar as the preposition "from" implies a relation to a material cause, or "from an agent cause," insofar as this preposition implies a relation to an efficient cause. The latter meaning seems to be more consistent with what he asserts in the proof of his comment.

The second proposition is the following: *Every substance that is abiding steadfastly in its essence is not generated from another thing*. He calls *a substance that is abiding steadfastly in its essence* that which subsists in itself. {125} But, since to subsist in itself is proper to substance, it accordingly follows that no substance is generated. So, we must say that the substance and essence of a thing is principally form, which a definition principally signifies. Therefore, whatever things have a form founded on matter are not the kind of substances that are abiding steadfastly in their essence. Rather, their essences, i.e., their forms, rest on the foundation of matter. Thus, those substances that are abiding steadfastly in their essence are those which are only forms, not in matter, and it is impossible for such to be generated. We should note, however, that the first proposition is the conclusion of the second proposition.[5] For he proved before that all intelligent substances are abiding steadfastly in their essence, which was held in Proposition 15, *Every knower knows* etc.[6] So, *if every substance that is abiding*

---

4. *incorruptio*.
5. *concluditur ex hac secunda*.
6. Cf. above, S{91}.

steadfastly in its essence is not generated, it follows that every intellectual substance is not generated.

The first of these two propositions is not found in Proclus's book, but only the second, which is [Proposition] 45 there: "Every *authypostaton*," i.e., what subsists in itself, "is ingenerable."[7] And only this proposition is subsequently proved here in the same way as in Proclus's book. For it is clear that everything that is generated is of itself imperfect because it is a being in potency and so *it requires to be completed* or perfected through *that from which it is generated,* i.e., through the one that generates, which reduces it from potency to act. The sign of this is that *generation* is nothing other than a certain *pathway* from the incomplete to the opposite complete, namely, to the incomplete thing that pre-exists, for the terms of generation are privation and form. Now, matter as it exists under privation has the character of the imperfect. But as it exists under form it has the character of the perfect. And so it is clear that *generation* {126} *is the pathway,* or process, from the imperfect to the opposite perfect. So, *if* there is something that does not require something other for its formation, but *is itself the cause of its own formation* because its substance is form, it follows that such a thing is *forever complete,* or perfect. And thus there cannot be a transition in it from the imperfect to the perfect, but it is at once in itself both a being and one, as is said in Book VIII of the *Metaphysics.*[8] It remains, therefore, that every substance that is a subsistent form is not generable.

But lest someone incorrectly understand by this that such substances have no cause of their being, though he said before[9] that *all things have essence through the first being,* he subsequently makes clear how one should understand what he has said. For what he has said, that it is [itself] *the cause of its own formation and completeness,* must not be understood as if it did not depend on some other higher cause. But he said that it is *the cause of its own formation* in the sense that it has a sempiternal *relation to its* first *cause.* Hence in relation[10] to its first cause it has *simultaneously,* i.e., at once, *formation and completeness.* In evidence of this we should note that each thing participates being according to the relation it has to the first principle of being. Now, a thing composed of matter and form has being only

---

7. Proclus, Prop. 45, Dodds, p. 46.12; Vansteenkiste, p. 283.
8. Aristotle, *Metaphysics,* VIII 6, 1045a26ff.
9. Cf. above, S{100}.
10. *comparationem.*

through the acquisition of its form. Hence through its form it has a relation to the first principle of being. But because matter temporally pre-exists form in a generated thing, it follows that it does not always and simultaneously have the above relation to the principle of being, since it was matter, but with form supervening afterwards. Therefore, if a certain substance {127} is form itself, it follows that it always has the above relation to the first cause and it does not come to it after a time but is *simultaneously* concomitant with its substance, which is form.

So, *therefore, it is has been made clear that every substance that is abiding steadfastly in its essence* is *not* generated *from* something.

PROPOSITION 26[1]

Every substance that is abiding steadfastly in itself does not fall under corruption.

But if someone should say, it is possible for a substance that is abiding steadfastly in itself to fall under corruption, we shall say, if it is possible for a substance that is abiding steadfastly in itself to fall under corruption, it would be possible for it to be separated from its essence and [yet] be fixed, abiding steadfastly in its essence without its essence. But this is absurd and impossible because, due to the fact that it is one, simple and incomposite, it is itself simultaneously both cause and effect. Now, the corruption of anything that falls under corruption happens only because of its separation from its cause. As long as a thing remains dependent upon its cause, which maintains and conserves it, it neither perishes nor is destroyed.[2] So, if this is so, the cause of a substance that is abiding steadfastly in its essence is never separated,[3] because it is inseparable from its essence, due to the fact that it is itself its cause in its formation.

And it becomes the cause of itself only because of its relation to its cause, and that relation is its formation. Furthermore, because it is always related to its cause and is itself the cause of that relation, it is cause of itself in the way we have described, because it neither perishes nor is destroyed, since it is simultaneously cause and effect, as we have just shown.

Therefore, it is already clear that every substance that is abiding steadfastly in itself is neither destroyed nor corrupted.

---

1. This proposition relates to Prop. 46 in Proclus's *Elements*. Cf. Dodds, p. 46.20–28. Here the author argues that the self-subsistent substance whose essence is identical with its formal cause is simple and incomposite, and consequently free from the corruption characterizing material composites. St. Thomas distinguishes two senses of "the cause of being," namely, the formal cause and the efficient cause. Only God is self-sufficient or characterized as "abiding steadfastly in itself" in both senses.

2. Though it does not affect the translation, we read *neque etiam destruitur* instead of Bardenhewer's and Saffrey's *neque destruitur*. In doing so we follow Latin manuscripts BS and Aosta in accord with the Arabic, which has *aidan*.

3. The Latin here is a mistranslation of the Arabic, which has, "If this is so, the substance subsistent through its essence never separates itself from its cause . . ."

COMMENTARY

[The author] treated things that are not generated before.[4] Here he treats corruptible and incorruptible things; first, incorruptible things [here]; second, corruptible things, in Proposition 27: *Every destructible substance* etc. Regarding the first, he asserts the following proposition: *Every substance that is abiding steadfastly in itself does not fall under corruption.* Proclus also asserts this in his book [as Proposition] 46, in these words, "Every authypostaton is incorruptible."[5]

{128} In evidence of this proposition we should note that, since the preposition "in"[6] denotes cause, that is said to be *abiding steadfastly,* or to subsist, *in itself* which has no cause of being other than itself. The cause of being is twofold: the form by which something is in act, and the agent that makes [it] to be in act. So, if "to be abiding steadfastly in itself" means that it does not depend upon a higher agent, then to be abiding steadfastly in itself applies only to God, who is the first efficient cause[7] on whom all second causes depend, as is clear from the [discussions] above. But if "to be abiding steadfastly in itself" means what is not formed through any other thing, but is itself form, then to be abiding steadfastly in itself applies to all immaterial substances. For a substance composed of matter and form is abiding steadfastly in itself only by reason of parts, because matter is in act through form and form is sustained in matter, just as something is said to move itself by reason of parts because one part of it moves while another part of it is moved. Thus, it is evident that to be abiding steadfastly in itself can apply only to a substance that is a form without matter. Such a substance is of necessity incorruptible. For it is clear that in corruptible things corruption occurs because something is separated from its formal cause, through which it[8] has being in act. For just as generation, which is the pathway to being, is through the acquisition of a form, so corruption, which is the pathway to nonbeing, is through the loss of a form. So, if a substance that is abiding steadfastly

---

4. Cf. above, S{124}.
5. *authypostaton,* i.e., self-subsistent. Proclus, Prop. 46, Dodds, p. 46.20; Vansteenkiste, p. 283.
6. *per.*   7. *causa agente.*
8. *aliquid.*

in its essence were to be corrupted, it would be necessary for it to be separated from its formal cause. But its form is its essence. Therefore, it would be separated from its essence, which is impossible. Therefore, it is not possible for a substance that is abiding steadfastly in itself to be corrupted.

But lest someone should think[9] that substances of this sort that abide steadfastly in their essence do not depend upon some higher efficient cause, {129} he subsequently excludes this, at: *And it becomes the cause of itself* etc. He says that this must not be understood in such a way that a substance of this sort would be the cause of itself, as if it were not dependent upon some higher efficient cause. Rather, he says this because such a substance in itself has *a relation to* the first *cause* insofar as [the first cause] is the cause of its *formation*. For we see that material things are referred to the first cause in order to receive being from it through their form. And for this reason a substance whose entire essence is form has in itself *always* a relation to its *cause*, and this relation is not caused in such a substance through some other form. And so he says that it is cause of itself in the way mentioned above. And so it is that it cannot be corrupted, as he has shown.[10]

Therefore, it is clear that every substance that is abiding steadfastly is incorruptible.

9. *credat.* 10. Cf. above, S{128}.

PROPOSITION 27[1]

Every destructible, nonsempiternal substance is either composed or supported by[2] another thing.

[This is] because a substance either needs[3] the things from which it is and it is composed from them, or it requires [something] supporting [it] in its stability and essence. Therefore, when it is separated from what supports it, it is corrupted and destroyed.

But if a substance is neither composed nor supported, it is simple and never destroyed or diminished[4] at all.

COMMENTARY

After showing what the condition of an incorruptible substance is, [the author] shows here the condition of a corruptible substance, asserting this proposition: *Every destructible, {130} nonsempiternal substance is either composed or supported by another thing.* And Proclus asserts this same proposition [as Proposition] 48 in his book.[5]

The proof for this proposition is that if everything that is abiding stead-

---

1. This proposition relates to Prop. 48 in Proclus's *Elements*. Cf. Dodds, p. 48.5–10. With this proposition, which is closely dependent on Proclus, the author clarifies his understanding of simple substances with a brief discussion of composite substance. Corruptible substances are either composites of parts or dependent on some subject (matter) for their sustenance. St. Thomas notes that this proposition is relevant to the understanding of both intelligences and the human intellectual soul. For he holds that the soul is not completely dependent upon matter, since it is not the case that all the activities of the soul involve matter.
2. *est delata super.*
3. The Latin translator apparently read *yakunu muntaqisan* instead of the correct reading, *yakunu muntaqidan*, "is dissoluble."
4. The Arabic is considerably clearer for this proposition: "Every destructible and non-perpetual substance either is composite or is present in something else, because the substance is either dissoluble into the things from which it is, such that it is composite, or it needs a substrate for its stability and subsistence, such that when it separates itself from its substrate, it corrupts and is destroyed. So if the substance is not composite and present [in something else, but] is simple and per se, then it is perpetual and altogether indestructible and indissoluble." See Taylor (1981).
5. Cf. Proclus, Prop. 48, Dodds, p. 48.5–6; Vansteenkiste, p. 283.

fastly in itself is incorruptible, as was proved,[6] then everything that is corrupted must not be abiding steadfastly in itself but must need something else to sustain it. This happens in two ways: in one way, when a whole needs parts for its constitution. So, when the parts separate from one another, corruption follows. In another way, when the form is not subsistent but needs for its stability a *supporting* subject. And so, when the *supporting* subject is not disposed to such a form, there must take place a separation of the form from the subject, and so corruption follows. Hence, it is clear that every corruptible substance either is composed of diverse parts, through whose dissolution the corruption of the whole follows (as is evident in compound bodies), or the form needs matter or a subject to sustain it, and so through the change of the subject corruption follows (as is evident in simple bodies and in accidents).

And for this reason we can accept the corollary that, *if a* certain *substance is* not *composed* but *is simple and is not supported* by a subject that it needs for it to be, as it were, but is abiding steadfastly in itself, it is entirely incorruptible. This is evident in both an intelligence and the intellectual soul. Regarding the latter, it is clear that [the intellectual soul] is not a form supported by the matter to which it gives being in such a way that [the intellectual soul] is totally dependent upon it, because it would then follow that none of its activities[7] would be without the involvement[8] of corporeal matter, which is clearly false from what is proved in Book III of *On the Soul*.[9]

---

6. Cf. above, S{127ff}. 7. *nulla eius operatio.*
8. *communione.*
9. Aristotle, *On the Soul*, III 7ff. For a more complete treatment of what St. Thomas says here, see *Quaest. Disp. de Anima*, Q. 1 and 2.

{131} PROPOSITION 28[1]

Every substance that is abiding steadfastly in its essence is simple and is not divided.

But if anyone should say, it is possible for it to be divided, we will say, if it is possible for a substance that is abiding steadfastly in itself to be divided and [yet] it is simple, then it would be possible for the essence of its part again to be through its essence, just as the essence of a whole [is]. So, if that is possible, the part would revert upon itself, and every part of it would revert upon itself, just as the reversion of a whole upon its essence is. But this is impossible. So, if this is impossible, then a substance that is abiding steadfastly in itself is indivisible and is simple.

If it is not simple but is composed, one part of it would be better than another part, while one part of it would be worse than another part. Thus, a better thing would be from a worse thing, and a worse thing from a better thing, when every part of it is separated from every other part of it.

Therefore, its totality is not sufficient in itself, since it needs its parts from which it is composed. And this belongs, not to the nature of a simple thing, but rather to the nature of composed substances.

Therefore, it is already established that every substance that is abiding steadfastly in its essence is simple and is not divided. And when it does not receive division and is simple, it receives neither corruption nor destruction.

COMMENTARY

After attending to the difference in substances according to generation and corruption, [the author] attends here to the difference in substances that can be considered according to simplicity and composition. To do this he introduces two propositions, the second of which seems to be the converse of the first. The first proposition, then, is the following: *Every substance that is abiding steadfastly in its essence is simple and is not divided.* Pro-

---

1. This proposition relates to Prop. 47 in Proclus's *Elements*. Cf. Dodds, p. 46.29–48.4. Here the author establishes the indivisible and simple nature of a self-subsistent substance through consideration of its reversion on itself and the relative ranking of its parts if it were composite. St. Thomas notes that the arguments presented here are much more fully and carefully presented in Proclus.

PROPOSITION 28

clus also asserts this proposition in his book [as Proposition] 47, in these words: "Every *authypostaton* is impartible[2] and simple."[3]

It seems that we should note here that "simple" and "impartible" are the same in subject, but differ in notion. For something is called "impartible" {132} through the privation of division because it is not divisible into many. But something is called "simple" through the privation of composition because it is not composed of many. So [the author] proves first that a substance that abides steadfastly in itself is indivisible, and second that it is simple.

Proclus better proves the first point than the author does here. For this is Proclus's proof. He says, "For, if it were partible, being *authypostaton*," i.e., subsistent in itself, "it would establish itself as partible, and the whole of it[4] would return to itself[5] and every [part] would be in every [part] of it. But this is impossible. Therefore, [anything] *authypostaton* [is] impartible."[6] In evidence of this we should note here that something is understood to be abiding steadfastly in itself, not by reason of a part, so that one part of it would abide through another [part], as happens in material substances, but by reason of the whole, so that the whole abides steadfastly in itself [as] a whole. Furthermore, everything is turned to that through which it abides steadfastly as an effect to a cause, and it must be in [its cause] as in its foundation. So, if something partible were abiding steadfastly in itself, each part of it would have to be abiding steadfastly through each [part] and each [part] would have to be founded in each [part]. But this is impossible because it would then follow that one and the same part of it would be simultaneously both cause and effect with respect to the same thing, which is impossible.

Now, in this book the author proves the matter in this way. What belongs to something in itself would, if it were partible, belong to each part of it. So, if something partible were to be abiding steadfastly in itself, each part of it would have to be abiding steadfastly in itself, and so not depend upon another [part] for the constitution of the whole. But this proof is

---

2. *impartibile*.
3. Proclus, Prop. 47, Dodds, p. 46.29; Vansteenkiste, p. 283. *Impartibile* ("impartible," i.e., without parts) is Moerbeke's translation of Proclus's term *ameres*. In the commentary St. Thomas explains this term to mean "not divisible into many."
4. *totum ipsum*.
5. *vertetur ad seipsum*.
6. Proclus, Prop. 47.30–33, Dodds p.46; Vansteenkiste, p.283.

not very effective, because whatever belongs to some whole in itself need not belong to each of its parts. For there is a type of whole that consists of similar parts, such as air or water, and another type of [whole] that consists of dissimilar [parts], such as an animal or a house.

{133} Now, he proves in a twofold argument that what is abiding steadfastly in itself is simple, i.e., not composed of many. In everything composed of many parts it is necessary to maintain that there be a certain order of parts, namely, that one *part of it* be *better and* another *worse*. For many come to constitute one thing in a certain order, just as multiplicity proceeds in a certain order from one. Hence we see that, in the composition of a natural body, form is more preeminent[7] than matter, and in the composition of a compound body, one element dominates, and in the composition of the parts of an animal, one member is more principal than another, and in the parts of a continuum, one part comes closer to a point, which is the principle of magnitude, than another. Therefore, if something composed of many parts is abiding steadfastly in itself, each part of it will have to be abiding steadfastly due to each other part, and so a *better* part will have to depend *upon a worse* part, and conversely.

The second argument is that everything that is abiding steadfastly in itself is sufficient to itself in its being, not needing another for its subsistence. Through this a dependency upon a formal and material cause that gives it subsistence is excluded, but not a dependency upon an efficient cause. But anything composed of parts *is not sufficient* to itself but *needs* for its subsistence *the parts of which it is composed*, which stand as the material cause in relation to the whole. Therefore, nothing composed of parts is abiding steadfastly in itself. Therefore, *every substance that is abiding steadfastly* in itself *is simple*. We should realize, however, that Proclus explicitly asserts this second argument in his book,[8] while the author of this book presents it by way of a conclusion.

7. *praestantior.*
8. Cf. Proclus, Prop. 47, Dodds, p. 46.32–48.4; Vansteenkiste, p. 283.

{134} PROPOSITION 29[1]

Every simple substance is abiding steadfastly in itself, namely, in its essence.

For it is created without time and is higher[2] in its substantiality than temporal substances. The indication of this is that it is not generated from something else, because it is abiding steadfastly through its essence. And substances generated from something else are composed substances that fall under generation.

Therefore, it is already clear that every substance that is abiding steadfastly in its essence is only atemporal, and that it is loftier and higher[3] than time and temporal things.

COMMENTARY

Here [the author] asserts the following proposition, which is the converse of the previous one: *Every simple substance is abiding steadfastly in itself, namely, in its essence.* But we should realize that he does not prove this proposition in his comment, but he inserts something else, which he proves, namely, that *a substance abiding steadfastly in itself is created without time and is in its substantiality higher than temporal substances.* And this is Proposition 51 in Proclus's book, in these words: "Every *authypostaton* is free from those things that are measured by time according to their substance."[4]

We should note here that when Proclus says, "according to their substance," this can refer either to temporal substances themselves, whose substantial being is subject to variation, whence they are said "to be measured by time according to their substance." Or it can refer to substances that are abiding steadfastly in themselves, which are according to their substance higher than temporal substances. {135}

---

1. This proposition relates to Prop. 51 in Proclus's *Elements*. Cf. Dodds, p. 50.1–6. This discussion of the atemporal nature of self-subsistent substances is little more than a translation of Proclus.
2. That is, more transcendent.
3. *altior et superior.*
4. Proclus, Prop. 51, Dodds, p. 50.1–2.

So, [the author] gives the following proof for this additional proposition. For it was shown before[5] that no substance that is abiding steadfastly in itself falls under generation. But all substances that are measured by time according to their substance fall under generation. For they are measured by time according to their substance because their substantial being changes[6] through generation and corruption. Therefore, it remains that no *substance that is abiding steadfastly in* itself falls under *time*; rather, [such a substance] *is higher* than all temporal substances.

From this proposition proved in this way, we can conclude to what [the author] stated. For, if it is proper to a substance that is abiding steadfastly in itself not to fall under time according to its substance, then this belongs to every simple substance, because every generable substance that falls under time is composed of matter and form. It remains that every simple substance is abiding steadfastly in itself, which is what he first proposed.

5. Cf. above, S{124ff}.
6. *variatur.*

PROPOSITION 30[1]

Every substance created in time either is always in time and time does not overreach[2] it, because it and time are created equally; or it overreaches time and time overreaches it, because it was created at a certain moment[3] of time.

This is because, if created things follow one another, and only that substance follows a higher substance which is like it, not a substance unlike it, then there are substances like the higher substance, and there are created substances that time does not overreach, which are before substances that are[4] made like sempiternal substances, and there are substances that are not continuous with time[5] [and] are created at a certain moment of time. Therefore, it is not possible for substances created at a certain moment of time to be continuous with sempiternal substances, because they are not at all made like them. Therefore, substances sempiternal in time are {136} *those which are continuous with sempiternal substances, and they are intermediaries between fixed substances and substances bounded by time.[6]*

And it is possible for sempiternal substances, which are above time, to follow

---

1. This proposition relates to Prop. 55 in Proclus's *Elements*. Cf. Dodds, p. 52.15–54.3. Here the author considers the hierarchy of substances with respect to their relation to time. The three sections of the hierarchy discussed here are: (1) the higher substances, which are above time both in substance and in activity; (2) the temporal substances, which are sempiternal in time and inseparable from it; and (3) substances that are not sempiternal and not continuous with time, i.e., separable from time, having perpetuity only through generation of like individuals.

2. *non superfluit*. For the Arabic text the Latin translator read *ghaira fadil* instead of the correct reading, *ghaira fasil*, "is inseparable." In Arabic the forms are distinguished only by the placement of one diacritical mark or point. This problem persists for the roots *f-s-l* and *f-d-l* throughout this proposition, with severe consequences for the Latin translation. Our translation is of the Latin, as it must be. But a complete translation of the Arabic text of this proposition is supplied in Appendix 1.

3. *in quibusdam horis*.

4. Pattin adds <*non*> to his edition of the *De Causis*. This addition is clearly required in the Arabic text. However, there is no evidence at all that *non* was in the original Latin translation.

5. *abscisae a tempore*. Literally, "cut off from time."

6. *substantias sectas in tempore*. Literally, this is "cut off in time," though the sense is that these are not coequal and continuous with time but rather bounded by it because they come into being and pass out of being.

temporal substances created in time only with the mediation of temporal substances sempiternal in time. And these substances become intermediaries only because they share[7] in permanence with more sublime substances and through generation they share in time with temporal substances that are not continuous with time.[8] For, although they are sempiternal, nevertheless their permanence is through generation and motion. And substances sempiternal with time are like sempiternal substances that are above time in durability, but they are not made like them in motion and generation. Substances bounded by time are not in any way[9] made like sempiternal substances that are above time. Therefore, if they are not made like them, then they cannot receive them or touch them.

Therefore, there are necessary substances that touch sempiternal substances, which are above time, and they will touch substances bounded by time. Therefore, through their motion they will assemble[10] between substances bounded by time and sempiternal substances, which are above time. And through their durability they will assemble between substances that are above time and substances that are under time, namely, [those] which fall under generation and corruption. And they will assemble between good substances and base substances, so that the base substances are not deprived of the good substances nor deprived of all that is good and fit,[11] nor be without endurance and stability.

Therefore, it has already been shown from this that there are two kinds of durability, one of which is eternal and the other temporal. But one of the two durabilities is abiding steadfastly and at rest, while the other durability is in motion. And one of them is united[12] and all its activities are simultaneous, [such that] one of [its activities] is not before another. But the other is flowing,[13] extended, [and] some of its activities are before others. And the totality of one of them is through its essence, while the totality of the other is through its parts, in which each [part] is separated from its counterpart in terms of first and last.[14]

Therefore, it is already clear that among substances there are some that are sempiternal above time. And among them there are sempiternal [substances] equal to time and time does not overreach them. And among them there are [some] that are bounded by time, and time overreaches them from the higher of them down to the lower of them, and [these] are substances that fall under generation and corruption.

7. communicant.
8. substantiis temporalibus abscisis.
9. per aliquem modorum.
10. aggregabunt.
11. omni bonitate et omni conveniente.
12. aggregatur.
13. currens.
14. per modum primum et postremum.

COMMENTARY

After attending to the difference in things according to generation and corruption, as well as simplicity and composition, [the author] here attends, in the third place, to the difference between what is temporal and what is eternal. Regarding this, he does two things. First, he shows how some things are in a twofold way both sempiternal and temporal. Second, he shows how the eternal and the temporal exist simultaneously, at: *Between a thing whose substance* etc.[15] Or, in the first he asserts the order of temporal things to one another; in the second the order of eternal things to one another, at: *Between a thing whose substance* etc. Regarding the first, he asserts the following proposition: {**137**} *Every substance created in time either is always in time and time does not overreach it, because it and time are created equally; or it overreaches time and time overreaches it, because it is created at a certain moment of time.*

In evidence of this we should note that, because time is the number of motion, every mobile substance is said to be created in time. Now, there are two kinds of mobile substance. One of them is motion in the whole of time, such as a heavenly body, whose motion is equivalent with time because time is in the first place and in itself the measure of the motion of the heavens and by that motion it provides the measure for[16] all other motions. And this [is so] whether we assert that the motion of the heavens always was and always will be, as Aristotle and certain other philosophers maintained, or also that the motion of the heavens was not always nor will always be, as the faith of the Church teaches, because in this way also the motion of the heavens is equal to time. For there was no time before the motion of the heavens began nor will there be time after the motion of the heavens ceases to be. Hence the substance of a heavenly body is in every way always in time by reason of its motion, and time does not surpass it, but both are equal to one another. But some substances are mobile and their being and motion are not in the whole of time but in some part of time, as is evident with generable and corruptible substances. And because such a substance does not have a relation to the whole of time but to a part of time, one part of time is found to be greater than their duration and another part less. Hence it is that such a substance

---

15. Cf. Prop. 31. 16. *mensurat*.

surpasses time with respect to that part [of time] which is less than the duration [of the substance]. In turn, it is surpassed by time with respect to that part [of time] which is greater than the duration [of the substance]. For in Proclus's book we find Proposition 55, [which states this] more plainly and briefly in this way: "Everything that subsists according to time [does so] either because it is always in time or for a time has [its] hypostasis[17] in a part of time."[18]

{138} Now, to clarify the stated proposition, [the author] first gives the proof. Second, he infers a certain corollary, at: *Therefore it has already been shown from this* etc. The same proof is given in both books. For the order of things proceeds in such a way that like things follow one another. But those things which are entirely dissimilar follow one another in the grades of things only through some intermediary. So we see that a complete animal and a plant are entirely dissimilar with respect to two things. For a complete animal has senses and moves with progressive motion. But a plant has neither of these. Therefore, nature does not proceed immediately from complete animals to plants but produces in between incomplete animals, which have senses, like animals, but do not move, like plants. Now, it is clear that spiritual substances, which are made equal to eternity, as was said before,[19] and generable and corruptible substances are entirely dissimilar. For spiritual substances both always are and are immobile, and neither of these [characteristics] belongs to generable and corruptible substances. Hence it is necessary to maintain that between these two extremes there is some intermediary, which is like both extremes, so that the grades of things proceed through like things.

Proclus proceeds by investigating the matter in this way. Between what is "always" and immovably a being and what is "for a time" and is movably, there can be found only three kinds of "intermediary," namely: (1) that "which always" is in motion, (2) that "which" immovably is "for a time," and (3) that "which" is "for a time." But this third kind cannot be an intermediary because that "which" is "for a time" is the same as what is in motion for a time, which we have called an extreme. So, too, what immovably is for a time cannot be an intermediary. For it is impossible for some such thing to be, for something ceases to be only

17. *hypostasim.* I.e., its being or reality.
18. Proclus, Prop. 55, Dodds, p. 52.8–10; Vansteenkiste, p. 286.
19. Cf. above, S{15}.

through some change. Hence what is immovably cannot be [something that is] a being for a time. Rather, it is always a being. So, it remains that an intermediary between what always is immovably and what for a time is movably, is that which is always {**139**} in motion. For this [nature] belongs to the higher [extreme], for the reason that it is always being, but to the lower extreme, for the reason that it is in motion.[20] Now, [the author] uses the word "generation" in general for any change whatsoever because in any motion both generation and corruption are involved, as is said in Book VIII of the *Physics*.[21] Thus, substances that are always in motion, namely, heavenly bodies, touch both extremes according to a certain likeness. And through them higher immobile substances are joined in a certain way to lower generable and corruptible substances, insofar as the power of higher substances is brought down to generable and corruptible things through the motion of the heavenly bodies.

Now, he infers subsequently a certain corollary from these things, namely, that "perpetuity" or perpetual *durability* is of two kinds: one by way of eternity, and the other by way of the whole of time. These perpetual durations differ in three ways. First, eternal perpetuity is fixed, abiding steadfastly, immobile. But temporal perpetuity is flowing and mobile insofar as time is the measure of motion, while eternity is understood as the measure of immobile being. Second, eternal perpetuity is all *at the same time*, "collected" into one, as it were. But temporal perpetuity has successive "extension according to before and after," which belong to the nature of time. Third, eternal perpetuity is simple, "a whole" existing "according to itself." But *the universality* or totality of temporal perpetuity is according to different *parts* succeeding one another.

20. I.e., it is becoming. Cf. Proclus, Prop. 55, Dodds, p. 52.20–29.
21. Aristotle, *Physics*, VIII 3, 254a11–12.

{140} PROPOSITION 31[1]

Between a thing whose substance and action are in the moment of eternity and a thing whose substance and action are in the moment of time there exists an intermediary, and it is that whose substance belongs to the moment of eternity, while [its] activity [belongs to] the moment of time.

This is because a thing whose substance falls under time because time contains it, falls under time in all its dispositions. For this reason its action also falls under time. Because when the substance of a thing falls under time, undoubtedly its action also falls under time. But a thing which falls under time in all its dispositions is separate from a thing which falls under eternity in all its dispositions. There is continuity only among like things. Therefore, there must be another third intermediary thing between the two, whose substance falls under eternity, while its action falls under time. For it is impossible that there be a thing whose substance falls under time but its action under eternity. For then its action would be better than its substance. But this is impossible.

Therefore, it is clear that between things which fall under time in both their substances and their actions and things whose substances and actions both fall under the moment of eternity there are things which fall under eternity in their substances, while they fall under time in their activities, as we have shown.

COMMENTARY

In the preceding proposition [the author] clarified the order of temporal things to one another. Here he clarifies the order of eternal things to one another. First, he asserts that among eternal things there is something which is eternal in every way and something which is both in a way eternal and in a way temporal. Second, he clarifies the condition of what is both in a way eternal and in a way temporal, in Proposition 32, at: *Every*

---

1. This proposition relates to Prop. 106 in Proclus's *Elements*. Cf. Dodds, p. 94.21–30. As St. Thomas notes, the previous proposition clarified the author's understanding of the order of temporal things, while this propostion does so for the order of eternal things. St. Thomas refers to it in *De Veritate*, Q. 28, A. 9, 3 s.c. and *Quodlibet*. V, Q. 4. A. 7c.

substance etc. Regarding the first, he asserts the following proposition: *Between a thing whose substance and action are in the moment of eternity and a thing whose substance and action are in the moment of time there exists an intermediary, and it is that whose substance belongs to the moment of eternity, while [its] activity [belongs to] the moment of time.*

{141} Here it seems that the "moment" of eternity or time is taken [to mean] "measure," so that what is measured by eternity he says is in the moment of eternity and what is measured by time he says is in the moment of time. Proclus also asserts this proposition [as Proposition] 106 in his book in these words: "Between everything that is in every way eternal according to substance and activity, and what has substance in time, there is an intermediary, which is in one way eternal but in another way measured by time."[2]

Now, it could appear to someone that this intermediary is a heavenly body, which is incorruptible in its substance, while its motion is measured by time. But this is not sound. For in the preceding proposition[3] what is always in motion is simply placed among temporal things. For as the Philosopher says in Book IV of the *Physics*:[4] "As time measures motion, so the 'now' of time measures what is mobile." Hence a heavenly body which is in motion is not in the moment of eternity but in the moment of time. Furthermore, motion is not the action of what is moved but rather something that it undergoes.[5] It is the action of the mover, as is said in Book III of the *Physics*.[6]

The principle of motion is the soul, as was held in Proposition 2.[7] So, because a noble soul is immobile in itself {142} but its action is motion, it follows that the soul in its substance is in the moment of eternity, while its action is in time. Both the substance and the activity of a body that is in motion is in time, while both the substance and action of an intelligence is in the moment of eternity.

Now, the proof of this proposition is similar to the proof of the preceding proposition. For it was said before[8] that the grades of beings are

---

2. Proclus, Prop. 106, Dodds, p. 94.21–23; Vansteenkiste, p. 493.
3. Cf. above, S{137}.
4. Aristotle, *Physics*, IV 11, 219b22–23.
5. *magis passio*.
6. Aristotle, *Physics*, III 3, 202a26–27.
7. Cf. above, S{15}.
8. Cf. above, S{138}.

continuous with one another according to a certain likeness. Hence those things that are totally dissimilar follow one another in the order of things through some intermediary which has a likeness to both extremes. But a thing whose substance and action is in time is totally unlike that whose substance and action is in eternity. *Therefore, there must be between* them *a third intermediary thing,* so that either its *substance falls under eternity, while* [its] *action under time,* or conversely. But it cannot be that *the substance* of something be in *time but* [its] *action* in *eternity,* because *then* [its] *action would be* higher and *better* than [its] *substance* and the effect than the cause, which *is impossible.* Therefore, it remains that that intermediary thing is in the moment of eternity with regard to its substance but in time with regard to [its] activity. And this is what we intended to prove.

{143} PROPOSITION 32[1]

Every substance that falls under eternity in some of its dispositions, while falling under time in other of its dispositions, is simultaneously a being and a coming to be.

For every thing that falls under eternity is truly a being and every thing that falls under time is truly a coming to be. Therefore, if this is so, then, if one thing falls under both eternity and time, it is a being and a coming to be not in one way but rather in different ways.[2]

Therefore, it is already clear from what we have said that everything that comes to be, falling under time in its substance, has a substance that depends on the pure being, which is both the cause of durability and the cause of all things, whether sempiternal or destructible.[3]

There must be a one causing the acquisition of unities while it is itself unacquired, though[4] all the rest of the unities are acquired. And the indication of this is what I say: If a one is found that causes acquisition [but is itself] unacquired, then what is the difference between it and the first thing that causes acquisition? For it can only be either that it is like it in all its dispositions or that there is a difference between the two. Therefore, if it is like it in all its dispositions, then one of them is not first and the other second. But if one of them is not like the other in all its dispositions, then one of them is first and the other second. Therefore, that in which there is a fixed unity not found to be from another is the first true one,

---

1. This proposition relates to Prop. 107 and Prop. 116 in Proclus's *Elements*. Cf. Dodds, pp. 94.32–96.7 and p. 102.13, 102.17–23, 102.25–26. This final proposition consists of two parts. The first half draws on Proclus's Prop. 107 for the teaching that a substance that is in both eternity and time is both a being as eternal and stable and a coming-into-being as temporal and changing. But all that has come into being and is substantially subject to time is ultimately linked to the Pure Being which is the cause of all perpetuity and all things, according to the author's exposition. The second half has little relation to the first and draws on Proclus's Prop. 116. Here it is argued that all unity ultimately derives from a "First True One" as the uncaused cause of the unity participated by all other things. This awkwardly formed concluding proof of the True One is especially interesting for its similarity to a proof found in al-Kindi's *On First Philosophy*. Cf. *Rasa'il al-Kindi al-falsafiyah*, ed. Muhammad 'Abdalhadi Abu Rida, I (Cairo, 1950), pp. 160–62.

2. *per modum et modum.*   3. The Arabic has "a true one."
4. *sed.*

as we have shown. But that in which unity is found to be from another is in addition to the first true one. So, if it is from another, it is a unity acquired from the first one. Therefore, it happens that unity again belongs to the true pure one and the remaining ones, and that there is unity only because of the true one, which is the cause of unity.

Therefore, it is already clear and plain that every unity after the true one is acquired and created. But the first true one creates unities, causing acquisition [but is] not [itself] acquired, as we have shown.

COMMENTARY

Because in the preceding proposition [the author] proved that there is some thing whose substance is in eternity but whose action in time, he shows subsequently the condition of such a substance in this last proposition, saying: *Every substance that falls under eternity in some of its dispositions, while falling under time in other of its dispositions, is simultaneously a being and a coming to be.* Proclus asserts this same proposition [as Proposition] {144} 107 in his book in these words: "Everything that is in one way eternal but in another way temporal is simultaneously both a being and a coming to be."[5]

Now, to clarify this proposition [the author] does three things. First, he states the proof of the proposition he has introduced, which [proof] depends wholly upon the meaning[6] of the terms. For, because eternity is all at the same time, lacking succession of past and future, as was held above,[7] he calls what is in eternity "a being" because it is always in act. But time consists in the succession of past and future. Hence what is in time is in [the state of] becoming, as it were, which the word "a coming to be" signifies. So, what is wholly in eternity is wholly a being. And what is wholly in time is wholly a coming to be. But what is in one way in time but in another way in eternity is simultaneously a being and a coming to be.

Second, at: *Therefore it is already clear* etc., he introduces a certain corollary. For the disposition among beings is such that lower things depend

---

5. Proclus, Prop. 107, Dodds, p. 94.32–33; Vansteenkiste, p. 493. Moerbeke translates Proclus's *genesis* as *generatio* ("coming to be").
6. *significatione*.
7. Cf. above, S{11ff}.

upon higher things. Hence what is wholly a coming to be, as having substance and activity in time, must depend upon what is simultaneously a being and a coming to be which has substance in eternity but activity in time. This must depend upon what is wholly in eternity with respect to substance and activity. And this further depends upon the first being above eternity, which is the principle of the duration *of all things* both *sempiternal* and corruptible.

Third, at: *There must be a one causing* etc., he shows that all things depend upon this first one. To understand what he says here, we ought to take Proposition 116 in Proclus, which is as follows: "Every god is participable, except one."[8] Proclus asserts this proposition to show how the Platonists {145} maintained that there are many gods. For they did not maintain that all [the gods] are equal[9] but that one is first, which participates nothing but is essentially the one and good. They maintained that the other lower gods participate the one and good itself. And he presents the proof of this because it is clear that the first and supreme God participates nothing, otherwise he would not be the first cause of all things. For what participates always presupposes something prior which is essentially. But he proves that all other gods participate through the fact that, if the first god is one essentially and not by way of participation, either one of the other gods is likewise one and thus in no way different from the first, or it must be one by way of participation. For, if one itself is the essence of the first, then, if something differs from it as a second that exists after it, it must not be such that its essence is one itself but that it participates [its] unity.

And this is what [the author] proposes here: that *it is* necessary to assert that there is *a* first *one which causes unities* to be acquired, i.e., from which whatever are one participate unity, *but it does not acquire*, i.e., it does not participate unity from some other. And what was stated he presents as a proof of this.

And so ends the entire Book of Causes. Thanks be to almighty God, who is the first cause of all things.

---

8. Proclus, Prop. 116, Dodds, p. 102.13; Vansteenkiste, p. 290.; cf. above, S{18}.
9. *omnes ex aequo.*

Appendices and Bibliography

APPENDIX 1

ANOTHER PROPOSITION 29
[Proposition 30(29) Translated from the Arabic][1]

Every substance originated in time is either perpetual in time and time is inseparable from it because it and time were equally originated; or it is separate from time and time is separate from it because it was originated in a certain moment of time.

For, if originated things follow one after another and the higher substance follows only the substance similar to it and not the substance dissimilar to it, then the substances similar to the higher substances (namely the originated substances from which time is not separate) are before the substances that are <not> similar to the perpetual substances (namely the substances not continuous with time and originated in certain moments of time). For it is impossible for substances originated in certain moments of time to be in contact with perpetual substances, because they are not at all similar to them. The substances perpetual in time are, then, those which are in contact with perpetual substances and are intermediate between the fixed substances and the substances that are not continuous with time.

It is impossible for perpetual substances above time to follow temporal substances that are not continuous with time except through the mediation of temporal substances perpetual in time. And these substances came to be intermediate because they share in perpetuity with higher perpetual substances and they share in time with temporal substances that are not continuous <with time> through generation. For, although they are perpetual, their perpetuity is through generation and motion. Substances perpetual with time are similar to perpetual substances above time in perpetuity and dissimilar to them in motion and generation. As for substances that are not continuous with time, these are in no way whatsoever similar to perpetual substances above time. And if they are not similar to them, then they cannot receive them or be in contact with them.

It is therefore necessary that there be substances that are in contact with perpetual substances above time so that they are in contact with substances that are

---

1. Revised translation based on Taylor (1981), pp. 330–32; Arabic text, pp. 260–68.

not continuous with time. So, through their motion they join temporal substances that are not continuous with time and perpetual substances that are above time. Through their perpetuity they join substances that are above time and substances that are under time, i.e., falling under generation and corruption. [In this way] they join noble substances and ignoble substances, lest ignoble substances destroy noble substances and so destroy all beauty and all goodness and not have any persistence and fixity.

It has become plain from these proofs, then, that there are two sorts of perpetuity, one eternal and another temporal. The perpetuity of one of the two [sorts of perpetual substance] is subsistent and quiescent, while the perpetuity of the other is mobile; one of them is concentrated, and all its activities are together without some being before others, while the other is flowing and protracted [through time] and some of its activities are before others; and the completeness of one of them is through its essence, while the completeness of the other is through its parts, every one of which is distinct from others in terms of priority and posteriority.

It has become clear and evident, then, that there are some substances perpetual above time, there are some substances equal with time and time is inseparable from them, and there are some that are not continuous with time and time is separate from them both above and below, and these [latter] are substances falling under generation and corruption.

APPENDIX 2

The following list of references to the works of St. Thomas in which he explicitly refers to the *Book of Causes* and its various propositions is taken from C. Vansteenkiste, O.P., "Il *Liber de Causis* negli scritti di San Tommaso," *Angelicum* XXXV (1958), pp. 325–74. The appendix is divided into two parts:

I. A numbered list of citations of the *Book of Causes* found in the works of St. Thomas.

II. A listing of these citation numbers under those propositions of the *Book of Causes* to which they refer. The summaries and divisions of the propositions are by Vansteenkiste. Citations that can refer to more than one proposition in the *Book of Causes* are given by him in parentheses. For example, in Proposition 2, numbers (96) and (97) also relate to Proposition 9.[1]

I. Explicit Citations of the *Book of Causes* in St. Thomas's Writings

A. Commentaries on Scripture

In Psalmos

1. Ps. XVII

B. Theological Commentaries

In Boethium de Trinitate

2. Q. 1, A. 1, 6a
3. Q. 1, A. 3, 2a
4. Q. 4, A. 1, 2a
5. Q. 6, A. 1, 3.2a

---

1. Vansteenkiste provides a third list, not reproduced here, of 89 implicit citations of the *Book of Causes* by St. Thomas, indicating that there are perhaps many, many more.

C. Theological Syntheses

Scriptum super Libros Sententiarum

6. I, D. 4, Q. 1, A. 2c
7. D. 8, Q. 1, A. 2 s.c.
8. D. 8, Q. 1, A. 3 s.c.
9. D. 12, Q. 1, A. 2, 1a
10. D. 14, Q. 1, A. 1, 3a
11. D. 14, Q. 2, A. 1, 2a
12. D. 17, Q. 1, A. 5, ad 3
13. D. 19, Q. 2, A. 1
14. D. 22, Q. 1, A. 1, 1a
15. D. 22, Q. 1, A. 1, ad 1
16. D. 33, Q. 1, A. 2c
17. D. 34, Q. 3, A. 2, ad 3
18. D. 35, Q. 1, A. 1, 1a
19. D. 35, Q. 1, A. 1, 2a
20. D. 37, Q. 1, A. 1, 1a
21. D. 38, Q. 1, A. 2c
22. D. 42, Q. 1, A. 2 s.c. 2
23. D. 43, Q. 1, A. 1c
24. D. 43, Q. 1, A. 2, 4a
25. D. 43, Q. 1, A. 2, ad 4
26. II, D. 1, Q. 1, A. 3, 1a
27. D. 1, Q. 1, A. 3c
28. D. 1, Q. 1, A. 4c
29. Ibid.
30. D. 1, Q. 1, A. 6, 5a
31. D. 1, Q. 1, A. 6, ad 5
32. D. 2, Q. 1, A. 1, 1a
33. D. 2, Q. 1, A. 1, ad 1
34. D. 2, Q. 2, A. 3c
35. D. 3, Q. 1, A. 1, 5a
36. D. 3, Q. 1, A. 1c
37. D. 3, Q. 1, A. 1, ad 5
38. D. 3, Q. 1, A. 2c
39. D. 3, Q. 3, A. 1 s.c. 2
40. D. 3, Q. 3, A. 1c
41. D. 3, Q. 3, A. 2 s.c. 2
42. D. 4, Q. 1, A. 1c
43. D. 13, Q. 1, A. 1, 2a
44. D. 17, Q. 1, A. 1 s.c. 1
45. D. 17, Q. 2, A. 1, 3a
46. D. 18, Q. 2, A. 2, 1a
47. D. 18, Q. 2, A. 2, 5a
48. D. 18, Q. 2, A. 2, ad 1
49. D. 18, Q. 2, A. 2, ad 2
50. D. 18, Q. 2, A. 2, ad 5
51. D. 19, Q. 1, A. 1c
52. Ibid.
53. D. 23, Q. 2, A. 1c
54. D. 32, Q. 2, A. 2c
55. D. 39, Q. 3, A. 1c
56. D. 41, Q. 1, A. 2c
57. D. 44, expositio, c
58. III, D. 10, Q. 1, A. 1, ql. 2, ad 3
59. D. 11, A. 2c
60. D. 13, Q. 1, A. 2, ql. 2c
61. D. 13, Q. 3, A. 1 s.c. 3
62. D. 14, A. 1, ql. 2, ad 1
63. D. 14, A. 2, ql. 2, 4a
64. D. 14, A. 3, ql. 4 s.c. 1
65. D. 22, Q. 1, A. 1 s.c. 3
66. D. 35, Q. 1, A. 1, 3a
67. D. 35, Q. 1, A. 1, ad 3
68. IV, D. 10, A. 4, ql. 5, 1a
69. D. 12, Q. 1, A. 1, ql. 1c
70. D. 17, Q. 1, A. 5, ql. 2, ad 3
71. D. 49, Q. 1, A. 2, ql. 3, 2a
72a. D. 49, Q. 2, A. 6, 5a
72b. D. 50, Q. 1, A. 1 c.

APPENDIX 2

Summa contra Gentiles

73. I, c. 26
74. II, c. 98
75. Ibid.
76. Ibid.
77. III, c. 61
78. III, c. 66

Summa Theologiae

79. I, Q. 3, A. 8 s.c. 2
80. Q. 5, A. 1, 2a
81. Q. 5, A. 1, ad 2
82. Q. 5, A. 2 s.c.
83. Q. 10, A. 2, 2a
84. Q. 10, A. 2, ad 2
85. Q. 14, A. 2, 1a
86. Q. 14, A. 2, ad 1
87. Q. 45, A. 4, 1a
88. Q. 45, A. 4, ad 1
89. Q. 45, A. 5c
90. Q. 50, A. 2, ad 4
91. Q. 55, A. 3 s.c.
92. Q. 56, A. 2, 2a
93. Q. 56, A. 2 s.c.
94. Q. 57, A. 3, 2a
95. Q. 58, A. 1, 3a
96. Q. 61, A. 2, 2a
97. Q. 61, A. 2, ad 2
98. Q. 84, A. 3, 1a
99. Q. 94, A. 2, 3a
100. I-II, Q. 2, A. 6, 2a
101. Q. 5, A. 5c
102. Q. 50, A. 6c
103. Q. 67, A. 5, 1a
104. Q. 67, A. 5, ad 1
105. II-II, Q. 23, A. 6, ad 1
106. Q. 37, A. 2, ad 3
107. Q. 45, A. 3, ad 1
108. Q. 52, A. 2, 2a
109. III, Q. 6, A. 4, 3a
110. Q. 75, A. 5, ad 1

D. Disputations

De Veritate

111. Q. 1, A. 1 s.c. 4
112. Q. 1, A. 4 s.c. 6
113. Q. 1, A. 9c
114. Q. 2, A. 1, 3a
115. Q. 2, A. 1, 11a
116. Q. 2, A. 2, 2a
117. Q. 2, A. 2, ad 2
118. Q. 2, A. 3c
119. Q. 3, A. 2, 3a
120. Q. 5, A. 2, 3a
121. Q. 5, A. 2, 9a
122. Q. 5, A. 8 s.c. 9
123. Q. 5, A. 9, 7a
124. Q. 5, A. 9, 10a
125. Q. 5, A. 9, ad 7
126. Q. 5, A. 9, ad 10
127. Q. 6, A. 6c
128. Q. 8, A. 3c
129. Q. 8, A. 5 s.c.
130. Q. 8, A. 6 s.c. 5
131. Q. 8, A. 7, 1.2a
132. Q. 8, A. 7, 2.1a
133. Q. 8, A. 7 s.c. 1
134. Q. 8, A. 7c
135. Ibid.
136. Q. 8, A. 8 s.c. 1

137. Q. 8, A. 8c
138. Q. 8, A. 10 s.c. 2
139. Q. 8, A. 14, 9a
140. Q. 8, A. 14, 12a
141. Q. 8, A. 14, ad 6
142. Q. 8, A. 15c
143. Q. 13, A. 2c
144. Q. 18, A. 4, 7a
145. Q. 21, A. 1, 7a
146. Q. 21, A. 2, 5a

147. Q. 21, A. 4, ad 9
148. Q. 21, A. 5c
149. Ibid.
150. Ibid.
151. Q. 22, A. 11c
152. Q. 24, A. 1, 4a
153. Q. 24, A. 8, 6a
154. Q. 24, A. 14c
155. Q. 28, A. 9 s.c. 3

De Potentia

156. Q. 3, A. 1c
157. Ibid.
158. Q. 3, A. 3, 1a
159. Q. 3, A. 4, 10a
160. Q. 3, A. 4, 11a
161. Q. 3, A. 4c
162. Ibid.
163. Ibid.
164. Q. 3, A. 4, ad 10
165. Q. 3, A. 5, 2a
166. Q. 3, A. 7c
167. Ibid.
168. Q. 3, A. 8, 19a
169. Q. 3, A. 8, ad 19
170. Q. 3, A. 9, 27a

171. Q. 3, A. 10, 8a
172. Q. 5, A. 1 s.c. 4
173. Q. 5, A. 8c
174. Q. 5, A. 10, 6a
175. Q. 6, A. 1, 5a
176. Q. 6, A. 3, 9a
177. Q. 6, A. 3, 10a
178. Q. 6, A. 3, ad 9
179. Q. 6, A. 6 s.c. 2
180. Q. 6, A. 6c
181. Q. 7, A. 2, 6a
182. Q. 7, A. 2 sol.
183. Q. 7, A. 2, ad 5
184. Q. 7, A. 5, 5a
185. Q. 7, A. 8c

De Malo

186a. Q. 2, A. 9, ad 18
186b. Q. 4, A. 6, ad 15
187. Q. 16, A. 1, 4a
188. Q. 16, A. 2, 10a
189. Q. 16, A. 2, ad 10
190. Q. 16, A. 4 s.c. 2

191. Q. 16, A. 4c
192. Q. 16, A. 4, ad 14
193. Q. 16, A. 6 s.c. 4
194. Q. 16, A. 7, 3a
195. Q. 16, A. 9, 8a
196. Q. 16, A. 9, ad 8

De spiritualibus Creaturis

197. A. 1 s.c. 7

De Anima

198. A. 7, 8a
199. A. 7, ad 1
200. A. 7, ad 5
201. A. 9c
202. A. 13, 9a

203. A. 17, 9a
204. A. 18c
205. A. 19, 10a
206. A. 20, 18a

Quodlibeta

207. II, A. 3 s.c.
208. V, A. 7c
209. VII, A. 3c

210. IX, A. 5c
211. IX, A. 5c

E. Special Treatises

De Ente et Essentia

212. C. 4
213. C. 5
214. Ibid.

215. C. 8
216. C. 18

Responsio ad Io. Vercellensem de Art. XLII

217. Art. 15

F. Works of Doubtful Authenticity

Quaestio de Immortalitate Animae

218. Arg. 18

De quatuor Oppositis

219. C. 4

De Natura Materiae

220. C. 1

Partes deletae ex Autographo S. c. Gentiles

221. I, C. 68
222. I, C. 73

Supplementum ad S. Theologiae, III

223. Q. 83, A. 3c

II. Propositions from the *Book of Causes* Cited by St. Thomas

Proposition 1

a. Every primary cause infuses its effect more powerfully than a second [universal] cause. The effect of the second cause is only through the power of the first cause.—Nos. 2, 3, 9, 29, 57, 69, 100, 109, 110, 122, 124, 125, 126, 127, 150, 152, 154, 163, 167, 173, 186 (2x), 210, 221, 222, 223

b. It is necessary that something first of all be a being, next a living thing, and afterward a man. Being is more powerfully the cause. When you remove living, being remains (see Prop. 4 a).—Nos. 19, 28, 54, 56, 65, 69, 103, 104, 110, 186, 201

Proposition 2

a. The first cause is before eternity, since it is the cause of it (see Prop. 9).—Nos. 13, 33, 83, 84

b. The soul is [lower] on the horizon of eternity and above time.—Nos. 70, 72a, 72b, 77, (96, 97), 170, 171

c. An intelligence is made equal to eternity (see Props. 7 b, 31).—Nos. 32, 84, 94 (96, 97), 216

Proposition 3

a. Every noble soul has three activities.—No. 123

b. [The soul's] divine activity is . . . from the power . . . of the first cause (see Props. 9 b, 23).—Nos. 89, 123, 125, 157, (169)

c. The first cause created the being of the soul with an intelligence mediating (see Props. 5 a, 8 d, 9 c, 14 b, 16 c).—Nos. 26, (46, 47, 48, 161, 164)

d. The soul [was placed as something] subject to an intelligence [on which it] carries out [its] intellectual activity.—Nos. 47, 50, 125

e. The soul impresses things only through motion (see Prop. 5 b).—Nos. 34, 71, 125

Proposition 4

a. The first of created things is being (see Props. 1 b, 18 a).—Nos. 4, 8, 27, 30, 31, 82, 87, 88, 111, 125, 146, 165, 169, 175, 182, 219

b. Created being . . . is composed of the finite and the infinite.—Nos. 35, 37

c. Intelligible forms are more extended [in higher intelligences] . . . and not as extended [in lower intelligences] (see Prop. 10 b).

d. Because intelligence is diversified, the intelligible form [there] becomes diversified . . . just as . . . individuals in the lower world.—No. 40

Proposition 5

a. [The first higher] intelligences impress steadfast forms.—Nos. 46, 48

APPENDIX 2

b. [The motion] of souls . . . is regular, continuous motion (see Prop. 3 e).—Nos. 66, 67, (71)

Proposition 6

a. The first cause transcends description, and language fails in describing it (see Prop. 22 a).—Nos. 1, 5, 6, 14, 15, 68

b. The first cause is signified [only] from a second cause . . . referred to by the name of its first effect, which is an intelligence.—Nos. 17, 18, 115, 184

Proposition 7

a. An intelligence is an undivided substance.—Nos. 179, 197

b. An intelligence is with eternity . . . above time; its substance and activity . . . are one thing (see Props. 2 c, 31).—Nos. 140, 155, 194

Proposition 8

a. Every intelligence knows what is above it . . . because it acquires from it as its cause . . . and what is below it . . . because it is its cause (see Prop. 13 c).—Nos. 42, 53, 72, 94, (99), 101, 118, (128), 131, (135), 143, (160, 192), 198, 206

b. An intelligence knows . . . things according to the mode of its substance . . . and not according to the mode of the things themselves (see Props. 11 b, 13 a).—Nos. (42), 74, 95, 101, 102, 128, 134, 135, 141, 160, 189, 203

c. Sensible things are intelligible in an intelligence (see Props. 12, 13 a).—Nos. 39, 136

d. An intelligence is the cause of the things [below it] (see Props. 3 a, 5 a, 9 c, 14 b).

Proposition 9

a. The stability and essence of every intelligence is through the pure goodness that is the first cause.—No. 172

b. An intelligence is the ruler of all the things [under it] . . . through the divine power because through it, it is the cause of the things. (For the soul see Prop. 3 b; see Props. 3 c, 23.)—Nos. 78, 89, 137, 166, 169, 182

c. The first cause . . . creates an intelligence without mediation and . . . the rest of things with the mediation of an intelligence (see Props. 3 c, 8 d).

d. An intelligence . . . is being and form.—Nos. 36, 207, 212

e. The first cause . . . is being alone; its being is infinite; its individuality is the pure goodness [that infuses . . . the rest of things].—Nos. 38, 73, 147, 148, 149, 183, 213

Proposition 10

a. Every intelligence is full of forms.—Nos. 39, 41, 62, 76, 98, 129, 136, 139, 142, 144, 199, 204

b. Among intelligences there are some that contain more universal forms and others that contain less universal forms (see Prop. 4 c).—Nos. 41, 63, 75, 91, 138, 191, 200, 209

c. The first intelligences have great power because [they possess] a more powerful unity [than the second, lower intelligences] (see Prop. 17 a, and elsewhere).

d. [Any] thing receives what is above it only through the mode according to which it can receive it, not through the mode according to which the received thing is. (For knowledge, see Props. 8 b, c; in general, see Props. 12, 20 b, 22 c, 24.)—Nos. 21, 45, 105, (137, 151), 153, 158, 193, 211

Proposition 11

a. Every intelligence understands sempiternal things, which things are neither destroyed nor fall under time.—Nos. 93, 133

b. An intelligence understands a thing through its being (see Prop. 13 b).

Proposition 12

All of the first things are in one another in the mode appropriate for one of them to be in another. An effect is in a cause in the mode belonging to the cause, and a cause is in the effect in the mode belonging to the effect (see Prop. 13 b).

Proposition 13

a. Things are . . . in an intelligence . . . in an intelligible mode (see Prop. 8 b & c).

b. When [an intelligence] knows its essence, it knows the rest of the things [that are under it] (see Props. 8, 11 b).—Nos. 99, 132, 188

Proposition 14

a. Sensible things are in every soul because it is their example (see Prop. 3).—Nos. (137), 205

b. The soul . . . is an effect of the intelligence [before it] (see Prop. 3 c).

Proposition 15

Every knower knows it essence. Therefore, it returns to its essence with a complete reversion. . . . abiding steadfastly, fixed *per se* (see Props. 7, 28).—Nos. 12, 52, 85, 86, 113, 116, 117, 130

Proposition 16

a. The power [of an intelligence] came to be infinite only with respect to the lower, not with respect to the higher. (With regard to the soul, see Prop. 5.)—Nos. 25, 49, 60, 90, 176, 178, 195, 196, 214, 217, 220

b. The first infinite . . . is the power of powers . . . pure power.—No. 23

c. The remaining . . . effects [are] . . . with an intelligence mediating (see Prop. 3 c).

Proposition 17
a. Every united power is more infinite than a multiplied power (see Prop. 10 c).—Nos. 22, (24, 44, 64), 106, 107, 108, 119, 120, 174, 177, 185, 202

b. The more [that power] is united, the [more] wondrous [its] effects.—No. 177

Proposition 18
a. The first being . . . the cause of causes, gives . . . being by way of creation.—Nos. 27, 43, 59, 156, 162, 168, 169

b. [The first] life gives [life to those under it], an intelligence [knowledge and] the remaining things [to those under it but only] by way of form.—Nos. 27, 59, 80, 111, 145, 156, 162

Proposition 19
Among intelligences . . . there is divine [intelligence] . . . and only intelligence. Among souls [there is] an intellectual [soul] and only soul.—Nos. 159, 187

Proposition 20
a. The first cause rules all [created] things without being mixed with them.—Nos. 7, 20, 79, 181.

b. The first goodness infuses [all things with goodnesses] in one infusion. But each thing receives that infusion according to the mode of its power and its being (see Props. 10 d, 12, 22 c, 24).

Proposition 22
a. The first cause is above every name by which it is named (see Prop. 6 a).—Nos. 15, 16, 33, 114

b. Neither diminution nor mere completeness belongs to it (see Prop. 9 e).

c. Every world receives [that goodness only] according to the mode of its potency (see Props. 10 d, 12, 20 b, 24).

Proposition 23
Every divine intelligence knows things inasmuch as it is an intelligence and rules them inasmuch as it is divine (see Prop. 9 b).

Proposition 24
The first cause exists in all things according to one disposition, but not all things exist in the first cause according to one disposition. . . . Each thing . . . receives it according to the mode of its potency (see Props. 10 d, 12, 20 b, 22 c).—Nos. 11, 61, 112, 121

Proposition 27
Every destructible substance . . . is either composed or supported by another thing.—Nos. 51, 180, 218

Proposition 29

Every simple substance . . . is loftier and higher than time [and temporal things] (see Props. 2 c, 7 b, 31).

Proposition 30

Created things follow one another, and only [that] substance follows [a higher substance] which is like [it] (see Prop. 31).—No. 55

Proposition 31

Between a thing whose substance and action are in the moment of eternity and a thing whose substance and action are in the moment of time there exists an intermediary . . . (see Props. 7 b, 30).—Nos. 10, (140, 155), 190, (194), 208

BIBLIOGRAPHY

Primary Sources

1. Latin Editions of St. Thomas's *Commentary on the Book of Causes*

Sancti Thomae de Aquino super Librum de Causis Expositio. Critical edition by Henri-Dominique Saffrey, O.P. Fribourg: Société Philosophique, 1954. [The text from which this translation has been made.]

S. Thomae Aquinatis in Librum de Causis Expositio. Edition by Ceslao Pera, O.P. Turin: Marietti, 1955. [English translation of Pera edition: "A Translation and Analysis of Thomas Aquinas' *Expositio super Librum de Causis*." Elizabeth Collin-Smith. Dissertation. Austin: University of Texas, 1991.]

2. Works of St. Thomas Aquinas Cited

References to the *Sancti Thomae de Aquino Opera Omnia iussu Leonis XIII P.M. Edita* (Rome: 1882–) are given where available. How the works of St. Thomas are designated in the footnotes is indicated in the left-hand column.

A. Theological Syntheses

I Sent.
II Sent. *Scriptum super Libros Sententiarum Magistri Petri Lombardi* (1252–56). Ed. P. Mandonnet, O.P. Vols. 1 & 2. Paris: P. Lethielleux, 1929. M. F. Moos, O.P. Vols. 3 & 4. Paris: P. Lethielleux, 1933.

ScG *Summa contra Gentiles* (1259–64). Leonine edition (1918–30). Vols. 13–15.
[English translation: *On the Truth of the Catholic Faith.* Trans. Anton C. Pegis (vol. 1); James F. Anderson (vol. 2); Vernon J. Bourke (vol. 3); Charles J. O'Neil (vol. 4). New York: Doubleday, 1955–56.]

ST *Summa Theologiae* (1266–73). Leonine edition (1888–1906). Vols. 4–12.
[English translations: *Summa Theologica.* Trans. English Dominican Fathers. 3 vols. New York: Benziger, 1947. *Summa Theologiae.* Ed. Thomas Gilby, O.P. Latin/English. 60 vols. & index. New York: McGraw-Hill, 1964–1980.]

B. Disputations

Quaest. Disp. de Anima	*Quaestiones Disputatae de Anima* (1269). Vol. 2. Turin: Marietti, 1953. [English translation: *Questions on the Soul.* Trans. James H. Robb. Milwaukee: Marquette University Press, 1984.]
De Potentia	*Quaestiones Disputatae de Potentia Dei* (1265–66). Vol. 2. Turin: Marietti, 1953. [English translation: *On the Power of God.* Trans. English Dominican Fathers. Westminster, Maryland: Newman Press, 1952.]
De Veritate	*Quaestiones Disputate de Veritate* (1256–59). Leonine edition (1970–76). Vol. 22. [English translation: *Truth.* Trans. Robert W. Mulligan, S.J., James V. McGlynn, S.J., Robert W. Schmidt, S.J. 3 vols. Chicago: Henry Regnery, 1952.]
Quaest. Disp. de spir. Creat.	*Quaestiones Disputatae de Spiritualibus Creaturis* (1267–68). Vol. 2. Turin: Marietti, 1953. [English translation: *On Spiritual Creatures.* Trans. Mary C. Fitzpatrick and John J. Wellmuth. Milwaukee: Marquette University Press, 1969.]
Quodlibet.	*Quaestiones Quodlibetales* (1256–59 & 1269–72). Ed. Raymundi Spiazzi. Turin: Marietti, 1949.

C. Theological Commentaries

In Boeth. de Trin.	*In Librum Boethii de Trinitate Expositio* (1258–59). In *Opuscula Theologica.* Vol. 2. Turin: Marietti, 1954. [English translations: *The Divisions and Methods of the Sciences.* (Questions V & VI.) Trans. Armand Mauer. Toronto: Pontifical Insitute of Mediaeval Studies, 1963.] *The Trinity and the Unity of the Intellect.* Sr. Rose Emmanuella Brown, S.H.N. St. Louis: Herder, 1946.
In Boeth. de Heb.	*In Librum Boethii de Hebdomadibus* (1256–59). In *Opuscula Theologica.* Vol. 2. Turin: Marietti, 1954.
In de div. Nom.	*In Librum Beati Dionysii de divinis Nominibus* (1265–67). Turin: Marietti, 1950.

D. Commentaries on Aristotle

In de Anima *In Aristotelis Librum de Anima Commentarium* (1269–70). Leonine edition (1984). Vol 45.1.
[English translation: *Aristotle's De Anima in the Version of William of Moerbeke and the Commentary of St. Thomas Aquinas*. Trans. Kenelm Foster, O.P., and Silvester Humphries, O.P. New Haven: Yale University Press, 1965. Reprinted as *Commentary on Aristotle's De anima*. Intro. Ralph McInerny. Notre Dame: Dumb Ox Books, 1994.]

In de Caelo *In Aristotelis Libros de Caelo et Mundo Expositio* (1272–73). Leonine edition (1886). Vol. 3.

In Eth. *In Decem Libros Ethicorum Aristotelis ad Nicomachum Expositio* (1271). Leonine edition (1969). Vol 47.
[English translation: *Commentary on the Nicomachean Ethics*. Trans. C. I. Litzinger, O.P. 2 vols. Chicago: Henry Regnery, 1964.]

In Met. *In Duodecim Libros Metaphysicorum Aristotelis Expositio* (1269–72). Turin: Marietti, 1950.
[English translation: *Commentary on the Metaphysics of Aristotle*. Trans. John P. Rowan. Chicago: Henry Regnery, 1961.

In Phys. *In Octo Libros Physicorum Aristotelis* (1269–70). Leonine edition (1884). Vol. 2.
[English translation: *Commentary on Aristotle's Metaphysics*. Trans. Richard J. Blackwell, Richard J. Spath, and W. Edmund Thirkel. New Haven: Yale University Press, 1963.]

In Pol. *Sententia Libri Politicorum* (1269–72). Leonine edition (1971). Vol. 48.

In post. Anal. *In Aristotelis Libros posteriorum Analyticorum* (1269–72). Second Leonine Edition (1989). Vol. 1.2.
[English translation: *Commentary on the Posterior Analytics of Aristotle*. Trans. F. R. Larcher, O.P. Albany: Magi Books, 1970.]

E. Scriptural Commentaries

In Ioan. *Super Evangelium S. Ioannis Lectura* (1269–72). Ed. Raphaelis Cai, O.P. Turin: Marietti, 1952.

F. Special Treatises

De Aet. Mundi *De Aeternitate Mundi contra Murmurantes* (1270). In *Opuscula Philosophica*. Turin: Marietti, 1954.

	[English translation: *On the Eternity of the World.* Trans. Vollert, Kendzierski, and Byrne. Milwaukee: Marquette University Press, 1964.]
De Ente et Essentia	*De Ente et Essentia* (1252–56). Turin: Marietti, 1948. [English translation: *Aquinas on Being and Essence.* Trans. Joseph Bobik. Notre Dame: University of Notre Dame Press, 1965.]
De Natura Materiae	*De Natura Materiae.* In *Opuscula Philosophica.* Turin: Marietti, 1954. (This work is of doubtful authenticity.)
De Subst. sep.	*De Substantiis separatis* (or *De Angelis*) (1271–73). Leonine edition (1967–68). Vol. 40. [English translation: *Treatise on Separate Substances.* Trans. Francis J. Lescoe. West Hartford, Conn.: St. Joseph College, 1959.]
De Unitate Intellectus	*De Unitate Intellectus contra Averroistas* (1270). In *Opuscula Philosophica.* Turin: Marietti, 1954. Also in Leonine edition (1976). Vol. 43. [English translation: *On the Unity of the Intellect against the Averroists.* Trans. Beatrice H. Zelder. Milwaukee: Marquette University Press, 1968.]

3. Arabic Editions of the *Book of Causes*

Bardenhewer, Otto. *Die pseudo-aristotelische Schrift Über das reine Gute bekannt unter dem Namen Liber de causis.* Freiberg-im-Breisgau: Herder, 1882.

Badawi, 'Abdurrahman. *Procli: Liber (Psuedo-Aristotelis) de expositione bonitatis purae.* In *Neoplatonici apud Arabes.* Islamica 19. Cairo, 1955; pp. 1–33.

4. Latin Edition of the *Book of Causes*

Adriaan Pattin, O.M.I. " Le *Liber de causis.* Édition établie à l'aide de 90 manuscrits avec introduction et notes." In *Tijdschrift voor Filosofie* 28 (1966), pp. 90–203. Also, as a separate publication: Louvain: Éditions du "Tijdschrift voor filosofie," n.d. [1966].
[English translation: *The Book of Causes.* Translated from the Latin with an Introduction by Dennis J. Brand. Milwaukee: Marquette University Press, 1984.]

5. Other Latin Commentaries on the *Book of Causes*

Albert the Great. *Liber de Causis et Processu Universitatis.* In *B. Alberti Magni Opera Omnia.* Ed. August Borgnet. Paris: Vivès, 1890–99. Vol. 10, pp. 361–619.

———. *De causis et processu universitatis a prima causa*. In *Alberti Magni Opera Omnia*. Munster: Aschendorff, 1993. Vol. 17, 2.

Roger Bacon. *Quaestiones supra Librum de Causis*. In *Opera hactenus inedita Rogeri Baconi*, Fasc. 12. Ed. Robert Steele. Oxford: Clarendon Press, 1935.

Giles of Rome. *Fundatissimi Aegidii Romani, Archiepiscopi Bituricensis, Doctorem praecipue, Ordinis Eremitarum Sancti Augustine, Opus super Authorem de Causis, Alpharabium*. Venice: J. Zoppin, 1550.

Henry of Ghent. *Les Quaestiones in Librum de Causis attribuées à Henri de Gand*. Critical edition by John P. Zwaenepoel, C.I.C.M. Louvain: Publications universitaires de Louvain, 1974.

Siger of Brabant. *Les Quaestiones super Librum de Causis de Siger de Brabant*. Critical edition by Antonio Marlasca. Louvain: Publications universitaires de Louvain, 1972.

6. Other Primary Works Cited

al-Kindi. *Rasa'il al-Kindi al-falsafiyah*. [*On First Philosophy*.] Ed. Muhammad 'Abdalhadi Abu Rida, I. Cairo, 1950.

Aristotle. *Aristoteles Graece* ex recensione Immanuelis Bekkeri. Berlin: Reiner, 1931.

[English trans: *The Basic Works of Aristotle*. Ed. Richard McKeon. N.Y.: Random House, 1941.]

St. Augustine. *De Genesi ad litteram libri XII*. In *Corpus Scriptorum Ecclesiasticorum Latinorum*, Vol. XXVIII ex recensione I. Zychia. Prague: PL Tempsky-Freitag, 1894. In *Patrologia Latina*. Ed. J. P. Migne. Paris, 1844–64. Vol. 34.

[English translation: *On the Literal Interpretation of Genesis*. Trans. Roland J. Teske, S.J. Washington, D.C: The Catholic University of America Press, 1991.]

———. *De civitate Dei libri XXII* ex recensione E. Hoffmann, pars I. Prague: Tempsky-Freitag, 1899. In PL, Vol. 41.

[English translation: *City of God*. Trans. Gerald Walsh, S.J., et al. New York: Doubleday, 1958.]

———. *De Trinitate*. CSEL, Vol. 50. Turnhout: Brepols, 1968.6. In PL, Vol. 42.

[English translation: *On the Holy Trinity*. Trans. A. West and W. Shedd. In Nicene and Post-Nicene Fathers of the Church. Vol. 3. Grand Rapids, Mich.: Wm. B. Eerdmans, 1976.]

Averroes. *Aristotelis Opera cum Averrois Commentarium*, Venetiis apud Iunctas, 1562–1574. Frankfurt-am-Main: Minerva, 1963.

Boethius. *Philosophiae Consolationis Libri quinque* recensuit G. Weinberger. CSEL, Vol. LXVII. Vienna: Hoelder & Pichler, 1934.

[English translation: *The Consolation of Philosophy.* Trans. W. V. Cooper. New York: Random House, 1943.]

St. Gregory the Great. *Dialogorum Libri quatuor.* In *Patrologia Latina.* Ed. J. P. Migne. Paris, 1849. Vol. 77.

Moerbeke's Latin Translation of Proclus. Vansteenkiste, C. "Procli *Elementatio theologica* translata a Guilelmo de Moerbeke." In *Tijdschrift voor filosofie* 13 (1951), pp. 263–302, 491–531.

Plato. *Platonis Opera.* Ed. J. Burnet. 5 vols. Oxford: Clarendon, 1905–13.

[English translation: *The Dialogues of Plato.* Trans. B. Jowett. 2 vols. New York: Random House, 1937.]

Plotinus. Plotini *Opera* ediderunt P. Henry & H. R. Schwyzer. Paris: Desclée de Brouwer, 1954–73.

[English translation: *The Enneads.* Trans. S. MacKenna; third edition revised by B. S. Page. London, 1962.]

Proclus. *Proclus: The Elements of Theology.* A Revised Text with Translation, Introduction and Commentary by E. R. Dodds. Greek/English. Oxford: Oxford University Press, 1963.

Pseudo-Dionysius. *Opera Omnia* quae extant. *Patrologia Graeca* (PG). Vol. 3. Ed. J. P. Migne. Paris, 1857–66, pp. 119–1120.

———. *Dionysiaca.* Recueil donnant l'ensemble des ouvrages attribués au Denys de l'Aréopage, et synopse marquant la valeur des citations. Ed. P. Chevallier et al. 2 vols. Paris: Desclée de Brouwer, 1937–50.

[English translations: *The Divine Names and Mystical Theology.* Trans. John D. Jones. Milwaukee: Marquette University Press, 1980. *Pseudo-Dionysius. The Complete Works.* Trans. Colm Luibheid. London: SPCK, 1987.]

Secondary Sources

1. On Proclus and Pseudo-Dionysius

Beierwaltes, W. *Proklos. Grundzüge seiner Metaphysik.* Frankfurt-am-Main: V. Klostermann, 1965.

Breton, S. "La théoreme de l'un dans les Eléments de Théologie de Proclus." *Revue de sciences philosophiques et théologiques* 58 (1974), pp. 561–82.

Brons, B. *Gott und Seienden: Untersuchungen zur Verhältnis von neuplatonischer Metaphysik und christlicher Tradition bei Dionysius Areopagita.* Göttingen: Vanderhoeck-Ruprecht, 1976.

Charles, A. "La raison et le divin chez Proclus." *Revue des sciences philosophiques et théologiques* 53 (1969).

Dondaine, H. F. *Le Corpus Dionysien de l'Université de Paris au XIIIe siècle.* Rome: Edizioni di Storia e Letteratura, 1953.

Gersh, S. E. Κίνησις ἀκίνητος. *A Study of Spiritual Motion in the Philosophy of Proclus.* Leiden: Brill, 1973.

———. *From Iamblichus to Eriugena. An Investigation of the Prehistory and Evolution of the Pseudo-Dionysian Tradition.* Leiden: Brill, 1978.

Grabmann, Martin. "Die Proklusübersetzung des Wilhelm von Moerbeke und ihre Verwertung in der lateinischen Literatur des Mittelalter." In *Mittelalterliches Geistesleben.* Munich: Max Hüber, 1926; vol. 2, pp. 413–23.

Klibansky, Raymond. *The Continuity of the Platonic Tradition during the Middle Ages.* London: The Warburg Institute, 1950.

Lloyd, A. C. "Procession and Division in Proclus." In *Soul and the Structure of Being in Late Neoplatonism. Syrianus, Proclus and Simplicius.* Ed. H. J. Blumenthal & A. C. Lloyd. Liverpool: Liverpool University Press, 1982; pp. 18–42.

Louth, Andrew. *The Origins of the Christian Mystical Tradition from Plato to Denys.* Oxford: Clarendon Press, 1981.

Lowry, J. W. P. *The Logical Principles of Proclus' Στοιχείωγις Θεολογική as Systematic Ground of the Cosmos.* Amsterdam: Rodopi, 1980.

Roques, René. *L'Univers dionysien. Structure hiérarchique du monde selon le Pseudo-Denys.* Paris: Les Éditions du Cerf, 1983.

Rutledge, Dom Denys. *Cosmic Theology. The Ecclesiastical Hierarchy of Pseudo-Denys: An Introduction.* London: Routledge & Kegan Paul, 1964.

Saffrey, H.-D. "Allusions antichrétiens chez Proclus, le Diadoque platonicien." *Revue des sciences philosophques et théologiques* 59 (1975), pp. 553–63.

———. "New Objective Links between the Pseudo-Dionysius and Proclus." In *Neoplatonism and Christian Thought.* Ed. Dominic J. O'Meara. Albany: State University of New York, 1982; pp. 64–74.

Sheldon-Williams, I. P. "Henads and Angels: Proclus and the Pseudo-Dionysius." *Studia Patristica* 11 (1972), pp. 65–71.

Sweeney, Leo, S.J. "The Origin of Participant and Participated Perfection in Proclus' *Elements of Theology.*" In *Wisdom in Depth. Essays in Honor of H. Renard.* Ed. V. F. Daues et al. Milwaukee: Bruce, 1966.

———. "Participation and the Structure of Being in Proclus' *Elements of Theology.* In *The Structure of Being. A Neoplatonic Approach.* Ed. R. Baine Harris (1982), pp. 140–55, 177–81.

Trouillard, J. L'un et l'âme selon Proclus." *Diotima* 2 (1974), pp. 117–25.

———. "Théologie négative et psychogonie chez Proclus." In *Plotino e il neoplatonismo in Oriente e in Occidente.* Rome: Academia Nazionale dei Lincei, 1974; pp. 253–264.

———. "Procession néoplatonicienne et création judéo-chrétienne." In *Néoplatonisme. Mélanges offerts à J. Trouillard.* Fontenay aux-Roses, 1981.

[Note: The above represent only a small portion of publications on Proclus by this Neoplatonist scholar.]

Von Ivánka, Endre. "Teilhaben, Hervorgang und Hierarchie bei Pseudo-Dionysios und bei Proklos. Der Neuplatonismus des Pseudo-Dionysios." *Actes du XI congrès international de philosophie.* Brussels, 1953. Vol. 12; Louvain (1953), pp. 153–58.

Whittaker, J. "The Historical Background of Proclus' Doctrine of the αὐθυπόστατα. In *De Jamblique à Proclus.* Geneva: Vandoeuvres, 1975.

2. On the *Book of Causes*

Alonso, M. A. "El *Liber de causis.*" *al-Andalus* 23 (1958), pp. 43–69.

———. "Las fuentes literarias del *Liber de causis.*" *al-Andalus* 10 (1945), pp. 345–82.

Anawati, G. C. "Prolegomènes à une nouvelle édition du *De causis* arabe." In *Mélanges Louis Massignon.* Paris: A. Maissonneuve, 1957. Reprinted in *Études de philosophie musulmane.* Paris: Vrin, 1974; pp. 117–54.

Badawi, A. *La Transmission de la philosophie grecque au monde arabe.* Paris: Études de philosophie médiévale, LVI, 1987.

Bédoret, H. "L'auteur et le traducteur du *Liber de causis.*" *Revue néoscholastique de philosophie* 41 (1938), pp. 519–33.

D'Ancona Costa, Cristina. "Causa prima non est yliatim." *Liber de Causis,* Prop. 8 (9): le fonte e la dottrina." *Documenti e studi sulla tradizione filosofica medievale* (Spoleto), I,2 (1990), pp. 327–51. French translation of this article appears on pp. 97–119 of *Recherches* (the next item).

———. *Recherches sur le Liber de causis.* Etudes de philosophie médiévale, vol. 72. Paris: Vrin, 1995.

De Vogel, Cornelia J. "Some Reflections on the *Liber de causis.*" *Vivarium* 4 (1966), pp. 67–82.

Doresse, J. "Les sources du *Liber de causis.*" *Revue de l'histoire des religions* 131 (1946), pp. 234–38.

Endress, G. *Proclus Arabus. Zwanzig Abschnitte aus der Institutio Theologica in arabischer Übersetzung.* Wiesbaden-Beirut: F. Steiner Verlag, 1973.

Frank, R. M. D. "The Origin of the Philosophical Term *anniyya.*" *Cahiers de Byrsa* 6 (1956), pp. 181–201.

Goichon, A.-M. *Lexique de la langue philosophique d'Ibn Sina (Avicenne).* Paris: Desclée de Brouwer, 1938.

Jolivet, J. "Intellect et Intelligence. Note sur la tradition arabo-latine des XII et XIII siècles." In *Mélanges H. Corbin.* Montreal: McGill University, 1977; pp. 681–702.

Magnard, Pierre, Olivier Boulnois, Bruno Pinchard, Jean-Luc Solère. *La demeure de l'être. Autour d'un anonyme. Étude et traduction de Liber de Causis.* Paris: Vrin, 1990.

Murari, R. "Il *De Causis* e la sua fortuna nel Medio Evo." *Giornale storico della letteratura italiana* 34 (1899), pp. 98–117.

Opelt, I. "Die Übersetzungstechnik des Gerhārd von Cremona." *Glotta* 38 (1959), pp. 135–70.

Pattin, A. "De hierarchie van het zijnde in het *Liber de Causis.*" *Tijdschrift voor Filosofie* 23 (1961), pp. 130–57.

———. "Over de schrijveren de vertaler van het *Liber de Causis.*" *Tijdschrift voor Filosofie* 23 (1961), pp. 503–26.

———. "De *Proclus Arabus* en het *Liber de Causis.*" *Tijdschrift voor Filosofie* 38 (1976), pp. 468–73.

———. "Auteur du *Liber de causis*: Quelques réflexions sur le récente littérature." *Freiburger Zeitschrift für Philosophie und Theologie* 41, 3 (1994), pp. 354–88.

Saffrey, H.-D. "L'État actuel des recherches sur le *Liber de Causis* comme source de la métaphysique au Moyen Age." In *Die Metaphysik im Mittelalter.* Berlin: W. de Gryte, 1963; vol. 2, pp. 267–81.

Serra, G. "Alcune osservazioni sulle traduzioni dell arabo in ebraico e in latino del *De generatione et corruptione* di Arisotele e dell pseudo-aristotelico *Liber de Causis.*" In *Scritti in onore di Carlo Diano.* Bologna: Patron, 1975; pp. 385–433.

Sweeney, Leo, S.J. "Doctrine of Creation in *Liber de causis.*" In *An Etienne Gilson Tribute.* Ed. Charles J. O'Neil. Milwaukee: Marquette University Press, 1959; pp. 274–289.

———. "Research Difficulties in the *Liber de causis. Modern Schoolman* 36 (1959), pp. 109–16.

Taylor, Richard C. "A Note on Chapter 1 of the *Liber de Causis.*" *Manuscripta* 22 (1978), pp. 169–72.

———. "The *Liber de causis (Kalam fi mahd al-khair)*: A Study of Medieval Neoplatonism." Ph.D. dissertation. University of Toronto, 1981.

———. "Neoplatonic Texts in Turkey: Two Manuscripts Containing Ibn Tufayl's *Hayy Ibn Yaqzan,* Ibn al-Sid's *Kitab al-Hada'iq,* Ibn Bajjah's *Ittisal al-'Aql bi-l-Insan,* the *Liber de causis,* and an Anonymous Neoplatonic Treatise on Motion." MIDEO 15 (1982), pp. 251–64.

———. "The *Liber de causis*: A Preliminary List of Extant MSS." *Bulletin de philosophie médiévale* 25 (1983), pp. 63–84.

———. "The Kalam fi mahd al-khair (*Liber de causis*) in the Islamic Philosophical Milieu" *Pseudo-Aristotle in the Middle Ages.* The *Theology* and other Texts. London: Warburg Institute Surveys and Texts, XI, 1986), pp. 37–52.

———. "Remarks on the Latin Text and the Translation of the *Kalam fi Mahd Al-Khair/Liber de Causis.*" *Bulletin de philosophie médiévale* (1989), pp. 75–83.

———. "The *Liber de Causis*: A Preliminary List of Extant Manuscripts." *Bulletin de philosophie médiévale* 25 (1993), pp. 63–84.

Vansteenkiste, C. "Intorno al testo del *Liber de causis.*" *Angelicum* 44 (1967), pp. 67–83.

Zimmermann, F. W. "The Origins of the So-Called *Theology of Aristotle.*" *Pseudo-Aristotle in the Middle Ages. The Theology* and other Writings. London: Warburg Institute Surveys and Texts, XI, (1986), pp. 110–240.

3. On St. Thomas and the *Book of Causes*

Antoniotti, M. L. "La prémotion divine: Saint Thomas d'Aquin et l'auteur du *Liber de Causis*. In *Atti dell'VIII Congresso Tomista Internazionale*. Vatican City: Pontifical Academy of St. Thomas, 1982.

Beierwaltes, W. "Der Kommentar zum *Liber de Causis* als neuplatonisches Element in der Philosophie des Thomas von Aquin." *Philosophische Rundschau* 11 (1963), pp. 192–215.

D'Ancona Costa, Cristina. "L'uso della *Sententia Dionysii* nel Commento di S. Tommaso e Egidio Romano alle propositioni 3, 4, 6 del *Liber de causis.*" *Medioevo* 8 (1982), pp. 1–42.

———. *Tommaso D'Aquino: Commento al "Libro delle cause."* Milan: Rusconi, 1986.

De Libera, Alain. "Albert le Grand et Thomas d'Aquin interprétes du *Liber de causis.*" *Revue des sciences philosophiques et théologiques* 3 (1990), pp. 347–77.

Elders, Léon. "Saint Thomas d'Aquin et la métaphysique du *Liber de Causis.*" *Revue Thomiste* 89 (1989), pp. 427–42.

Fabro, Cornelio. "The Overcoming of the Neoplatonic Triad of Being, Life and Intellect by Thomas Aquinas." In *Neoplatonism and Christian Thought*. Ed. Dominic J. O'Meara. Albany: State University of New York Press, 1982; pp. 97–108.

Ho, J. C. Y. "La doctrine de la participation dans le commentaire de Saint Thomas sur le *Liber de Causis.*" *Revue philosophique de Louvain* 70 (1972), pp. 360–83.

Mansion, A. "Saint Thomas et le *Liber de causis.*" *Revue philosophique de Louvain* 53 (1955), pp. 54–72.

Kremer, Klaus. "Die creatio nach Thomas von Aquin und dem *Liber de Causis.*" *Ekklesia*. Festscrift für M. Wehr. Trier: Paulinusverlag, 1962, pp. 321–44.

Oshika, K. "Thomas Aquinas and the *Liber de causis.*" *Studies in Medieval Thought* (Tokyo) 9 (1967), pp. 102–22.

Selner, Susan Canty. "The Metaphysics of Creation in Thomas Aquinas' *De*

Potentia Dei." Dissertation. Washington, D.C.: The Catholic University of America, 1992.

Strasser, Michael. "Saint Thomas' Critique of Platonism in the *Liber de Causis.*" Dissertation. Toronto: University of Toronto, 1963.

Stypinski, Andreze-Bobola. "Aquinas on the "Communicability" of Creation: The *Scriptum* and the *Liber de Causis.*" Dissertation. Toronto: University of Toronto, 1983.

Taylor, Richard C. "St. Thomas and the *Liber de causis* on the Hylomorphic Composition of Separate Substances." *Medieval Studies* 41 (1979), pp. 506–13.

Vansteenkiste, C. "Notes sur le Commentaire de Saint Thomas du *Liber de causis.*" *Études et recherche. Cahiers de théologie et de philosophie* 8 (1952), pp. 171–91.

———. "Il *Libro de causis* negli scritti di San Tommaso," *Angelicum* 35 (1958), pp. 325–74.

4. Other Related Literature on St. Thomas

Annice, M. "Historical Sketch of the Theory of Participation." *The New Scholasticism* 26 (1952), pp. 49–79.

Berti, E. "Aristotelismo e neoplatonismo nella dottrina tomistica di Dio come 'Ipsum esse.'" In *Studi aristotelici*. Ed. L. U. Japadre. Aquilla, 1975; pp. 347–352.

Blanchette, Oliva. *The Perfection of the Universe according to Aquinas: A Teleological Cosmology.* University Park, Penn.: The Pennsylvania State University Press, 1992.

Booth, Edward. "A Confrontation between the Neo-Platonisms of St. Thomas and Hegel." *Angelicum* 63 (1986), pp. 56–89.

Brady, Ignatius. "John Pecham and the Background to the *De aeternitati mundi* of St. Thomas Aquinas." In *St. Thomas Aquinas Commemorative Studies*. Toronto: Pontifical Institute of Mediaeval Studies, 1974.

A. Campodonico. "Il carattere immediato della presenza di Dio nel mondo secondo Tommaso D'Aquino." *Rivista di filosofia neoscolastica* 76 (1984), pp. 245–68.

Chenu, M.-D. "Un vestige du stoicisme." *Revue des sciences philosophiques et théologiques* 27 (1938), pp. 63–68.

———. *Toward Understanding Saint Thomas*. Trans. Albert M. Landry, O.P., and Dominic Hughes, O.P. Chicago: Henry Regnery, 1964.

Clarke, W. Norris, S.J. "The Limitation of Act by Potency: Aristotelianism or Neoplatonism." *New Scholasticism* 26 (1952), pp. 167–94.

———. "St. Thomas and Platonism." *Thought* 32 (1957), pp. 437–44.

Corrigan, Kevin. "A Philosophical Precursor to the Theory of Essence and Existence in St. Thomas Aquinas." *The Thomist* 48 (1984), pp. 219–40.

De Couesnongle, C. "La causalité du maximum. Pourquoi saint Thomas a-t-il mal cité Aristote?" *Revue des sciences philosophiques et théologiques* 38 (1954), pp. 658–80.

De Vogel, Cornelia J. "*Deus Creator Omnium*. Plato and Aristotle in Aquinas' Doctrine of God." In *Graceful Reason: Essays in Ancient and Medieval Philosophy Presented to Joseph Owens, C.S.S.R.* Toronto: Pontifical Institute of Mediaeval Studies, 1983.

Dewan, Lawrence, O.P. "St. Thomas and the Causality of God's Goodness." *Laval théologique et philosophique* 34 (1978), pp. 291–304.

Dondaine, H.-F. "Le premier instant de l'ange d'apres Saint Thomas." *Revue des sciences philosophiques et théologiques* 39 (1955), pp. 213–27.

Ducoin, G. "L'homme comme conscience de soi selon saint Thomas d'Aquin." in *Sapientia Aquinatis*. Comunicationes IV Congr. Thom. Int., I. Rome: Officium Libri Catholici, 1955.

Fabro, Cornelio. *La nozione metafisica di partecipazione secondo S. Tommaso*. Milan: Vita e Pensiero, 1939.

———. *Partecipazione e causalità secondo S. Tommaso d'Aquino*. Turin: SEI, 1960. (*Participation et causalité selon saint Thomas d'Aquin*. Louvain: Universitaires de Louvain, 1961.)

———. "Platonismo, neoplatonismo e tomismo, convergenze e divergenze." *Aquinas* 12 (1969), pp. 217–42.

———. "The Intensive Hermeneutics of Thomistic Philosophy: The Notion of Participation." *Review of Metaphysics* 27 (1974), pp. 449–91.

Farre, Luis. *Tomas de Aquino y el Neoplatonismo*. La Plata: Instituto de Filosofia, Universitad Nacional de La Plata, 1966.

Faucon, P. *Aspects néoplatoniciens de la doctrine de saint Thomas d'Aquin*. Paris: Honoré Champion, 1975.

Fauser, Winfried, S.J. "Albert the Great's Commentary on the *Liber de causis*." *Bulletin de philosophie médiévale* 36 (1994), pp. 38–44.

Fay, T. "The Transformation of Platonic and Neoplatonic Thought in the Metaphysics of Thomas Aquinas." *Divus Thomas* 76 (1973), pp. 50–64.

Fetz, R. L. *Ontologie der Innerlichkeit. Reditio completa und processio interior bei Thomas von Aquin*. Freiburg: University of Freiburg, 1975.

Geiger, Louis-Bertrand, O.P. *La participation dans la philosophie de S. Thomas d'Aquin*. Paris: Libraire Philosophique J. Vrin, 1953.

Gomez-Nogalez. "Santo Tomás y los Arabes. Bibliografía." *Miscellanea Comillas* 33 (1975), pp. 205–50.

Hankey, W. J. "Theology as System and as Science: Proclus and Thomas Aquinas." *Dionysius* 6 (1982), pp. 83–93.

Hayen, André. *La communication de l'être d'après saint Thomas d'Aquin.* 2 vols. Paris: Desclée de Brouwer, 1957, 1959.

Henle, R. J. "St. Thomas' Methodology in the Treatment of 'Positiones' with Particular Reference to 'Positiones Platonicae.'" *Gregorianum* 36 (1955), pp. 391–409.

———. *Saint Thomas and Platonism. A Study of "Plato" and "Platonici" Texts in the Writings of St. Thomas.* The Hague: Martinus Nijhoff, 1956.

Huit, C. "Les éléments platoniciens de la doctrine de saint Thomas." *Revue thomiste* 19 (1911), pp. 724–66.

Imbach, R. "Le (néo-)platonisme médiéval, Proclus latin et l'ecole dominicaine allemande." *Revue de théologie et de philosophie* 110 (1978), pp. 427–48.

Johnson, Mark F. "Did St. Thomas Attribute a Doctrine of Creation to Aristotle?" *New Scholasticism* 63 (1989), pp. 129–55.

Jones, John D. "The Ontological Difference for St. Thomas and Pseudo-Dionysius." *Dionysius* 4 (1980), pp. 119–32.

Jordan, Mark D. "The Grammar of *Esse*: Re-reading Thomas on the Transcendentals." *The Thomist* 44 (1980), pp. 1–26.

Jossua, Jean-Pierre, "L'Axiome *Bonum diffusivum sui* chez S. Thomas d'Aquin." *Revue des sciences religieuses* 40 (1966), pp. 127–53.

Kainz, H.P. *Active and Passive Potency in Thomistic Angelology.* The Hague: Martinus Nijhoff, 1972.

Kremer, Klaus. *Die neuplatonische Seinsphilosophie und ihre Wirkung auf Thomas von Aquin.* Leiden: Brill, 1972.

Lescoe, F. J. *Saint Thomas on the Separate Substances.* West Hartford: St. Joseph College, 1963.

Lapointe, E. "Le problème de *l'esse* chez saint Thomas." *Archives de philosophie* 26 (1963), pp. 59–70.

Litt, T. *Les corps célestes dans l'univers de saint Thomas.* Louvain: Publ. Univ.-B. Nauwelaerts, 1963.

Little, Arthur, S.J. *The Platonic Heritage of Thomism.* Dublin: Golden Eagle Books, 1950.

Lohman, J. "Saint Thomas et les arabes (Structures linguistiques et formes de pensée)." *Revue philosophique de Louvain* 74 (1976), pp. 30–44.

Montagnes, Bernard. "L'axiome de continuité chez saint Thomas." *Revue des sciences philosophiques et théologiques* (1968), pp. 201–21.

Moreau, J. "La platonisme dans la Somme Théologique." In *Tommaso d'Aquino settimo centenario*, I, *Le fonte del pensiero di S. Tommaso*. Naples: Edizioni Domenicane Italiane, 1975.

Neidl, Walter N. *Thearchia. Die Frage nach dem Sinn von Gott bei Pseudo-Dionysius Areopagita und Thomas von Aquin.* Regensburg: Josef Habbel, 1976.

Oeing-Hanhoff, Ludger. *Ens et Unum Convertuntur. Stellung und Gehalt des Grund-*

satzes in der Philosophie des Hl. Thomas von Aquin. Münster: Aschendorffsche Verlag, 1953.

O'Rourke, Fran. *Pseudo-Dionysius and the Metaphysics of Aquinas.* Leiden: E. J. Brill, 1992.

Owens, Joseph. *The Doctrine of Being in the Aristotelian Metaphysics.* Toronto: Pontifical Institute of Mediaeval Studies, 1978.

Pera, Ceslao. "Il Tomismo di fronte alle correnti Platoniche e neo-Platoniche." *Aquinas* 3 (1960), pp. 279–90.

Reichmann, James B. "Immanently Transcendent and Subsistent *Esse*: A Comparison." *The Thomist* 38 (1974), pp. 332–69.

Riesenhuber, Klaus. "Partizipation als Strukturprinzip der Namen Gottes bei Thomas von Aquin." In *Sprache und Erkenntnis im Mittelalter* (Miscellanea Mediaevalia XIII, 2). Berlin: Walter de Gruyter, 1981; pp. 969–82.

Santeler, Josef. *Der Platonismus in der Erknenntnis des Heiligen Thomas von Aquin.* Innsbruch: F.Rauch, 1939.

Schenk, Richard, O.P. *Die Gnade vollendeter Endlichkeit. Zur transzendentaltheologischen Auslegung der thomanischen Anthropologie.* Freiburg-im-Breisgau: Herder, 1989.

Solignac, A. "La doctrine de l'*esse* chez saint Thomas est-elle d'origine néoplatonicenne?" *Archives de philosophie* 30 (1967), pp. 439–52.

Steel, Carlos. "*Omnis corporis potentia est finita*. L'interprétation d'un principe aristotélicien: de Proclus à S. Thomas." In *Philosophie im Mittelalter.* Ed. Jan P. Beckman et al. Hamburg: Meiner, 1987; pp. 213–24.

Sweeney, Leo, S.J. "*Esse primum creatum* in Albert the Great's *Liber de causis et processu universitatis.*" *The Thomist* 44 (1980), pp. 599–646.

Taylor, A. E. *Philosophical Studies.* London: Macmillan, 1934.

Torrell, Jean-Pierre. *Initiation à saint Thomas d'Aquin: sa personne et son ouevre.* Fribourg: Editions universitaires; Paris: Cerf, 1993. English translation by Robert Royal, *Saint Thomas Aquinas: The Man and His Work,* forthcoming, spring 1996 from The Catholic University of America Press.

Vansteenkiste, C. "Autori arabi e giudei nell'opera di San Tommaso." *Angelicum* 27 (1950), pp. 336–401.

———. "Platone e S. Tommaso." *Angelicum* 34 (1957), pp. 318–28.

Verbeke, G. "Guillaume de Moerbeke traducteur de Proclus." *Revue philosophique Louvain* 51 (1953), pp. 349–73.

———. "Man as 'Frontier' according to Aquinas." In *Aquinas and Problems of His Times.* The Hague: Martinus Nijhoff, 1976; pp. 195–223.

Von Ivánka, Endre. "S. Thomas Platonisant." In *Tommaso d'Aquino nel suo settimo centenario, I, Le fonti del pensiero di Tommaso.* Naples: Edizioni Domenicane Italiane, 1975; pp. 256–57.

Wallis, R. T. "Divine Omnipotence in Plotinus, Proclus, and Aquinas." In *Neo-*

Platonism and Early Christian Thought. Essays in Honor of A. H. Armstrong. Ed. H. J. Blumenthal & R. A. Markus. London: Variorum, 1981; pp. 223–35.

Weisheipl, James, O.P. "The Celestial Movers in Medieval Physics." *The Thomist* 24 (1961), pp. 286–326.

———. "Thomas' Evaluation of Plato and Aristotle." *New Scholasticism* 48 (1974), pp. 100–124.

———. *Friar Thomas D'Aquino: His Life, Thought and Works.* Washington, D.C.: The Catholic University of America Press, 1983.

Westra, Laura. "The Soul's Noetic Ascent to the One in Plotinus and to God in Aquinas." *New Scholasticism* 44 (1970), pp. 98–126.

Wilhelmsen, Frederick D. "Existence and Esse." *New Scholasticism* 50 (1976), pp. 20–45.

Zum Brunn, Émilie. "La 'métaphysique de l'Exode' selon Thomas d'Aquin." In *Dieu et l'être.* Paris: Études Augustiniennes, 1978; pp. 245–69.

Commentary on the Book of Causes was composed in
Meridian by Brevis Press, Bethany, Connecticut; printed on
60 lb. Booktext Natural and bound by BookCrafters, Chelsea, Michigan;
and designed and produced by Kachergis Book Design,
Pittsboro, North Carolina.